QUITO

BETHANY PITTS

CONTENTS

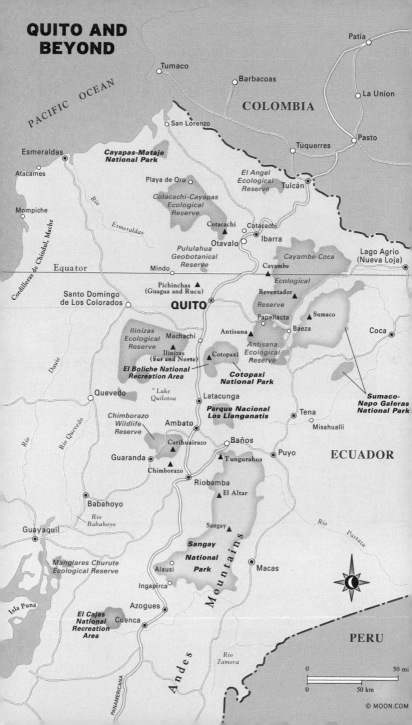

1. food vendor at Otavalo's textile market

2. colonial buildings in Old Town Quito

3. encebollado, a fish stew and typical Ecuadorian dish

4. Itchimbía Cultural Center in Quito

5. Plaza Grande in Quito

6. the two steeples of La Basílica del Voto Nacional

DISCOVER
QUITO

At 2,850 meters (9,350 ft) above sea level, Ecuador's dramatic capital city is the second highest in the world after Bolivia's La Paz. Built on the ashes of the northern Inca capital following the 1533 Spanish conquest, Quito is nestled in a valley surrounded by majestic Andean peaks, among them the restless Volcán Pichincha.

This spectacular backdrop adds to the joy of exploring the cobblestone streets, stately plazas, and lavish churches of Quito's Old Town, one of the best-preserved colonial cities in Latin America and a UNESCO World Heritage Site. Amid the spires and cupolas, rows of pastel-colored houses with flower-decked wrought-iron balconies sit beside lovingly restored mansions with tranquil inner courtyards. Looking further back in time, museums provide fascinating insights into Ecuador's pre-Columbian ancestral cultures, some dating back to 4000 BC. The vibrant, living city is as intriguing as its rich history. Stop at a sidewalk café and watch formally dressed Quiteños hurrying to work alongside shoe shiners, street vendors, and indigenous women in traditional dress.

A short hop from Old Town are the modern streets and shining office blocks of New Town, where some of the country's best hotels, restaurants, and nightlife are found. Historically known for its conservative values, these days Quito is home to Ecuador's most vibrant alternative art, music, and theater scene. Relief from the city noise can be found in the welcome green spaces of the capital's well-kept parks.

Despite its proximity to the equator, Quito is spared the oppressive heat of the lowlands by its altitude. Locals are fond of saying that their city gives you four seasons in one day—a statement supported by the spring-like mornings, summery afternoons, autumnal evenings, and wintry nights. The Quiteños themselves are welcoming, helpful, and speak a beautifully clear Spanish, great for visitors who are practicing their language skills.

Take the time to wander the streets and talk with the people and you will discover for yourself how captivating the city really is.

6 TOP
EXPERIENCES

1 **Get a Condor's Eye View:** The climb up the tower of **La Basílica del Voto Nacional** isn't for the faint of heart, but those who dare are rewarded with a spectacular view of the Old City (page 32).

2 **Wander amid Colonial Architecture:** Stroll along the streets of 16th-century **Plaza Grande,** where elegant buildings provide a beautiful backdrop for the bustle of everyday life (page 26).

∧
∧
∧

3 **Find Adventure at Cotopaxi National Park:** On your own or with a guide, hike, bike, or climb throughout this magnificent park (page 110).

4 **Go Bird-Watching:** Andean cocks-of-the-rock and colorful toucans are just a few of the stunning species of birds you'll find in **Mindo,** 2.5 hours from Quito (page 73).

<<<

5 **Explore the Otavalo Textile Market:** Enjoy the festival atmosphere, admire the brightly colored woven fabrics, and learn about the tradition behind this world-famous textile market (page 88).

6 **Visit Chigüilpe:** 3 hours from Quito, this indigenous Tsáchila community is known for ancestral healing ceremonies and tree hugging (page 117).

PLANNING YOUR TRIP

WHERE TO GO

QUITO

A dramatic backdrop of Andean peaks and snowcapped volcanoes adds to the delight of exploring the cobblestone streets and elegant plazas of Quito's Old Town, one of the best-preserved colonial cities in Latin America and a **UNESCO World Heritage Site.** For a condor's-eye view, brave the climb to the top of the basilica's tower. The capital also hosts the country's best restaurants, museums, and nightlife, with a vibrant cultural scene. North of Quito, the village of **Mindo,** set amid lush cloud forest, is paradise for birders and nature lovers, while Maquipucuna is the best place in the world to see spectacled bears.

EXCURSIONS
OTAVALO

The northern Sierra's most famous attraction is the Otavalo **textile market,** one of the oldest and largest on the continent. Throughout the region, indigenous

courtyard café in the Palacio Arzobispal

artisans practice traditional crafts such as weaving and embroidery, and villages such as San Clemente offer the chance to share the Andean Kichwa way of life.

CENTRAL SIERRA
The **Avenue of the Volcanoes** is a jaw-dropping procession of some of the world's highest peaks, with the snowy flanks of picture-perfect Cotopaxi and colossal Chimborazo easily accessible as day trips.

SANTO DOMINGO AND VICINITY
The **indigenous Tsáchila** people near Santo Domingo keep their unique ancestral traditions alive and hold shamanic ceremonies in a candlelit underground chamber.

KNOW BEFORE YOU GO

WHEN TO GO
Ecuador's climate is so varied that it's impossible to make sweeping generalizations. Different regions have their own climates, and within these are countless **microclimates,** often depending on altitude. The good news is that there is no bad time to visit.

Broadly speaking, it's often sunny during the day and chilly at night. Daytime temperatures average 15-20°C (59-68°F), occasionally peaking at 25°C (77°F), with nights falling to 7-8°C (45-46°F) and sometimes dropping to freezing. The driest, warmest months are June to September, with December to May the wettest. Whatever the season, Andean weather can change very quickly. Rainstorms tend to be torrential and brief.

There are no national high or low tourism seasons, but accommodations are likely to be booked up—and may be double in price—around New Year's Day, Carnival, and Easter.

PASSPORTS, VISAS, AND ENTRY REQUIREMENTS
Travelers from the vast majority of countries do not require a **visa** to enter Ecuador and will be given a 90-day **permit stamp** upon arrival. This permit can only be issued once per year (i.e., if you are granted one on April 1, 2019, you cannot request another until April 1, 2020). A **passport** with validity of at least six months is required. You may be asked for proof of onward travel (a reservation for a bus ticket to Peru or Colombia is sufficient). If you are traveling from a country with a risk of yellow fever transmission, including Peru, Colombia, Brazil, Argentina, and Bolivia, you may be asked for a **vaccination certificate,** which is valid for life. Check with the **World Health Organization** for the current list of affected countries.

If you know beforehand that you would like to stay in Ecuador beyond 90 days, consider applying for a longer visa with your local

Ecuadorian embassy before your trip, to avoid formalities in Ecuador. Alternatively, the 90-day visa can be extended once, by paying a fee. After that, it's possible to apply for various longer-term tourist and resident visas. Since February 2018, overstaying involves a fine.

See the *Visas and Officialdom* section of the *Essentials* chapter for more details.

VACCINATIONS

All visitors should make sure their routine immunizations are up to date, along with **hepatitis A** and **tetanus.** Those whose activities may put them at extra risk should also consider hepatitis B, rabies, typhoid, and tuberculosis vaccinations. A yellow fever vaccination certificate is required when entering Ecuador from a country where it is present and is valid for life. There is a low risk of malaria; bite avoidance is advised, rather than antimalarial medication.

Ecuador is considered high risk for the **Zika virus,** which is usually mosquito-borne. The official advice is that pregnant women should postpone non-essential travel to Ecuador. Women should avoid becoming pregnant while in Ecuador and for eight weeks after leaving.

TRANSPORTATION

Modern and efficient **Mariscal Sucre International Airport** is located near the town of Tababela, about 12 kilometers (7.5 mi) east of Quito. A network of domestic airports across the country can be accessed in under an hour by plane from Quito. With some exceptions, mainland flights are generally economical (from $40 one way).

Ecuador's **bus system** is comprehensive and economical, and the roads are generally good. For short journeys, taxis are readily available and affordable. For longer journeys, hiring a driver is an option, but it's not cheap. Car rental is more budget friendly, but driving in urban areas can be quite alarming and tough to avoid, as rental companies are only present in the largest cities.

EXPLORE
QUITO

QUITO AND BEYOND

With cobblestone streets, stately plazas, and lavish churches, Ecuador's capital city is an adventure in itself. Expand your trip by taking excursions to an authentic market town, legendary volcanoes, or an indigenous community and get a taste of the magic of Ecuador.

DAYS 1 & 2
QUITO

Arrive in Quito, check into your hotel, and then explore **Old Town,** taking in the churches, plazas, and museums of the historical center, before heading to the **Museo Fundación Guayasamín** and **Capilla del Hombre,** just north of New Town. While in Quito, dine on the beautifully preserved colonial street of **La Ronda.**

DAYS 3-5
OPTION 1: MINDO

Take an early morning bus northwest from Quito to **Mindo,** where you can visit a **butterfly farm** and **hummingbird garden,** or go hiking, birding, or biking in the cloud

Quito's Old Town

ADRENALINE RUSH

There are plenty of thrills to be had in a country that boasts such dramatically changing terrain. Whether you want to zoom downhill on a bike, raft through river rapids, or scale a peak, you'll find what you're looking for here.

rafting in Mindo

- In **Mindo,** adventure seekers will enjoy **zip-lining** through the forest canopy, **tubing** down pristine rivers, or exploring the area on two wheels.
- The countryside around **Otavalo** offers wonderful **hiking, biking,** and **horseback riding,** including spectacular descents into the Intag Valley. Tour agencies offer **climbing, rafting,** and **kayaking.**
- For **mountaineering,** "starter peak" **Fuya Fuya** is a popular climb as acclimatization practice for higher peaks **Cotopaxi, Chimborazo,** and **Cayambe. Rumiñahui** and **Iliniza Sur** are less challenging. Chimborazo and Cayambe offer thrilling **downhill biking.**

forest. In the evenings, choose one of the excellent restaurants on Gourmet Avenue. When you're done exploring Mindo, head back to Quito early enough to continue to Machachi in the central Sierra.

OPTION 2: OTAVALO

Take an early morning bus from Quito to Otavalo, and spend time exploring the surrounding countryside or visiting a **Kichwa village.** If you're in Otavalo on a Saturday, don't miss the **textile market.** Head back to Quito and continue to Machachi.

DAYS 6 & 7
OPTION 1: COTOPAXI NATIONAL PARK

Machachi is a good access point for adventure-filled **Cotopaxi National Park.** On your own or with a guide, bike, hike, climb and enjoy Ecuador's natural splendor. Spend the night in the park and head back to Quito the next day.

OPTION 2: CHIGÜILPE

From Machachi, head to the indigenous **Tsáchila community** of **Chigüilpe** just outside Santo Domingo for an ancestral healing ritual in an underground shamanic chamber. Stay overnight with the community and head back to Quito the next day for your last day in Ecuador.

QUITO

Quito extends over 50 kilometers

(31 mi) north-south, and about 8 kilometers (5 mi) across. Fortunately, it's easily divided into zones: one for historical sights (**Old Town**); one for the majority of restaurants, accommodations, nightlife, and visitor services (**New Town**); and then everything else. Its long, narrow geography and abundance of transport options make the capital quite easy to get around.

In Old Town, El Centro Histórico, most of the plazas, churches, and other religious buildings are situated within a few blocks of the

HIGHLIGHTS

✪ **PLAZA GRANDE:** Find a quiet bench alongside Quiteño elders in the heart of Old Town to watch city life swirl past, surrounded by lily-filled flower beds, elegant colonial architecture, and magnificent mountain scenery (page 26).

✪ **LA COMPAÑÍA:** The epitome of golden grandeur, this extravagant chapel is the most dazzling of Quito's many beautiful churches (page 27).

✪ **LA CASA DE ALABADO:** Learn about Ecuador's ancient indigenous cultures at this museum, with beautifully arranged exhibits of pre-Columbian artifacts and fascinating displays on the underworld and shamanism (page 30).

✪ **LA BASÍLICA DEL VOTO NACIONAL:** With its mystical animal gargoyles, the country's tallest church is a striking sight. Even more spectacular is the condor's-eye view of the historical district from the spire, for those who dare to make the climb (page 32).

✪ **MINDO:** A world-class birding and ecotourism destination, this village nestled in the cloud forest is heaven for nature lovers and adventure seekers (page 73).

✪ **MAQUIPUCUNA BIOLOGICAL RESERVE:** Protecting over 6,000 hectares (14,800 acres) of pristine rainforest in the heart of one of the earth's top five biodiversity hot spots, this is the best place in the world to see the Andean or spectacled bear (page 82).

original heart of the city, Plaza de la Independencia or **Plaza Grande.** This is also where most of the museums and theaters are located. You may choose to head straight for the sights that are of most interest or to forget itineraries and simply wander the cobbled streets. There are several spectacular viewpoints to admire Old Town from a bird's eye view, from the gothic spires of the *basílica* to the even loftier heights of the **TelefériQo** (cable car).

Old Town is cleaner, safer, and a joy to explore following a multimillion-dollar regeneration. The blue-uniformed Metropolitan Police have a visible presence and are generally friendly, helpful, and happy to give directions. The municipality of Quito has put together an excellent map of themed historical walks, available at the Plaza Grande tourist office, where it is also possible to book **multilingual tours** given by municipal police.

Northeast of the historical center, **La Alameda** and **El Ejido** parks form a buffer between Old and New Town. Linking the two districts are the major thoroughfares **Avenida América** and **Avenida 10 de Agosto.**

The hub of New Town is Plaza Quinde, commonly known as **Plaza Foch,** and the surrounding area, Mariscal Sucre, or simply **La Mariscal.** Here you'll find most of the visitor amenities: hotels, restaurants, bars, Internet cafés, banks, shops, and tour agencies. The nightlife is particularly raucous Thursday-Saturday. The contrast with Old Town is striking; this sector has a decidedly modern, international feel. North of New Town is **Parque La Carolina,** a popular park with impressive facilities and a botanical garden. To the east of the park, the **Museo Fundación Guayasamín,** formerly the home of master painter and sculptor Oswaldo Guayasamín, is also the location of his unfinished masterpiece, the **Capilla del Hombre (Chapel of Man).**

North and east of La Mariscal are quieter neighborhoods such as arty, bohemian **La Floresta** and **Guápulo,** worth a visit for the spectacular views and lovely park.

Most visitors, especially backpackers, stay in New Town, mainly because there are so many amenities. However, following the regeneration, there is an increasing number of good accommodation and dining options in Old Town, offering a more authentic and picturesque experience. Wherever you stay, it's only a short cab or bus ride between the two districts. Traffic is overwhelming everywhere, though it's noticeably lighter on the weekends, when the lack of commuter traffic makes taxi journeys quicker and cheaper.

If you only have a couple of days in Quito, spend most of it in Old Town and perhaps half a day in New Town. Four days is a good amount of time to take in the key sights of both areas, by which time you may be ready to head out of the city for the welcome tranquility of **Mindo.**

CLIMATE

Quito is famed for its spring-like climate, with daytime temperatures usually 10-22°C (50-72°F), though a sunny day can feel hotter. Mornings tend to be chilly, but it can heat up considerably around midday. Temperatures drop quickly on rainy afternoons and in the evenings, with nighttime as low as 7°C (45°F). There is generally more sun in the mornings, so sightseeing early is a good idea. Locals say that the city can experience all four seasons in a single day, and that isn't far off the mark. The two rainy seasons are February-April and, to a lesser extent, October-November.

Even on a sunny day, Andean people are much more formal in dress than their coastal counterparts. Long shorts with a T-shirt is fine, but skimpy clothes should be avoided. The weather can change suddenly, so bring lots of layers and a light waterproof jacket. Jeans, a T-shirt, and a light sweater are usually fine for the daytime, but you'll want to add a jacket for the evening. Closed shoes rather than sandals are recommended. Don't underestimate the strength of the equatorial sun, and wear sunscreen, even on a cloudy day.

Bear in mind that the elevation may leave you breathless and lightheaded. Dizzy spells, stomach upsets, insomnia, headaches, and fatigue can also occur. It is best not to overexert yourself and to minimize caffeine and alcohol in favor of plenty of water and light food, at least for the first couple of days.

SAFETY

The majority of visitors to Quito experience no difficulties with security. However, as with most countries, extra precaution is needed in Ecuador's big cities. The high concentration of foreigners in the capital has led to an increased number of criminals targeting them, but if you stay alert and

Quito

© MOON.COM

0   0.5 mi
0   0.5 km

SEE "OLD TOWN QUITO" MAP

SEE "NEW TOWN QUITO" MAP

OCCIDENTAL/ SUCRE

BAHÍA DE CARÁQUEZ

24 DE MAYO

LA CASA DE ALABADO

LA COMPAÑÍA

PLAZA GRANDE

El Panecillo

GUAYAQUIL

Plaza del Teatro

LA BASÍLICA DEL VOTO NACIONAL

Cumandá

Recoleta

Santo Domingo

MALDONADO

Ómandá Urban Park

Ómandá

Marín

PICHINCHA

Santa Prisca

Consejo Provincial

COLOMBIA

Marín Central

MOSAICO

Parque La Alameda

ITCHIMBÍA PARK AND CULTURAL CENTER

LIBERTADOR

EL TREBOL

SIMÓN

GRAL

BOLÍVAR

RUMIÑAHUI

NUCANCHI PEÑA

UNIVERSITARIA

UNIVERSIDAD CENTRAL

LA GASCA

TELEFÉRICO

Seminario Mayor

AMERICA

HOSPITAL CARLOS ANDRADE MARÍN

Espejo

Pérez Guerrero

El Ejido

Parque

TARQUI

PATRIA

10 DE AGOSTO

POST OFFICE

ORELLANA

ELOY

AMAZONAS

PLAZA FOCH

COLÓN

12 DE OCTUBRE

INSTITUTO GEOGRÁFICO MILITAR

LADRÓN

COLISEO RUMIÑAHUI

DE

GUEVARA

IGLESIA GUÁPULO

Guápulo

Río Machángara

AVE CUMANDÁ

To Quitumbe Terminal and Chimbacalle Train Station

To Machachi Latacunga and South

To Los Chillos

TROLE LINE
ECOVIA LINE
TROLE/METROBUS
ECOVIA STOP
METROBUS

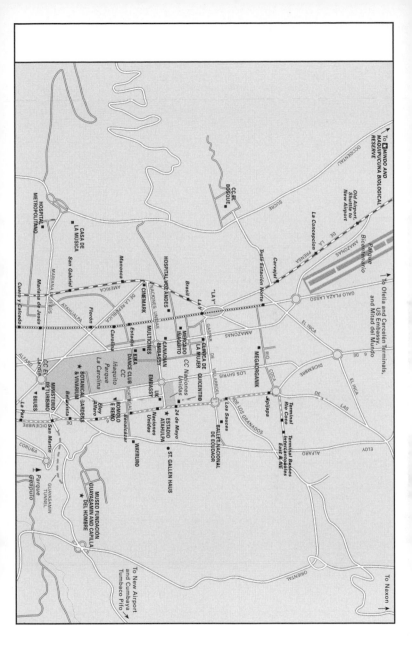

ONE DAY IN QUITO

MORNING

Start your day with a wander round the Plaza de la Independencia or **Plaza Grande,** the heart of Old Town, taking in the impressive facades of the buildings that flank the square: the **Palacio Presidencial,** the **Plaza Grande Hotel,** the **Palacio Arzobispal,** the **Palacio Municipal** (with a quick stop at **El Quinde Visitors Center** to pick up a walking map of central Quito), and the **Catedral Metropolitana de Quito.** Find a quiet spot on a bench alongside the Quiteño elders to sit for a few minutes and people watch, or eat breakfast at one of the little cafés with outdoor seating under the cathedral.

From the corner of Plaza Grande where the cathedral meets the presidential palace, walk a few hundred meters southwest along García Moreno and turn right onto Avenida José de Sucre to find La Iglesia de la Compañía de Jesús, or simply **La Compañía.** Spend some time inside marveling at the most opulent of Quito's churches. Leaving La Compañía, keep walking half a block along Avenida José de Sucre and you'll be at the eastern corner of **Plaza San Francisco.** Diagonally opposite, at the western corner, turn onto Cuenca to reach the **Casa de Alabado,** a museum of pre-Columbian art, in an immaculately restored 17th-century mansion with fascinating displays on Ecuador's ancestral indigenous cultures.

From the museum, head back to the Plaza San Francisco, passing the facade of the **Iglesia San Francisco** to stop for a late-morning drink at the **Tianguez Café Cultural** at the northern corner of the square. Browse for souvenirs at the attached fair trade store, where you'll find *paja toquilla* or "Panama" hats, ceramics, masks, woven goods, Tigua paintings, embroidered shirts, *tagua* jewelry, wooden bowls, coffee, and chocolate. Make your way back to the Plaza Grande and then past it for seven blocks along García Moreno to get to **La Basílica del Voto Nacional.** If you're feeling fit and have a head for heights, make the ascent to the top of the church tower for some truly spectacular views. Even without the climb, the basilica is worth a visit, for the mystical animal gargoyles, colorful stained-glass windows, and peaceful interior.

AFTERNOON

When you've had your fill at the basilica, take a taxi and enjoy a well-deserved lunch at one of the many **excellent restaurants in New Town** or, to eat with the locals, try the food court at New Town's **Mercado Santa Clara,** near the Central University. After lunch, walk to the **Mindalae Ethnic Museum** at the north end of New Town, to once again immerse yourself in the fascinating world of Ecuador's indigenous cultures, with displays on shamanism and replicas of ceramic artifacts from Ecuador's ancient civilizations, some dating back to 4000 BC. The attached fair trade store is one of Quito's best spots to pick up souvenirs and handicrafts.

Travel by taxi to the **Museo Fundación Guayasamín** and **Capilla del Hombre.** Take a guided tour around the former house of Ecuador's most famous artist and then admire his works, which have themes such as motherly love, anger, and the oppression of indigenous peoples. You don't have to be an art aficionado to find these deeply moving. Note that the museum closes at 5pm. Take one of the taxis waiting by the museum exit and head for the **Mirador de Guápulo.** Watch the sunset from one of the cafés perched on the hillside (such as **Tandana**), for spectacular views over the valley spread out below.

EVENING

Head back to your hotel or hostel to freshen up and rest. Ask your hotel to call you a taxi and go out either for dinner and dancing in **La Mariscal** or for mulled wine and typical Ecuadorian food at the beautifully preserved colonial street of **La Ronda** in Old Town.

take some common-sense precautions, your visit will likely be incident-free.

If you feel unsafe or are lost, Quito's Metropolitan Police are the most friendly and helpful in the country. They wear blue uniforms and are out in force in the main tourist areas.

Watch out for pickpockets and bag-slashers in crowded areas, at tourist spots, and on public transport. The trolley bus services (Trole, Ecovia, and Metrobus) are perhaps the worst for pickpockets. Don't go into any parks after dark. It is a good idea to seek current advice from your hotel about places to go and places to avoid.

La Mariscal in New Town is the most risky area for foreign visitors. Walk just a couple of blocks from the main drag and the police presence is replaced by groups of thieves or drug dealers. Unlike in the rest of the country, drunken street violence is common. Always use a prebooked taxi to get to and from La Mariscal after dark, even if your hotel is only a few blocks away. Drink spiking is prevalent, so don't leave your beverage unattended. Don't accept flyers from anyone on the street, as they may be dusted with scopolamine, a substance that leaves victims in a docile state, vulnerable to robbery or assault.

The area around El Panecillo (the hill with the Virgin Mary on top) is not safe, so take a taxi there and back. If walking to La Tola neighborhood from Old Town, take Manabí rather than Esmeraldas, as the latter street is the red-light district and can feel pretty sketchy even during the day. At the *teleférico* (cable car), assaults and muggings have been reported on the hike to Rucu Pichincha, although there are now police patrols on the weekend. Do not attempt this climb alone, and ideally don't take valuables.

Rather than flagging taxis down on the street, especially at night, ask your hotel, restaurant, or bar to call you a radio (prebooked) taxi. If you have a phone, save the number of a reliable taxi company and call one yourself (see the *Getting Around* section for some numbers). It might seem like an inconvenience to wait the few extra minutes for it to arrive, but it's a sure way to avoid "express kidnappings," where shady drivers relieve passengers of cash, valuables, and PIN numbers. Victims are usually released unharmed, but these incidents are terrifying and can turn violent. This type of crime is common in Quito, especially in La Mariscal. See the *Crime* section of the *Essentials* chapter for more information on how to travel safely by taxi in these cities.

Sights

OLD TOWN

Keep in mind that opening hours fluctuate regularly; those provided here are the latest available.

TOP EXPERIENCE

✪ PLAZA GRANDE AND VICINITY

The ornate 16th-century **Plaza Grande** (Venezuela y Chile) is the focal point of colonial Quito. Officially called the Plaza de la Independencia, it features a winged statue to independence atop a high pillar. The surrounding park is a great place for people watching; it's bustling with activity but there is always a quiet bench from which to take in the city life and beautiful surroundings. Join the locals in getting your shoes expertly shined under the arches on the northeastern side of the square.

On the plaza's southwest side, the **Catedral Metropolitana de Quito,** or simply **La Catedral** (Venezuela y Espejo 715, tel. 2/257-0371, www.catedraldequito.org/en, mass 7am and 8:30am daily), is actually the third to stand on this site since the founding of the city in 1534. Buried here is hero of independence Antonio José de Sucre, along with Ecuador's first president, Juan José Flores, and President Gabriel García, who died on August 6, 1875, after being attacked with machetes outside the presidential palace. The adjoining **Museo de la Catedral** (9am-5pm Mon.-Sat., $3) houses religious artifacts and paintings.

Next door, the **Iglesia El Sagrario** (tel. 2/228-4398, 7:30am-6pm Mon.-Fri., 7:30am-noon Sat., 8am-1pm and 4pm-6pm Sun.) was begun in 1657 and completed half a century later. Originally built as the cathedral's chapel, it is considered one of the city's most beautiful churches. Unlike at La Compañía, photography is allowed inside.

The northwest side of the plaza is taken up by the long, columned facade of the seat of government, the **Palacio Presidencial** (9am-5pm Tues.-Sat., 9am-4pm Sun.), also known as El Carondelet. Entrance is only possible with a free tour and upon presentation of ID. Tours leave every 15-20 minutes and last 80 minutes.

The **Palacio Arzobispal** (Archbishop's Palace) on the northeast side of the plaza leads to a three-story atrium housing a number of small shops and eateries. The cobbled courtyard, thick whitewashed walls, and wooden balconies make it worth a look.

The church of **La Concepción** (7am-11am daily) stands at the corner of Chile and García Moreno. The attached convent is Quito's oldest, dating to 1577, and is closed to visitors.

At the corner of Benalcázar and Espejo, the **Centro Cultural Metropolitano** (tel. 2/395-2300, ext. 15508, 9am-4:30pm daily) houses the collection of the **Museo Alberto Mena Caamaño** (tel. 2/395-2300, ext. 15535, 9am-5pm Tues.-Sat., 10am-4pm Sun., $1.50). There are displays of colonial and contemporary art, a set of wax figures depicting the death throes of patriots killed in 1810 by royalist troops, and a gallery space for temporary art exhibits.

✪ LA COMPAÑÍA

La Iglesia de la Compañía de Jesús (Benalcázar 562 y Sucre, tel. 2/258-4175, 9:30am-6pm Mon.-Thurs., 9:30am-5:30pm Fri., 9:30am-4pm Sat., 12:30pm-4pm Sun., $5, free visits 12:30pm-4pm 1st Sun. of the month) is one of the most beautiful and extravagant churches in the Americas. Built by the wealthy Jesuit order between 1605 and 1765, it is a glorious example of both human endeavor and opulence gone mad, with seven tons of gold reportedly decorating the ceiling, walls, and altars. Night visits can be arranged in advance.

Across Sucre from La Compañía is the **Museo Numismático** (tel. 2/393-8600, https://numismatico.bce.fin.ec, 9am-5pm Tues.-Fri., 10am-4pm Sat.-Sun., $1), which traces the history of Ecuador's various currencies, from indigenous bartering systems to the adoption of the U.S. dollar. Also housed here is the national music library, where there are often free concerts in the evenings. On the opposite side of García Moreno from the museum is the **Casa de María Augusta Urrutia** (tel. 2/258-0103, 10am-6pm Tues.-Fri., 9:30am-5:30pm Sat.-Sun., $2). This well-preserved 19th-century mansion provides a glimpse into the life of one of the city's wealthiest former inhabitants, with luxurious accoutrements from all over the globe and a gallery of Victor Mideros paintings. Visitors are accompanied by a Spanish-speaking guide.

Heading east on Sucre brings you to the **Casa de Sucre** (Venezuela 573 y Sucre, tel. 2/295-2860, 9am-5:30pm daily, free), former home of Antonio José de Sucre, the hero of Ecuadorian independence who led the decisive victory of the Battle of Pichincha.

the ornate ceiling of La Compañía

Old Town Quito

© MOON.COM

CHIMBORAZO

LÓPEZ

ROCAFUERTE

BAHÍA DE CARAQUEZ

MARISCAL SUCRE

LOJA

BOLÍVAR

IMBABURA

MIDEROS

CHILE

LA CONCEPCIÓN

TANGUEZ CAFE & FAIR TRADE STORE

PORTAL DE CANTUÑA

CASA DE ALBADO

CAPILLA DE CANTUÑA

IGLESIA SAN FRANCISCO

MERCADO CENTRAL

HOSTAL SUCRE

Plaza San Francisco

MUSEO FRAY PEDRO GOCAL

CENTRO CULTURAL METROPOLITANO

PALACIO PRESIDENCIAL

CATHEDRAL

ARCHBISHOP'S PALACE

Plaza Grande

EL CAFETO

IGLESIA SAN AGUSTÍN

PLAZA GRANDE

El Panecillo

AMBATO

MONASTERIO EL CARMEN ALTO

MUSEO DE LA CIUDAD

LA RONDA

24 DE MAYO

CASA MARÍA AUGUSTA URBUTIA

CASA DE SUCRE

MUSEO NUMISMÁTICO

IGLESIA EL SAGRARIO

LA COMPAÑÍA

ESPEJO

TOURIST OFFICE

TEATRO BOLÍVAR

HOTEL BOUTIQUE PLAZA SUCRE

SANTA CATALINA

Santo Domingo

LEÑA QUITEÑA

HOTEL SAN FRANCISCO DE QUITO

IGLESIA SANTO DOMINGO

Plaza Santo Domingo

MALDONADO

La Recoleta

To Trolé Estación Sur

Cumandá

5 DE

JUNÍN

TEXEIRA

MAMACUCHARA

Cumandá Urban Park

24 DE MAYO

Marín Terminal

PICINCHA

To Playón, el Trébol, and el Censo

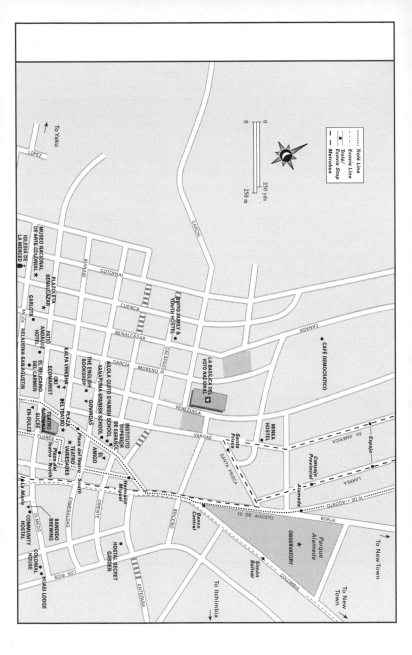

The building has been preserved in its original state from the early 1800s. Tours in English are available.

PLAZA SAN FRANCISCO AND VICINITY

Turn right up the hill past La Compañía to reach the **Plaza San Francisco,** flanked by Calles Bolívar, Benalcázar, Sucre, and Cuenca. At the time of writing, the center of the square was closed for the construction of a Metro station with an anticipated completion date of 2019. It is still possible to walk around the outside of the plaza and to visit the **Iglesia San Francisco** (on the west side of Plaza San Francisco on Cuenca, 6:30am-6:45pm Mon.-Sat.), the oldest colonial edifice in the city and the largest religious complex in South America. It was begun on the site of an Inca royal house within weeks of the city's founding in 1534. The first wheat grown in Ecuador sprouted in one of its courtyards, and Atahualpa's children received their education in its school. Inside the church, many of the design motifs come from indigenous cultures, including the smiling and frowning faces of sun gods, and harvest symbols of flowers and fruit.

To the right of the church's main entrance, the **Museo Fray Pedro Gocial** (Sucre, tel. 2/295-2911 or 98/729-9479, www.museofraypedrogocial.com, 9am-5:30pm Mon.-Sat., 9am-1pm Sun., $2.50) houses one of the city's finest collections of colonial art, dating from the 17th and 18th centuries. Guided tours are included in English, Spanish, and French. On the other side, the **Capilla de Catuña** (Cuenca y Bolívar, 8am-noon and 3pm-6pm daily) also has displays of colonial art. The story goes that this chapel was constructed by an indigenous man named Catuña who promised to have it completed in a certain amount of time. When it became obvious that he wasn't going to meet his deadline, he offered his soul to the devil in exchange for help getting the job done. Catuña finished the chapel but had a sudden change of heart, begging the Virgin Mary to save him from his hasty agreement. Sure enough, a foundation stone was found to be missing during the inauguration, negating his deal with the devil.

Under the church on the plaza is the **Tianguez Café Cultural** (tel. 2/257-0233, www.tianguez.org, 9:30am-6:30pm Mon.-Tues., 9:30am-11:30pm Wed.-Sun.), a great place to sample Ecuadorian cuisine from the coast, Amazon, and Andes. The attached Tianguez fair trade store is one of Quito's best spots to pick up souvenirs and handicrafts. Both the café and the shop are run by the Sinchi Sacha Foundation, a nonprofit set up to support indigenous Amazon communities.

✪ LA CASA DE ALABADO

Just off the Plaza San Francisco is the **Casa de Alabado** (Cuenca y Bolívar, tel. 2/228-0940, www.alabado.org, 9am-5:30pm daily, $4), a museum of pre-Columbian Ecuadorian art in an immaculately restored 17th-century house. The exhibition is organized with the aim of communicating the indigenous cosmovision or world view. Rather than being arranged by chronology or region, the artifacts are grouped by themes such as "Underworld," "Spiritual World of the Shaman," and "World of the Ancestors." Some ceramic sculptures are from civilizations as ancient as 4000 BC. The exhibits are exquisitely presented and the museum is an oasis

pre-Columbian pottery at La Casa de Alabado

of tranquility. All signage is in Spanish and English. Guided tours and audio guides are available. The café in the courtyard by the entrance is a pleasant spot to take a break from museum hopping and doesn't require an entrance fee.

PLAZA SANTO DOMINGO AND VICINITY

Down the hill southeast of Plaza San Francisco, bounded by Bolívar, Guayaquil, and Rocafuerte, is the elegant **Plaza Santo Domingo,** decorated with a statue of Sucre pointing to the site of his victory on the slopes of Pichincha. Built between 1581 and 1650, the interior of the **Iglesia Santo Domingo** (7am-6:45pm daily), on the west side of the plaza, is an ornate and atmospheric mix of styles, including colonial and Moorish. It is possible to quietly enter the church during the daily services (7am-1pm and 5pm-6:45pm), but tours are only possible between 1pm and 5pm. The attached **Museo Fray Pedro Bedon** (tel. 2/228-0518, 9am-1:30pm and 2:30pm-5pm Mon.-Fri., 9am-2pm Sat., $3) allows entry to the church cupolas and terraces.

From the western corner of Plaza Santo Domingo, turn onto Guayaquil to reach one of the best-preserved colonial streets in Old Town. Also called Calle Juan de Dios Morales, **La Ronda** was nicknamed for the evening serenades (*rondas*) that once floated through the air. The narrow lane is lined with painted balconies, craft shops, tiny art galleries, and cafés. During the day, it's a charming place to wander and relish the lack of traffic (it's a pedestrian-only zone). At night, it's a popular and safe spot for Quiteños and visitors to soak up the atmosphere with a drink of *canelazo* and some traditional music.

Directly below La Ronda, the urban park **Cumandá** (Av. 24 de Mayo, tel. 2/257-3645, Facebook @ quitocumanda, 7am-8pm Mon.-Fri.,

8am-6pm Sat.-Sun., $1-5) is a master-piece of urban renewal. Located in a refurbished former bus station, the park has green spaces and gardens, six swimming pools, a climbing wall, cycling and jogging paths, covered indoor soccer and *ecuavolley* courts, exhibition spaces, children's areas, exercise studios, a gym, a table tennis area, and a chess area. The three-story complex also acts as a cultural center. Check Facebook for event listings. Art and photography exhibits are displayed on the lower levels alongside a sprawling satellite map of Ecuador and a 3-D sculpture of Quito.

MUSEO DE LA CIUDAD AND MONASTERIO EL CARMEN ALTO

Just up from La Ronda is **Museo de la Ciudad** (García Moreno *y* Rocafuerte, tel. 2/228-3883, www.museociudadquito.gob.ec, 9:30am-4:30pm Tues.-Sun., $3), which traces Quito's history from precolonial times to the beginning of the 20th century, with scale models of the city at different periods. Tours in English can be arranged for $1.

Opposite the Museo de la Ciudad, the **Monasterio y Museo del Carmen Alto** (tel. 2/281-513, 9:30am-5:30pm Wed.-Sun., $3), was the home of Santa Mariana de Jesús from 1618 to 1645. Abandoned children were once passed through a small window in the patio to be raised by the nuns. Exhibitions focus on religious art, the history of the monastery, and the life of Santa Mariana de Jesús. A small adjacent shop sells cookies, chocolate, honey, creams, and herbs. The **Arco de la Reina** (Queen's Arch) over García Moreno marks the original southern entrance to Quito's center.

IGLESIA DE LA MERCED AND VICINITY

The entrance to one of Quito's most modern churches, **Iglesia de la Merced,** completed in 1742, is on Chile, just up from the corner of Cuenca. The 47-meter (154-ft) tower contains the city's largest bell. The church is dedicated to Our Lady of Mercy, whose statue inside is said to have saved the city from an eruption of Pichincha in 1575. To the left of the altar is the entrance to the **Monasterio de la Merced,** housing Quito's oldest clock, built in London in 1817. There are many paintings by Victor Mideros depicting the catastrophes of 1575.

Across Mejía is the **Museo Nacional de Arte Colonial** (Cuenca *y* Mejía, tel. 2/228-2297, 9am-5pm Tues.-Sat., $2), home to Quito's finest collection of colonial art, including works by Miguel de Santiago, Caspicara, and Bernardo de Legarda.

TOP EXPERIENCE

✪ LA BASÍLICA DEL VOTO NACIONAL

Walk eight blocks northeast from Plaza Grande on Venezuela to reach **La Basílica del Voto Nacional** (Carchi 122 *y* Venezuela, tel. 2/228-9428, 8am-6pm daily, $2). Even though construction began in 1892, the church is still officially unfinished. Inside, the gray interior is illuminated by dappled colored light from the stained-glass windows, making a peaceful change from the gaudiness of many other churches. The basilica is famous for its mystical gargoyles in the form of pumas, monkeys, penguins, tortoises, and condors, and for the spectacular views from the spire. Its two imposing 115-meter (377-ft) towers make this the tallest church in Ecuador, and the climb to the top isn't for the faint of heart, but those that dare are rewarded with a wonderful panorama of the Old City. A separate ticket, available from the window labeled "Administración General Boletería" in the square in front of the church, is required to enter the tower (9am-4pm daily, $2). An elevator goes as far as a café and gift shop; those wishing to go higher must rely on their legs and nerves. If you're feeling brave, head through the gift shop, then across a narrow wooden bridge over the nave of the church and up a series of metal ladders. It's also possible to climb a small metal staircase to look inside the clock tower.

IGLESIA SAN AGUSTÍN AND VICINITY

If you've seen enough ornate gold to last a lifetime, the **Iglesia San Agustín** (Chile *y* Guayaquil, 7:30am-noon and 2pm-5pm Tues.-Fri., 8am-noon Sat.-Sun.) offers something different, with its pastel frescoes and elegant chandeliers. The adjoining **Convento y Museo de San Agustín** (tel. 2/295-1001, 9am-12:30pm and 2pm-5pm Mon.-Fri., 9am-1pm Sat., $2) features a feast of colonial artwork on the walls and surrounds a palm-filled cloister. Ecuador's declaration of independence was signed in the *sala capitular* on August 10, 1809. Many of the heroes who battled for independence are buried in the crypt.

PLAZA DEL TEATRO AND VICINITY

This small plaza at Guayaquil and Manabí is surrounded by restored colonial buildings, including the **Teatro Nacional Sucre** (tel. 2/295-1661, www.teatrosucre.com, Facebook @ TeatroSucreQ). Erected in 1878, it's

pastel frescoes in the Iglesia San Agustín

one of the country's finest theaters, hosting frequent plays and concerts, including opera, jazz, ballet, and international traveling groups. Tucked in the far corner is the renovated **Teatro Variedades** (tel. 2/295-1661, ext. 125, Facebook @TeatroVariedadesQuito), part of the same organization as the Teatro Sucre. Check Facebook for listings. Next door is the popular **Café Teatro.**

TEATRO BOLÍVAR

Built in 1933, the 2,200-seat **Teatro Bolívar** (Pasaje Espejo 847 *y* Guayaquil, tel. 2/228-5278, www.teatrobolivar.org) was designed by the famous American theater architects Hoffman and Henon in a lavish eclectic style, combining art deco, Spanish, and classical motifs. Sadly, the theater was scorched by a fire in 1999, only two years after an extensive restoration. After appearing on the World Monuments Watch's "100 Most Endangered Sites" list in 2004, funds were raised for another restoration, which was 85 percent complete at the time of writing. The theater reopened to the public in early 2016, and ticket prices help to fund the remaining work.

SANTA CATALINA

The **Convent Museo Santa Catalina** (Espejo *y* Flores, tel. 2/228-4000, 1pm-5pm Mon.-Fri., 9am-1pm Sat., $2.50) is attached to the church of the same name. The remains of assassinated president Gabriel García Moreno rested here secretly for many years before being buried under the cathedral. His heart is still buried in the private chapel. There is also an extensive display of religious art and artifacts. A guided tour is included.

ABOVE OLD TOWN
EL PANECILLO

Old Town's skyline is dominated by a 30-meter (98-ft) statue of the **Virgen del Panecillo** (Calle Palestina, tel. 2/317-1985, www.virgendelpanecillo.com) on the hill at the southern end. The Virgin Mary is depicted preparing to take flight, with a chained dragon at her feet. You can climb up inside the base (9am-5pm Mon.-Wed., 9am-9pm Thurs.-Sun., $1) to an observation platform for views of the city from an altitude of 3,027 meters (9,931 ft) above sea level. The neighborhood at the foot of the hill and on the way up is dangerous, so take a taxi and ask the driver to wait. A round-trip taxi ride from Old Town is $5-8, including a short wait.

ITCHIMBÍA PARK AND CULTURAL CENTER

The old Santa Clara market building—imported from Hamburg in 1899 and brought to the highlands by mule, in sections—has been transported from Old Town and rebuilt in all its glory on top of a hill to the east. The glass structure, known as the Palacio de Cristal (Crystal Palace), is now the **Itchimbía Cultural Center** (José María Aguirre, tel. 2/322-6363, Facebook @ItchimbiaCentroCultural). It hosts occasional exhibitions and events, but the more common reason to come here is the view. The vicinity is more pleasant than around El Panecillo, and it's not as hair-raising as climbing the basilica. The center is surrounded by 34-hectare (84-acre) **Itchimbía Park** (*entre* Av. Velasco Ibarra *y* José María Aguirre), which is being reforested and laced with footpaths. Just below on Samaniego is the restaurant **Mosaico** (www.cafemosaicoecuador.com), along with other bars and cafés offering wonderful views. A taxi from Old Town costs $3.

BETWEEN OLD TOWN AND NEW TOWN
PARQUE LA ALAMEDA

Ornamental lakes and a monument to Simón Bolívar sit at opposite ends of this triangular park. Parque La Alameda is bounded by Avenidas Gran Colombia, 10 de Agosto, and Luis Sodiro. Many of the large trees were planted in 1887, when it was a botanical garden. In the center stands South America's oldest astronomical observatory, **Observatorio Astronómico de Quito** (tel. 2/257-0765, http://oaq.epn.edu.ec, 9am-5pm Mon.-Sat., $2), inaugurated in 1864. Night visits can be arranged Tuesday-Thursday via the website. The beautiful old building also houses a **museum** (9am-5pm Mon.-Sat.) filled with books, photos, and antique astronomical tools.

PARQUE EL EJIDO

Quito's most popular central park is all that remains of the common grazing lands that once stretched for more than 10 kilometers (6.2 mi) to the north. **El Ejido** (bounded by Avenidas 6 de Diciembre, Patria, 10 Agosto, and Tarqui) played its part in one of the most infamous moments in Ecuador's history, when liberal president Eloy Alfaro's body was dragged here and burned following his assassination. These days, it's a great spot for people watching. Courts for *ecuavolley* (the local version of volleyball) occupy the northwest corner of the park, and there is often a game to watch. A children's playground takes up the northeast corner. On weekends, the area near the arch at Amazonas and Patria becomes an outdoor arts and crafts market. At the time of writing,

a section of the park was closed for the construction of a Metro station, anticipated to be finished in 2019.

CASA DE LA CULTURA

On the northern edge of Parque El Ejido, the **Casa de la Cultura** (Av. 6 de Diciembre *y* Av. Patria, www.casadelacultura.gob.ec) may look like a convention center but in fact houses some of Ecuador's most well-known museums. At the time of writing, the main museums were closed for refurbishment and no reopening date had been set. This affects the **Museo del Banco Central,** the **Sala de Arqueología,** and the **Sala de Arte Colonial.**

Still open are the **Museo Etnográfico** (Ethnographic Museum, Facebook @museoetnograficocce) and the **Museo de Arte Moderno e Instrumentos Musicales** (Museum of Modern Art & Musical Instruments) (both 9am-4:45pm Mon.-Fri., free). The **Agora,** a huge concert arena in the center of the building, still hosts concerts, and the Casa de la Cultura exhibition space is open. Check the website for upcoming events and exhibits. There's also a cinema showing art and cultural films most evenings.

NEW TOWN
MUSEO ABYA-YALA

The small **Abya Yala** complex (12 de Octubre *y* Wilson, tel. 2/396-2899, www.abyayala.org) contains a bookstore with the city's best selection of works on the indigenous cultures of Ecuador. Shops downstairs sell snacks, crafts, and natural medicines, while the second floor is taken up by the small but well-organized **Museo Abya-Yala** (previously Museo Amazónico, 8:30am-1pm and 2pm-5:30pm Mon.-Fri., $2). The museum has two areas: archaeological

New Town Quito

To Old Town

LARREA

Pérez Guerrero

Mariscal

San Gregorio

VERSAILLES

DÁVALOS

MARCHENA

ULLOA

MERCADILLO

MARCHENA

CORDERO

SANTA CLARA MARKET

CRISTÓBAL COLÓN SPANISH SCHOOL

CARRIÓN

CAMARI

DARQUEA

10 DE AGOSTO

MINISTERIO DE RELACIONES EXTERIORES

Parque El Ejido ART FAIR

Parque El Ejido

AV. PATRIA

Casa de la Cultura

PÉREZ GUERRERO

CARRIÓN

ROCA

PÁEZ

Santa Clara

Park

VEINTIMILLA

Colón

COLÓN

AZCÚNUBI

18 DE SEPTIEMBRE

JORGE WASHINGTON

OCTUBRE

CULTURA MANOR

AMAZONAS

MÍDGENS POD HOSTEL

YOGA CHAI

TEATRO PATIO DE COMEDIAS

CASA DE LA CULTURA

UNIVERSIDAD CATÓLICA

POLITÉCNICA

LA MARISCAL

GALERÍA BELTRÁN

REINA VICTORIA

ROBLES

RINCÓN DE FRANCIA

HOSTEL LUZ ROBLES

LA COUPOLE

SAKTI

TOURIST POLICE

CHANDANI TANDOORI

SANTA MARÍA

ORELLANA

SOUTH AMERICAN LANGUAGE CENTER

PARRILLADAS COLUMBIA

NINA

FOCH

TAMAYO

PLAZA FLORA

Galo Plaza

NUEVO MUNDO EXPEDITIONS

9 DE DICIEMBRE

VEINTIMILLA

BAALBEK

Plaza Foch

Plaza Manuela Cañizares

MANOSALVAS

CALAMA

DIEGO DE ALMAGRO

JUAN LEÓN MERA

CASA DE MI ABUELA

LA BODEGUITA DE CUBA

LA PINTA

LA RÁBIDA

HOSTAL DE LA RÁBIDA

CROSS BAR

LA LENGUA SPANISH SCHOOL

ADAM'S RIB

MINDALAE ETHNIC MUSEUM

CEVICHERÍA

LA NIÑA

BIKING DUTCHMAN

MANOLO

To La Disco Bitch, Zazu, La Paella Valenciana

MERA

ORELLANA

Café Libro

12 DE OCTUBRE

MUSEO ABYA-YALA

MADRID

GALICIA

ANDALUCÍA

VALLADOLID

BOTÁNICA

ISABEL LA CATÓLICA

SIMÓN BOLÍVAR SPANISH SCHOOL

ANAHÍ BOUTIQUE HOTEL

EL HUECO, TERCER MILENIO EVOLUTION

LA PETITE MARISCAL

ALADDIN

COSA NOSTRA

ILIANA

PLAZA CLARON

BAQUEDANO

CORDERO

MORENO

Baca Ortiz

SURTREK

FOLKLORE OLGA FISCH

SAN IGNACIO

ALMAGRO

PINZÓN

COLÓN

ORELLANA

CORUÑA

GONZÁLEZ SUÁREZ

MORA

URKO

NOE SUSHI BAR

ALEIDA'S HOSTAL

SALAZAR

CORUÑA

To Guápulo

HOTEL QUITO

MIRADOR DE GUÁPULO

TANDANA

To Chez Jérôme, Trattoria Sol e Luna

Tranvía
- .... Ecovía Line
- — — — Trole Line
- ■ Trol e/ Ecovía Stop
- Metrobús

0   150 yds
0   150 m

© MOON.COM

SEE "MARISCAL SUCRE" MAP

replicas of pre-Columbian ceramic masks at Mindalae Ethnic Museum

and ethnographic. The latter is the most interesting, focusing entirely on Amazonian cultures. Two rooms exhibit instruments, clothing, and ceramics from various indigenous nationalities; the third is dedicated to the Shuar people and is the only exhibition in Quito with permission to display real *tsantsas* (shrunken heads). One impactful display contrasts photos of rainforest flora and fauna with images of oil spills to raise awareness of the biggest threat faced by the Ecuadorian Amazon: oil exploitation.

MINDALAE ETHNIC MUSEUM

Run by the Sinchi Sacha Foundation, which promotes indigenous cultures, fair trade, and responsible tourism, the **Mindalae Ethnic Museum** (Reina Victoria *y* La Niña, tel. 2/223-0609, www.mindalae.com.ec, 9am-5:30pm Mon.-Sat., $3) has five floors with comprehensive collections of ethnic clothing, artifacts, and pottery from all regions, with signage in English. The shamanic-themed room on the top floor is especially interesting, with displays showing the ceremonial altars of contemporary shamans from the coast, Andes, and Amazon. The ceramics are replicas of ancient pieces, lovingly recreated by the descendants of the original cultures. The attached fair trade store, beautifully arranged by region, is one of the best places in Quito to pick up souvenirs and crafts, with items such as coffee, chocolate, "Panama" hats, ceramics, woven goods, embroidered shirts, jewelry, and wooden bowls. There is also a restaurant.

NORTH OF NEW TOWN
PARQUE LA CAROLINA

To escape the concrete of New Town without actually leaving the city, head for Quito's largest park, **Parque La Carolina,** bounded by Avenidas de los Shyris, Naciones Unidas, Amazonas, de la República, and Eloy Alfaro. Popular with early morning joggers and families, it's a great spot for people watching and sampling typical street food. The impressive facilities include courts for tennis, basketball, football, and *ecuavolley*; athletics and cycle tracks; a skate park; a children's play area; a lake with paddleboats; and a gym. Like most of Quito's parks, it's not safe after dark.

Three museums are located on Rumipamba, one of the two boulevards that bisect the park. The **Vivarium** (tel. 2/227-1820, www.vivarium.org.ec, 9:30am-1pm and 1:30pm-5:30pm Tues.-Sun., $3.75) houses more than 100 reptiles and amphibians, including boa constrictors, in relatively spacious tanks with plenty of vegetation. To retreat farther from the city bustle and get your nature fix, visit the **Jardín Botánico** (tel. 3/332-516, www.jardinbotanicoquito.com, 8am-4:45pm daily, $3.50), which showcases Ecuador's vast array of flora, including a bonsai exhibition and 500 species of orchid. Natural history is the focus of the recently refurbished **Instituto Nacional de Biodiversidad** (tel. 2/244-9824, 8am-4:45pm Mon. and Fri., 9am-4:45pm Tues.-Thurs., 10am-4pm Sat.), next to the botanical gardens.

MUSEO FUNDACIÓN GUAYASAMÍN AND CAPILLA DEL HOMBRE

East of Parque La Carolina, up a steep hill in the Bellavista neighborhood, the former home of Ecuador's most famous artist has been converted into the **Museo Fundación Guayasamín** (Mariano Calvache *y* Lorenzo Chávez, tel. 2/244-6455, www.guayasamin.org, 10am-5pm daily, $8). Guayasamín designed the house himself and filled it with pre-Columbian, colonial, and contemporary art. His own large-scale paintings are alternately tender

and tortured, but always deeply emotive. The artist is buried beneath the Tree of Life in the garden just above the museum.

Completed three years after his death in 1999 by the Guayasamín Foundation, the **Capilla del Hombre (Chapel of Man)** is dedicated to the struggles endured by the indigenous peoples of the Americas. Huge paintings fill the open two-story building. In the center is a circular space beneath an unfinished dome mural portraying the workers who died in the silver mines of Potosí, Bolivia. Other works cover topics both heartwarming and wrenching, from the tenderness of a mother and child's embrace in *La Ternura* to the gigantic *Bull and Condor,* symbolizing the struggle between Spanish and Andean identities.

A guided tour in Spanish or English is obligatory in the museum, but visitors are free to wander the Chapel of Man unattended. Entrance to both is included in the ticket. To get there, take a bus bound for Bellavista from Parque La Carolina (marked "Batan-Colmena") or hail a taxi ($2-3). Taxis wait by the main entrance for the return journey.

OTHER AREAS
GUÁPULO

Just behind Hotel Quito is the **Mirador de Guápulo,** a viewing platform looking down over the charming hillside neighborhood of Guápulo, where the cobblestone streets and lush green park provide a welcome break from the noise and bustle of the city. Take the precipitous Camino de Orellana down the hill to reach the beautiful **Iglesia de Guápulo,** built between 1644 and 1693.

A 15-minute walk up the road

behind the church is **Parque Guápulo** (Av. de los Conquistadores, 6am-6:30pm daily) Previously a wealthy banker's estate, the park has attractive running and walking paths, a lake, an exhibition area, a camping ground, and a children's play area. There is an exit near the lake and parking lot where it is possible to flag down a bus or taxi.

TELEFÉRIQO CABLE CAR

Completed in 2005, the **TelefériQo** (tel. 2/222-2996 or 99/736-0360, www.teleferico.com.ec, 8am-8pm daily, $8.50) ascends the slope of the Pichincha volcano. It departs from above Avenida Occidental, where a tourist center with restaurants, go-karting, and a small theme park has been built. The 2.5-kilometer (1.6-mi) ride to the top takes about 10 minutes, and the views over the city and the Andes from 4,050 meters (13,285 ft) make it worth the entrance fee. On a clear day, it is possible to see an impressive chain of volcanoes, including Cayambe, Chimborazo, and Cotopaxi. Adrenaline seekers can bring a mountain bike and make the return descent on two wheels, or hike to the volcano Rucu Pichincha. Those making the hike should bring an experienced guide, start early, and allow five hours for the round-trip. Assaults and muggings have been reported on the way, although there are now police patrols on the weekend. Do not attempt this climb alone, and don't take valuables. See the *Sports and Recreation* section of this chapter for recommended guides.

There are no public transport options for the TelefériQo. Take a taxi ($3) from the closest trolley station at Mariana de Jesús to Avenida Occidental at the bottom of the hill, then continue on foot, by taxi (another $2), or on the free shuttle bus for the VulQano Park theme park, which is next to the TelefériQo. It's cold at the top so bring warm clothes.

Entertainment and Events

NIGHTLIFE

Quito has a thriving nightlife scene centered around Plaza Foch, Reina Victoria, and Calama in the **Mariscal Sucre** neighborhood. These blocks heave with locals and visitors on Thursday, Friday, and Saturday evenings. The party doesn't really get going until after 11pm, but live music usually starts earlier, between 9pm and 10:30pm. Although the sale of alcohol is officially illegal after midnight Monday-Thursday and after 2am Friday-Saturday, almost no drinking establishments respect this law, though most close before 3am. Many bars and clubs (and even some restaurants) are closed on Sunday and/or Monday. Remember to take your ID, whatever your age, as many places won't let you in without it. Clubs usually have a small cover charge ($3-5), which includes a drink. Bars often have happy hours 5pm-8pm to bring in the early crowds, and several have ladies' nights with free drinks before 10pm. The opening hours listed here were correct at the time of writing; check Facebook pages for updates before venturing out.

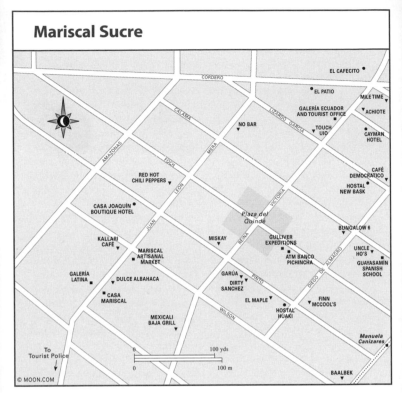

Mariscal Sucre

As well as the most popular nightlife spot, Mariscal Sucre is the most risky area for foreign visitors. Walk just a couple of blocks from the main drag and the police presence is replaced by groups of thieves or drug dealers. After dark, it's recommended to take a pre-booked taxi from your hotel to your destination, even if it's only a few blocks away. Ask a hotel or bar in La Mariscal to call you a taxi for the return journey, rather than flagging one down in the street. This is a hotspot for "express kidnappings," where shady taxi drivers rob passengers and leave them by the side of the road, usually unharmed. Don't take valuables, credit cards, or more cash than necessary. Drink spiking is common, so don't leave your beverage unattended. Don't accept flyers from anyone on the street, as they may be dusted with scopolamine, a substance which leaves victims in a docile state, vulnerable to robbery or assault.

BARS, PUBS, AND LATE-NIGHT CAFÉS

A block from Plaza Foch, Irish-run **Finn McCool's** (Diego de Almagro *y* Joaquín Pinto, tel. 2/252-1780, www.irishpubquito.com, noon-1am Mon.-Wed., noon-3am Thurs., 11am-3am Fri.-Sat., 11am-7pm Sun.) is an eternal favorite with visitors and locals alike. It has friendly staff, a warm fire, filling Irish pub food, pool, darts, foosball, and live sports on the TV. It's a good spot to meet people in the early evening, and the party gets lively as the night goes on. **Dirty Sanchez** (Joaquín Pinto *y* Reina Victoria, tel. 2/255-1810, www.dirtysanchez-bar.com, 5pm-12:30am Mon., 3pm-12:30am Tues.-Thurs., 3pm-2:30am Fri.-Sat.) has an eclectic, alternative vibe with live music and DJs. The "We Love Mondays" DJs nights are popular, when many other places are closed. Another café/bar with live music is **Garúa** (Joaquín Pinto *y* Reina Victoria, tel. 99/713-2226, www.garuacafe.com, 5pm-9:30pm Tues., 5pm-11:45pm Wed.-Fri., 5:30pm-11:45pm Sat.).

Poetry, tango, art, and salsa nights attract an arty crowd to **Café Libro** (Leonidas Plaza *y* Wilson, tel. 2/250-3214, www.cafelibro.com, noon-2pm Mon., noon-2pm and 5pm-11:30pm Tues.-Thurs., noon-2pm and 5pm-2am Fri.-Sat.), one of Quito's most established cultural cafés, opened in 1992.

La Mariscal is not the only option in New Town. If you want a quieter evening, head to the neighborhood of Guápulo, where the stunning view makes any night out special. Perched on a steep hillside, **Ananké** (Camino de Orellana 781, tel. 2/255-1421, 6pm-midnight Mon.-Thurs., 6pm-1am Fri.-Sat., www.anankeguapulo.com) is a bohemian pizzeria and bar with regular live music ranging from jazz to funk, dancehall to blues. On the same street is **Café Arte Guápulo** (tel. 2/513-2424, Facebook @CafeArteGuápulo, 6pm-midnight Mon.-Thurs., 6pm-2am Fri.-Sat.). With good food, hot wine, and *canelazo* (spiced hot fruit punch with *aguardiente*), it's a good place to warm up on chilly nights. There is often live music on weekends and the venue has hosted some big names in the past, including Manu Chao.

Founded over three decades ago,

Ñucanchi Peña (Av. Universitaria *y* Armero, tel. 2/254-0967, Facebook @ Niucanchi, 7:45pm-2:45am Fri.-Sat.) is Quito's most famous *peña*, or traditional music club, where live acts from around Ecuador play every weekend. It's not exactly the hippest scene, though Ecuadorian roots music fans can catch everything from Pacific coast *amorfino* songs to *pasillo* waltzes and Andean panpipes. The interior is small, informal, and often crowded, with blacked-out decor and folk art on the walls.

In Old Town, there are a few good cafés and bars along the regenerated **La Ronda,** several of which offer live music at the weekends. The cobbled street's many small establishments serve empanadas, hot mulled wine, hot chocolate, and *canelazo*. **Leña Quiteña** (tel. 2/228-9416, noon-midnight daily) has wonderful views of the Panecillo from the top floor—a great spot for a romantic evening. Thanks to police presence, La Ronda is safe to walk around at night. **Bandido Brewing** (Olmedo *y* Pedro Fermín Cevallos, tel. 2/228-6504, www.bandidobrewing.com, 4pm-11pm Mon.-Thurs., 4pm-midnight Fri., 2pm-midnight Sat.) is Old Town's first microbrewery, with a rotating variety of craft beers served in a converted chapel by its three friendly, expat owners. There is regular live music.

Wherever you go out, you cannot help but notice that Ecuadorians' salsa-dancing skills leave the rest of us looking like we have two left feet. You can do something about this; take the plunge and get some classes at one of these **dancing schools: Ritmo Tropical Dance Academy** (Amazonas *y* Calama, tel. 2/255-7094, www.ritmotropicalsalsa.com), **Tropical Dancing School** (Veracruz *y* Villalengua,

The cobbled streets of La Ronda are full of little bars and cafés.

tel. 2/245-9991, and Plaza Kendo, República del Salvador *y* Portugal, tel. 2/226-8999, www.tropicaldance.com. ec), and **Son Latino** (Reina Victoria N24-211 *y* Lizardo García, tel. 2/223-4340). Prices start at around $10 pp per hour for one-on-one or couples' lessons.

NIGHTCLUBS

Clubbing in La Mariscal tends to be aimed at the mass market, with a herd mentality. It's noisy and hectic, and you'll either love it or hate it. By far the most popular spot is the American- and British-run **Bungalow 6** (Diego de Almagro *y* Calama, tel. 99/751-0835, www.bungalow6ecuador.com, 8pm-3am Wed.-Sat.), playing mostly electronic and pop. Local students mix with backpackers on three dance floors. Another option is the **No Bar** (Calama *y* Juan León Mera, tel. 2/245-5145, 8pm-3am Wed.-Sat.), one of La Mariscal's most well established clubs. Open since 1994, it plays commercial music over two floors. **Blues** (República 476 *y* Pradera, tel. 99/985-1138, Facebook @ClubBlues, 9pm-3am Wed. and Fri.-Sat.) plays a mix of electronic and rock.

With one location in La Mariscal and another on the edge of Old Town just north of the basilica, **Café Democrático** (www.cafedemo-cratico.wordpress.com, Facebook @ DemocraQuito) offers a different late-night experience, catering to Quito's alternative crowd. There are cultural events, DJs, and live music several times a week. The La Mariscal location (Lizardo García *y* Diego de Almagro, tel. 2/603-4775, 6pm-3am Tues.-Sat.) has a café menu, and the Old Town location (in the Centro de Arte Contemporáneo, Montevideo *y* Luis Dávila, tel. 2/315-0008, 10am-1am Tues.-Sat., 10am-9pm Sun.) has a full restaurant menu.

There are a few **gay bars and clubs** in Quito. One of the best known confusingly has three names: **El Hueco / Tercer Milenio / Evolution** (Veintemilla *y* Av. 12 de Octubre, tel.

98/729-9228, Facebook @discotecat-ercermilenio, 10pm-3am Fri.-Sat.) and mostly plays pop music. **TOUCH Uio** (Joaquín Pinto *y* Juan León Mera, tel. 98/304-6843, 6pm-2am Tues.-Wed., 6pm-3am Thurs., 8am-3am Fri.-Sat.) is primarily a lesbian club. By Parque La Carolina is **Kika Dance Club** (Japón E569 *y* Av. Amazonas, tel. 99/750-8228, Facebook @fedearguel-lok, Thurs.-Sat. 9pm-4am). It's smaller than El Hueco and more trendy. It has an open bar with $10 entry before midnight and then turns into a disco playing Latino pop music, as does **La Disco Bitch** (Av. 6 de Diciembre *y* Av. República, tel. 99/966-4311, Facebook @EsLaDiscoB, 10pm-2:30am Fri.-Sat.).

THEATER, DANCE AND MUSIC

The municipality's website **Quito Culture** (www.quitocultura.info) is the best place to find cultural events, including music, theater, exhibitions, cinema, and festivals.

The **Casa de la Cultura** (6 de Diciembre *y* La Patria, tel. 5/352-8014, www.casadelacultura.gob.ec) is the city's leading venue for theater, dance, and classical music. The colorful, indigenous-themed **Jacchigua Ecuadorian Folklore Ballet** (tel. 2/295-2025, www.eng.jacchigua.org) performs here at 7:30pm every Wednesday ($35, $82 with dinner). **Casa de la Música** (Valderrama *y* Av. Mariana de Jesús, tel. 2/226-7093, www.casadelamusica.ec) is an excellent venue for classical music, jazz, and ballet, hosting regular concerts for as little as $5-10.

The **Ballet Nacional de Ecuador** (Manuel Abascal N40-63 *y* Gaspar de Villarroel, Facebook @balletnacionalecuador) puts on shows in a variety of styles, from urban to traditional ballet. Shows are often at their own theater, at Casa de la Música or Casa de la Cultura.

Quito has several excellent theaters. The 19th-century **Teatro Sucre** (Plaza del Teatro, tel. 2/295-1661, www.teatrosucre.com, Facebook @TeatroSucreQ) is Ecuador's national theater and one of the best. Also on Plaza del Teatro and part of the same organization is **Teatro Variedades** (tel. 2/295-1661, ext. 125, Facebook @TeatroVariedadesQuito). Check Facebook for listings. The iconic **Teatro Bolívar** (Pasaje Espejo *y* Guayaquil, tel. 2/228-5278, www.teat-robolivar.org) has been reopened following a devastating fire, and ticket prices help fund the remaining refurbishment work. The **Patio de Comedias** (18 de Septiembre *entre* 9 de Octubre *y* Av. Amazonas, tel. 2/256-1902, www.patiodecomedias.org) is a good spot to catch a play Thursday-Sunday in a more intimate atmosphere with dinner options available.

Quito's biggest rock and pop concerts take place at the **Coliseo Rumiñahui** and **Estadio Olímpico.** A good website for tickets to upcoming events is Ecutickets (www.ecutickets.ec).

FESTIVALS

The annual week-long **Fiestas de Quito** celebrate the founding of the city, culminating on December 6. The festivities include parades, fireworks, street parties, and concerts.

The **Verano de las Artes Quito** (Summer of Arts) is an annual cultural program that takes place in August, incorporating musical and theater events and light shows.

Sports and Recreation

CLIMBING AND MOUNTAINEERING
CLIMBING COMPANIES

A few of Quito's tour companies specialize in climbing, with the experience to get you back down in one piece should anything go wrong. Prices vary from $70 per person for easier climbs, such as the Pichinchas, to $220-350 per person for a two-day ascent of Cotopaxi.

The **Ecuadorian Association of Mountain Guides** (tel. 2/254-0599, www.aseguim.org) is a guide and mountain rescue cooperative that trains and certifies mountain guides. On its Members page are listed the contact details of guides who speak English, German, French, and Italian. **Andean Face** (Luis Coloma y Av. El Inca, tel. 2/245-6135, www.andeanface.com) is a Dutch-Ecuadorian company specializing in climbing and trekking in Ecuador. They can arrange anything from a Cotopaxi trek to a weeks-long tour of all the country's peaks. Andean Face supports the Daniëlle Children's Fund, an NGO working with Ecuador's street children. **Ecuadorian Alpine Institute** (Ramírez Dávalos y Amazonas, 1st floor, Oficina 102, tel. 2/256-5465, www.volcanoclimbing.com) has well-organized, professionally run climbs and treks in English, German, French, and Spanish.

CLIMBING AND CAMPING EQUIPMENT

Quito has by far the best selection of outdoor gear stores in the country. Everything from plastic climbing boots and harnesses to tents, sleeping bags, and stoves is readily available, although not always of the highest quality. Large-size footgear (U.S. size 12 and up) may be hard to find. Be aware that imported items will come at a high markup.

Equipos Cotopaxi (6 de Diciembre y Jorge Washington, tel. 2/225-0038, www.equiposcotopaxi.com) sells equipment for mountaineering, fishing, camping, trekking, cycling, swimming, astronomy, bird-watching, and canoeing. The company makes its own sleeping bags, backpacks, and tents for less than you'd pay for imported items. Equipos Cotopaxi also owns the following stores, which sell a similar range of products: **Antisana Sport** (tel. 2/246-7433, www.antisana.com.ec) in the El Bosque Shopping Center; **Camping Sport** (Av. Colón y Reina Victoria, tel. 2/252-1626, Facebook @CampingSport); and **Aventura Sport** (tel. 2/292-4372, Facebook @ AventuraSportEc) in the Quicentro mall. The various **Marathon Sports** outlets in the malls stock light-use sportswear.

CYCLING & MOUNTAIN BIKING

The **Aries Bike Company** (Av. Interoceanica km 22.5, Vía Pifo, La Libertad, tel. 2/389-5712, www.ariesbikecompany.com) near the airport offers 1- to 14-day biking and hiking tours all over Ecuador. Popular options include the cloud forest near Quito, Papallacta hot springs, Otavalo, Pichincha, Cotopaxi National Park, Chimborazo, and Quilotoa. The guides speak English, Dutch, and Spanish.

Biking Dutchman (La Pinta y Reina Victoria, tel. 2/254-2806, www.bikingdutchman.com) runs well-reviewed day trips to Cotopaxi, Papallacta, and the Tandayapa-Mindo area. The 30-kilometer (19-mi) descent of Cotopaxi is thrilling! Longer trips range 2-8 days.

Every Sunday 8am-2pm, a 30-kilometer (19-mi) north-south section of road through Quito is closed to motorized vehicles and open only to cyclists, skateboarders, skaters, runners, and walkers. For a map of the **CicloPaseo** route, which includes Parque La Carolina, Parque Ejido, and Plaza Grande, see www.ciclopolisecuador.wixsite.com/ciclopolis/ciclopaseo-quito. **Ciclopolis** (tel. 2/604-2079) rents bicycles from one hour ($2.50) to a morning ($8). Their rental locations at Tribuna del Sur and the Bicentennial Park are marked on the map. Two forms of ID are required. Another option is the **Quito Bike Rental Network** (tel. 98/401-4852, Facebook @ QuitoBikeRentalNetwork), which has 3 locations: Dulce Albahaca (Juan León Mera y Wilson); El Cafecito (La Reina Victoria y Cordero); and Lord Guau (Cumbayá, one block from the Chaquiñán entrance).

RAFTING AND KAYAKING

The **Río Blanco** and **Río Toachi** provide the nearest year-round white water to Quito, 3 hours from the capital. The Toachi (Class III-III+) is closest to the city and is therefore Ecuador's most rafted river, though not its most pristine. It's navigable all year and is particularly good during the high water season from January to the end of May. Much cleaner and more beautiful is the Upper Río Blanco (Class III), though the water

CicloPaseo

can be too low to navigate June-December. Kayakers can take on **Río Mindo** (Class III-IV), **Río Saloya** (IV-V), **Río Pilatón** (IV-V), and the upper **Río Toachi** (IV-V), depending on the time of year and their ability. A highly recommended company is **Torrent Duck** (Gonzáles Suárez *y* Eloy Alfaro, Tumbaco, tel. 99/867-9933, www.torrent-duck.com), for their excellent customer service and environmental responsibility. **Rios Ecuador** (www.riosecuador.com) is the most well-established operator of white-water trips out of Quito, charging $87 for a rafting day trip to Ríos Toachi and Blanco, $299 for 2 days. Customized itineraries are possible, as are kayak rentals and courses.

Only a 90-minute drive from the capital, but more seasonal, is **Baeza** on the **Río Quijos** (Class III-IV), where there is excellent rafting and kayaking between October and February. Class III-V kayaking is also available on the nearby **Ríos Oyacachi** and **Cosanga,** with the Cosanga Gorge a highlight. Local family-run **Baeza Tours** (Facebook @BaezaToursEcuador) offers rafting and kayaking for $65-75 pp per day and kayaking courses ranging from two days/one night ($180 pp) to four days/three nights ($360 pp), including accommodations. Companies in Quito also offer tours in the Baeza area.

HORSEBACK RIDING

Ride Andes (tel. 9/973-8221, www.rideandes.com) offers top-quality riding tours through the highlands, using local horse wranglers, support vehicles, and healthy animals. Options range from $110 pp for a one-day tour for two people to 7- to 10-day trips

staying in some of the country's plushest haciendas.

Green Horse Ranch (tel. 8/612-5433, www.horseranch.de) offers riding trips starting from the Pululahua Crater for people of all experience levels. Prices range from $95 pp for one day, to $250 pp for two days, and up to $1,550 pp for the eight-day Secrets of the Andes tour. Multilingual guides accompany all trips.

SPECTATOR SPORTS

Soccer (*fútbol*) is by far the most popular sport in Ecuador. The best place to see a game in Quito is the **Estadio Atahualpa** (6 de Diciembre *y* Naciones Unidas) when the national team plays. Check www.elnacional.ec for details of the next match. Tickets can be bought at the stadium. Take the Ecovia to the Naciones Unidas stop to get there. The **Casa Blanca,** which is the stadium of **Liga de Quito,** the city's most successful club, has home games several times per month. Buy tickets ahead of time at the stadium, which is a few minutes' walk from the Ofelia bus terminal.

YOGA

Yoga Chai (9 de Octubre *y* Jerónimo Carrión, tel. 99/452-9962, http://yogachaivegan.com) is a yoga and dance studio and vegan café in La Mariscal.

CITY TOURS

The municipality of Quito has put together an excellent map of themed historic walks through Old Town, available at the Plaza Grande tourist office, where it is also possible to book **multilingual tours** given by municipal police.

Carpe Diem Adventures offers a free **Old Town Walking Tour** (Antepara *y* Los Ríos, tel. 2/295-4713,

ETHICAL TOUR AGENCIES

Quito has many excellent tour agencies that offer expertise, local knowledge, and the peace of mind that comes with knowing that accommodations, food, and logistics are taken care of. The following companies are recommended for their quality, professionalism, and policies of **environmental** and/or **social responsibility.** Please note that most are closed on weekends. Don't be surprised if you're asked to pay in advance by Western Union or PayPal.

- **Neotropical Nature & Birding Trips** is based at El Quinde Visitors Center on the corner of the Plaza Grande (Palacio Municipal, Venezuela y Espejo, tel. 99/252-5251, www.neotropicalecuador.com). Tours include Quito day trips, Amazon lodges, Galápagos cruises, and the Avenue of the Volcanoes. This Ecuadorian-owned, family-run ecotourism agency supports sustainable development in fragile and threatened ecosystems throughout Ecuador, working with locally managed ecotourism projects.

- **GreenGo Travel** (Española 161 y Rumiñahui, tel. 2/603-4262, www.greengotravel. com) is an Ecuadorian-owned ecotour agency offering a broad range of experiences, from city day tours to extensive two-week programs all over mainland Ecuador and the Galápagos.

- **Enchanted Expeditions** (De las Alondras N45-102 y Los Lirios, tel. 2/334-0525, www.enchantedexpeditions.com) covers the entire country, with a focus on the Galápagos—the boats *Cachalote* and *Beluga* receive frequent praise.

- **Gulliver Expeditions** (Juan León Mera N24-156 y José Calama, tel. 2/252-8030, www.gulliver.com.ec) offers a huge range of climbing, biking, horseback riding, and sightseeing tours nationwide, including many one-day options. Gulliver's supports a day-care center for Ecuadorian children.

- **Nuevo Mundo Expeditions** (Vicente Ramón Roca N21-293 y Leonidas Plaza, tel. 2/450-5412, www.nuevomundoexpeditions.com) was started in 1979 by a founder and former president of the Ecuadorian Ecotourism Association. Among the offerings are an Amazon cruise and a Shamanism & Natural Healing Tour.

- **Happy Gringo Travel** (Oficina 207, Edificio Catalina Plaza, Aldaz N34-155 y Portugal, tel. 2/512-3486, www.happygringo.com) offers a wide variety of tours all over Ecuador. Best known for their Cuyabeno trips, they have also designed an eight-day Responsible Traveler tour of the Andes that includes several eco- and community tourism destinations. The agency was given the UNESCO-recognized Smart Voyager award for its ecological practices.

- **Surtrek** (Calle San Ignacio E10-114 y Plácido Caamaño, tel. 2/250-0660, www.surtrek-adventures.com) offers a wide range of high-end ecotourism and adventures tours. The agency is Rainforest Alliance Certified.

- **Destination Ecuador** (U.S. tel. 888/207-8615, https://destinationecuador.com) is an ecotourism company specializing in responsible, community-based tourism. Best-sellers include Galápagos land-based tours and cruises, a Cotopaxi hiking tour, and an Andes to Amazon wildlife adventure. Headed by Andy Drumm of the Ecuadorian Ecotourism Association, their trips have won awards for socially responsible tourism.

www.carpedm.ca, 10:30am Mon.-Fri.) that explores plazas, churches, and other colonial sights. Tours leave from the Secret Garden hostel. **Quito Street Tours** (Guipuzcoa y Coruña, tel. 99/886-0539, www.quitostreettours. com) focuses on local food and street art on their walking tours of La Floresta and Guápulo (free, but donations of $5-10 are appreciated).

The **Quito Tour Bus** (tel. 2/245-8010, www.quitotourbus.com, 8:30am-4pm daily, 7pm Fri.-Sat., $15) provides a hop-on hop-off bus service with 12 stops across the city, including Plaza Grande, La Compañía, El Panecillo, La Basílica, the TelefériQo, and the major parks. The nighttime tour includes a one-hour stop at La Ronda. Audio is available in English, Spanish, French, and German. Tickets can be bought online or at various points across the city, including Plaza Foch and Plaza Grande. There are also daily tours to Otavalo, Papallacta, Cotopaxi, and Quilotoa.

Ecuador Freedom Bike Rentals (Finlandia *y* Suecia, tel. 98/176-2340, www.freedombikerental.com, 10am-6pm daily) offers self-guided GPS tours of the city and surrounding area by motorbike, scooter, or bicycle, plus longer guided or self-guided tours that go farther afield.

Shopping

CRAFTS, SOUVENIRS, ART, JEWELRY, AND ACCESSORIES

In Old Town, one of the best options for souvenirs is **Tianguez** (underneath the Iglesia San Francisco, Plaza San Francisco, tel. 2/257-0233, www.tianguez.org, 9:30am-6:30pm daily). The fair trade store has an excellent selection of high-quality products and handicrafts from around the country, including *paja toquilla* or "Panama" hats, ceramics, masks, woven goods, Tigua paintings, embroidered shirts, *tagua* jewelry, wooden bowls, coffee, and chocolate. An outdoor café serves good Ecuadorian food. Tianguez is run by the Sinchi Sacha Foundation, a nonprofit supporting sustainable development in Ecuador, specializing in ecotourism, fair trade, the restoration of natural and cultural heritage, and the generation of income for populations with scarce resources.

In New Town, **Mindalae Ethnic Museum** (Reina Victoria *y* La Niña, tel. 2/223-0609, www.mindalae.com/ec, 9am-5:30pm Mon.-Sat.) is also operated by the Sinchi Sacha Foundation. The museum houses a large fair trade store selling an even more extensive range of products than Tianguez, beautifully arranged by region.

Another fair trade store in New Town is the **Camari Cooperative** (Antonio de Marchena *y* Versalles, tel. 2/252-3613, www.camari.org), offering a wide selection of handicrafts, clothing, jewelry, and food. Camari is dedicated to providing high-quality Ecuadorian products while helping to better the living conditions of small-scale producers.

A couple of blocks from Plaza Foch, **Galería Ecuador** (Reina Victoria *y* Lizardo García, tel. 2/223-9469, www.galeriaecuador.com, 9am-9pm Mon.-Sat., 10am-8pm Sun.) sells chocolate, coffee, perfumes, handicrafts, clothes, jewelry, books, and music. An official tourist information office and an organic bistro are attached. Another branch of Galería Ecuador can be found in Old Town at El Quinde Visitors Center on the Plaza Grande. The organization works with over a hundred indigenous communities, associations of small-scale producers, and entrepreneurs with organic and fair trade certifications.

Hungarian-born Olga Fisch came to Ecuador to escape the war in Europe in 1939, becoming a world-renowned expert on South American crafts and folklore. **Folklore Olga Fisch** (Av. Colón y Caamaño, tel. 2/254-1315, www.olgafisch.com, 9am-7pm Mon.-Fri., 10am-6pm Sat.), which was her house until her death in 1991, is now a fair trade store selling handmade products, including *paja toquilla* or "Panama" hats, handbags, home decor items, jewelry, and woven goods.

Beautiful, high-quality Andean wool textiles with *tagua* nut buttons can be found at **Hilana** (6 de Diciembre y Veintimilla, tel. 2/254-0714, www.hilana.ec, 9am-7pm Mon.-Fri., 10am-1pm Sun.), with designs inspired by pre-Columbian art.

There is a cluster of art galleries and stores selling handicrafts and antiques on Juan León Mera and Veintimilla. Try **Galería Latina** (Juan León Mera y Veintimilla, tel. 2/222-1098, www. galerialatina-quito.com, 10am-7pm Mon.-Sat., 11am-6pm Sun.) for alpaca clothing, ceramics, and jewelry. **Casa Mariscal** (Juan León Mera y Baquedano, tel. 2/515-3800, @ Facebook CasaMariscalQuito, 10am-7pm Mon.-Sat.) is a fair trade store for hand-made decorative items and fine crafts, including a wide range of jewelry. **La Mariscal Artisanal Market** (Jorge Washington *entre* Juan León Mera y Reina Victoria, tel. 2/512-4716, www.mercadoartesanal.com.ec, 8am-7pm Mon.-Sat., 8am-6pm Sun.) sells just about every souvenir and handicraft available in Ecuador, plus artisanal food items. Quality is variable, and haggling is obligatory.

Hugo Chiliquinga (Huachi y Av. Bernardo de Legarda, tel. 2/259-8822, www.guitarrashugochiliquinga.com, 9am-6pm daily) is considered by many to be the best guitar maker in Ecuador. He may have a waiting list.

For exclusive jewelry designs, stop by the **Museo Fundación Guayasamín** (Mariano Calvache y Lorenzo Chávez, tel. 2/244-6455, www.guayasamin.org, 10am-5pm daily).

A popular place to buy paintings is the **Parque El Ejido Art Fair** (Patria y Amazonas), open all day Saturday-Sunday. Many pieces are imitations of famous works, but you may find some original gems. Haggling is advised. Just north of the park, **Galería Beltrán** (Reina Victoria y Jorge Washington, tel. 2/222-1732, www.galeriabeltran. jimdo.com) has a good selection of paintings by Ecuadorian artists.

On Saturday, dozens of artisans and artists gather in Plaza Foch from 10:30am to 8pm to sell work in wood, *tagua,* glass, fabric, leather, and recycled paper. Organic products such as jams, chocolate, and honey-based cosmetics are also available.

MALLS

Remember that if you want your visit to benefit Ecuadorians, it's much better to shop at locally owned businesses, but if you're looking for big supermarkets, international chain stores, and movie theaters, you'll find them in Quito's many *centros comerciales* (malls). Major malls include **El Bosque** (Al Parque y Alonso de Torres), **El Jardín** (República and Amazonas), **CCI (Centro Comercial Iñaquito)** (Amazonas y Naciones Unidas), **Multicentro** (6 de Diciembre y La Niña), **CC Nu** (Naciones Unidas y Amazonas), and **Quicentro** (6 de Diciembre y Naciones Unidas).

BOOKS

For great deals on secondhand books in English and other languages, have a free cup of tea at the friendly

English-run **English Bookshop** (Venezuela *y* Manabi, tel. 98/424-1707, Facebook @The English Bookshop, 10am-6:30pm daily). Mark, the owner, is a great source of information on Ecuador.

Food

Quito has the widest range of international restaurants in Ecuador as well as many excellent local eateries. A lot of restaurants outside New Town close by 9 or 10pm, and throughout the city many are closed on Sunday.

OLD TOWN
BAKERIES, CAFÉS, AND SNACKS

There is a row of nice little cafés with outdoor seating under the cathedral on the Plaza Grande. At the entrance of San Agustín monastery is Ecuadorian-owned **El Cafeto** (Chile *y* Guayaquil, tel. 2/257-2921, Facebook @CafetoQuito, 8am-8pm Mon.-Sat., 8am-4pm Sun.), specializing in coffee and hot chocolate served with *humitas* (ground corn mashed with cheese, onion, garlic, eggs, and cream and steamed in corn leaves), tamales, empanadas, and cakes. **En-Dulce** (Guayaquil N6-56 *y* Olmedo, tel. 2/228-8000, http://endulce.com.ec, 7:30am-7:30pm Mon.-Fri., 8:30am-7:30pm Sat., 8:30am-5pm Sun.) has excellent cakes, pastries, and desserts, as well as breakfasts and sandwiches.

ECUADORIAN

For cheap, good quality Ecuadorian food, eat with the locals at the food courts of Quito's markets, where you'll find Andean specialties such as *hornado* (roasted pork) and *fritada* (crispy fried pork) served with *mote* (white corn), *llapingachos* (fried potato cakes), and avocado. Set lunches are also available. Meals cost $2.50-3.50 with a fresh juice for $1. In Old Town, the best food court is found at the ✪ **Mercado Central** (Av. Pichincha, 6am-5pm daily), a few blocks from Plaza Grande.

Heladería San Agustín (Guayaquil 1053 *y* Mejia, tel. 2/228-5082, http://heladeriasanagustin.net, 10am-3:30pm Mon.-Fri., $8.50-12.50) serves a wide range of typical Ecuadorian dishes. The attached ice cream parlor (10am-5:30pm Mon.-Fri.) is the oldest in the city, having made *helados de paila* sorbets in copper bowls for 150 years.

On Plaza San Francisco, ✪ **Tianguez Café Cultural** (tel. 2/257-0233, www.tianguez.org, 9:30am-6:30pm Mon.-Tues., 9:30am-11:30pm Wed.-Sun., $6-12) serves good quality Ecuadorian cuisine from the coast, Amazon, and Andes. The café is run by the Sinchi Sacha Foundation, a nonprofit set up to support indigenous Amazon communities.

Inside the Teatro Bolívar is **La Purísima** (Espejo *y* Guayaquil, tel. 98/301-1740, Facebook @lapurisimaec, noon-10pm Mon.-Sat., noon-5pm Sun., $12-15), a very well-reviewed restaurant serving innovative takes on traditional Ecuadorian dishes. Vegetarian options are available. The complimentary infused spirits at the end of the meal will put hairs on your chest!

INTERNATIONAL

On the hill beneath the Itchimbía Cultural Center is ✪ **Mosaico** (Samaniego N8-95 *y* Antepara, tel. 2/254-2871, 4pm-11pm Mon.-Wed., 1pm-11pm Thurs.-Sat., 1pm-10:30pm Sun., www.cafemosaicoecuador.com, $10-18). Start with pre-dinner drinks at sunset, when the views of Old Town from the terrace are wonderful. Arrive early to secure a table. The menu is a mix of Ecuadorian and international, with vegetarians and vegans catered for. Pets are welcome and there are even a couple of dishes for your four-legged companions! The house band is live every Friday and Saturday 8:30pm-11:30pm, playing music from the 1940s to the 1990s. A taxi from Old Town is $2.

VEGETARIAN

Vegetarian food is harder to come by in Old Town than in La Mariscal, but there are three places clustered together a few blocks from Plaza Grande toward the basilica. All three adhere to Hare Krishna principles. **Govindas** (Esmeraldas Oe3-119 *y* Venezuela, tel. 2/295-7849, Facebook @GovindasQuito, 8am-4pm Mon.-Sat., $2-3) has a wide range of lunches, including a filling set menu. Part of the same complex is the **Oki Ecomarket** (tel. 2/295-7849, Facebook @okiecomarket.ecuador, 9am-7pm Mon.-Sat., 8am-3pm Sun.), a shop selling fresh produce, health supplements, snacks, and light meals. The desserts and sweets are yummy. Next door is the ✪ **Restaurant Kalpa Vriksha / Tree of Desire** (tel. 2/258-1280, 11am-3pm Mon.-Sat., $2.80), a small, friendly place serving imaginative, healthy set lunches that include soup, main course, drink, and dessert.

NEW TOWN

ASIAN

Noe Sushi Bar (Isabel La Católica N24-6274 *y* Coruña, tel. 2/322-7378, 12:30pm-11:30pm Mon.-Thurs., 12:30pm-midnight Fri.-Sat., 12:30pm-10pm Sun., $10-20) has excellent combination platters and sashimi. For curries, you can't beat ✪ **Chandani Tandoori** (Juan León Mera *y* Cordero, tel. 2/222-1053, 11am-11pm Mon.-Thurs., 11am-2am Fri., 1pm-2am Sat., $4-8). Everything from *dopiaza* to korma, tikka masala, and *balti* is done well here, with some great veggie options. For Vietnamese, Thai, and Asian fusion specialties, head to **Uncle Ho's** (Calama *y* Almagro, tel. 2/511-4030, 11am-11pm Mon.-Sat., $5-14). Choose from a wide range of tasty rolls, soups, and curries.

CAFÉS, BAKERIES, AND SNACKS

El Cafecito (Luis Cordero *y* Reina Victoria, tel. 2/223-0922, www.cafecito.net, $3-8) is a long-standing Mariscal favorite for breakfasts, Sunday brunches, coffee, and cakes. Service is friendly, it's peaceful during the day, and the Wi-Fi works well, so it's a good spot for digital nomads. Chocoholics should head to **Kallari Café** (Wilson E4-266 *y* Juan León Mera, tel. 2/223-6009, www.kallari.com.ec, 9am-6pm Mon.-Fri., $3-8), run by a cooperative of 850 Kichwa families from the Ecuadorian Amazon who cultivate heirloom organic cacao trees to create their award-winning chocolate. Not surprisingly, the hot chocolate is wonderful. In La Floresta, family-run **Botánica** (Guipúzcoa E14-125 *y* Coruña, tel. 2/222-6512, www.botanicaquito.com, 12:30pm-9pm, Tues.-Fri., 2pm-9pm Sat.) is a treat, offering a small but freshly prepared organic menu of Ecuadorian coffee, sandwiches ($6), desserts ($4), and great cocktails. The interior decor is artsy recycled chic, and there is a plant-filled outdoor patio.

BURGERS AND STEAKS

Burgers, grilled plates, and barbecue are the specialties at **Adam's Rib** (La Niña *y* Reina Victoria, tel. 2/222-3086, noon-11pm Mon.-Fri., noon-5pm Sat.-Sun., $7-18). For Argentinian steak try **La Casa de Mi Abuela** (Juan León Mera 1649 *y* La Niña, tel. 2/256-5667, noon-11pm Mon.-Sat., $8-12), a Quito institution in the renovated house of the owner's grandmother. For beer, burgers, and wings, head to **King's Cross Bar** (La Niña *y* Reina Victoria, tel. 2/252-3597, 6pm-midnight Mon.-Thurs., 5:30pm till late Fri.-Sat., $5-8), where the Ecuadorian/Canadian owner dishes up her two menu items and tends bar.

CUBAN

La Bodeguita de Cuba (Reina Victoria 1721 *y* La Pinta, tel. 2/254-2476, noon-10pm Sun.-Tues., noon-midnight Wed., noon-1am Thurs., noon-2am Fri.-Sat., $8-10) is popular for its *bocaditos* (appetizers) as well as the live Cuban music.

ECUADORIAN

For cheap, good quality Ecuadorian food, eat with the locals at the food courts of Quito's **markets** ($2.50-3.50). In New Town, try ✪ **Mercado Santa Clara** (Antonio de Ulloa, near the Central University, 7am-5pm Mon.-Fri., 8am-2pm Sat.-Sun.) or **Mercado Iñaquito** (Iñaquito Bajo, 6am-5pm daily), north of Carolina Park.

✪ **La Petite Mariscal** (Diego de Almagro N24-304 *y* Juan Rodríguez, tel. 2/604-3303, www.lapetitemariscal.com, noon-3pm and 6pm-9:30pm Mon.-Fri., $12-22) serves excellent Ecuadorian cuisine with service to match. There is also an international menu with a couple of vegetarian options. The ambience is cozy with a fireplace. ✪ **Miskay** (Joaquín Pinto 312 *y* Reina Victoria, 3rd Fl., tel. 2/255-2872, https://miskayrestaurant. wordpress.com, noon-10:30pm daily, $8-19) consistently receives rave reviews for its top quality national cuisine and service. Vegetarians are catered to. Another consistently well-reviewed option is family-run **Achiote** (Juan Rodríguez 282 *y* Reina Victoria, tel. 2/250-1743, Facebook @ AchioteEcuador, noon-10pm daily, $15-28), which offers organic, gourmet Ecuadorian cuisine with vegetarian options.

At the top end of the scale, both **Urko** (Isabel La Católica N24-862 *y* Julio Zaldumbide, tel. 2/256-3180, www.urko.rest) and **Zazu** (Mariano Aguilera 331 *y* La Pradera, tel. 2/254-3559, http://zazuquito.com) offer exquisite tasting menus (each $75 not including drinks). Vegetarian menus are available.

FRENCH

Chez Jérôme (Whymper 3096 *y* Coruña, tel. 2/223-4067, www.chezjeromerestaurante.com, 12:30pm-3pm and 7:30pm-11pm Mon.-Fri., $10-33) offers top-notch food, decor, ambience, and service. A six-course tasting menu is available. Vegetarians are accommodated. **Rincón de Francia** (Vicente Ramón Roca N21-182 *y* Av. 9 de Octubre, tel. 2/222-5053, www. rincondefrancia.com, noon-3pm and 7pm-11pm Mon.-Fri., 7pm-11pm Sat., $20-25), has been in business for over 40 years.

ITALIAN

Sol y Luna (Whymper N31-29 *y* Coruña, tel. 2/223-5865, www.trattoriasoleeluna.com, 12:30pm-3:30pm and 7pm-11pm Mon.-Fri., 12:30pm-4:30pm Sat., $14-20), offers traditional dishes, including carpaccio, pasta, and gnocchi. Good service and generous portions make the prices more bearable, as does the delicious tiramisu.

Cosa Nostra Trattoria Pizzería (Moreno and Almagro, tel. 2/252-7145, http://pizzeriacosanostra.ec, 12:30pm-11pm Mon.-Sat., 12:30pm-10pm Sun., $12-18) has a wide selection of pizza, spaghetti, ravioli, and gnocchi. All the vegetables are organic. The owner, Simone, is from Italy and brought not only his family recipes to Quito but their hospitality as well. Home delivery is available. Close to Parque La Carolina, **Romolo e Remo** (República de El Salvador *y* Portugal, Edificio Rosanía, tel. 2/600-0683, 9am-8pm Mon.-Fri., 10am-5pm Sat.-Sun., $8-10) is friendly and has a small, inexpensive menu of pizzas, pastas, and focaccia. There is a three-course set menu with a glass of wine for $14.

MEXICAN

A plate of fajitas at **Red Hot Chili Peppers** (Foch *y* Juan León Mera, tel. 2/255-7575, Facebook @red.hot.mexican.food, noon-11pm Mon.-Sat., $6-10) will easily fill two people. A tiny place with a big TV and graffiti covering the walls, it serves top-notch Tex-Mex food and margaritas. Nearby is the ✪ **Mexicali Baja Grill** (Reina Victoria N23-69 *y* Wilson, tel. 2/290-8277, Facebook @mexicalibajagrill, 2pm-midnight Mon.-Sat., noon-8pm Sun.), which uses fresh, locally sourced ingredients for their expansive menu, from fish tacos to two-for-one frozen margaritas.

MIDDLE EASTERN

Shawarma (grilled meat in warm pita bread with yogurt sauce and vegetables) is increasingly popular in Ecuador. The patio at **Aladdin** (Almagro *y* Baquerizo Moreno, tel. 2/222-9435, 10:30am-midnight daily, $2-4) can get packed at night. The shisha pipes and 16 kinds of flavored tobacco probably have something to do with it, along with the cheap falafel and *shawarma.* **Baalbek** (Av. 6 de Diciembre N23-103 *y* Wilson, tel. 2/255-2766, http://restaurantbaalbek.com, noon-5pm Sun.-Tues., noon-10:30pm Wed.-Sat., $6-14) stands out for its hummus, *mansafh, fatush,* and other Lebanese favorites. There are plenty of veggie options and a belly-dancing show on Thursday at 8:30pm.

SEAFOOD

Cevichería Manolo (Diego de Almagro 1170 *y* La Niña, tel. 2/256-9254, Facebook @ CevicheriaManolosQuito, 8am-6pm Mon.-Sat., $7-15) is popular, with a wide selection of Ecuadorian and Peruvian ceviches.

SPANISH

La Paella Valenciana (Alpallana E7-294 *y* Diego de Almagro, tel. 2/250-1018, noon-3pm and 7pm-9pm Mon.-Sat., noon-3pm Sun., $10-20) has a wide range of Spanish entrées and tapas.

VEGETARIAN

New Town has the best selection of meat-free restaurants in the country (alongside Cuenca). Veggies and vegans are advised to make the most of this cornucopia of excellent options!

Sakti (Jerónimo Carrión E4-144 *y* Amazonas, tel. 2/252-0466, http://sakti-quito.com, 9am-6pm Mon.-Fri.,

vegan food at Tandana

$4-6) is a vegetarian restaurant, bakery, and hostel with decent set lunches. **Dulce Albahaca** (Juan León Mera N23-66 *entre* Baquedano *y* Wilson, tel. 2/510-3881, Facebook @dulcealbahacaec, 8am-8pm Mon.-Fri., 10am-6pm Sat.-Sun., $7-9) has great food, ambience, and service. The fruit tea infusion is such a work of art, it is a shame to drink it. There is also a health food store and deli selling fair trade and organic products. **El Maple** (Joaquín Pinto *y* Diego de Almagro, tel. 2/290-0000, Facebook @elmaplerestaurante, noon-10pm Mon.-Wed., noon-midnight Thurs.-Sat., noon-6pm Sun.) has a wide-ranging menu of national and international dishes. Especially recommended is the *sustento de altiplano,* a plate of meat-free versions of Andean specialties. **Mile Time** (Baquerizo Moreno *y* Reina Victoria, tel. 2/604-1475, Facebook @miletimeecuador, 9am-11am and noon-4:30pm Mon.-Sat.) has good set lunches ($3.75), breakfasts, and Chinese food. **Yoga Chai**

(9 de Octubre *y* Jerónimo Carrión, tel. 99/452-9962, http://yogachaivegan.com, $3-6) is a vegan café and yoga studio open daily for breakfast, lunch, and dinner.

✪ **Flora** (Leonidas Plaza N21-22 *y* Jorge Washington, tel. 2/603-5008, noon-9pm Mon.-Fri., noon-4pm Sat., $6.50-10) is a vegan, organic, non-GMO restaurant that uses local products from farmers that practice permaculture, agro-ecology, and fair trade. The decor is stylish and the service friendly. The set menu is imaginative, delicious, and beautifully presented. Flora is also a community center that aims to establish an urban example for conscious, regenerative, and harmonic living, with regular workshops on permaculture, natural medicines, and vegan cooking.

✪ **Tandana** (Mirador de Guápulo, tel. 2/323-8234, www.tandanaecuador.com, 12:45pm-7pm Wed.-Thurs., 12:45pm-10pm Fri.-Sat., 10am-4pm Sun., $5-9) is an excellent vegan restaurant with spectacular views over Guápulo. All proceeds go to Fundación Libera Ecuador, an organization working for the rights of nature and vulnerable local people. Chairs, tables, and glasses are made from reclaimed and recycled materials. There is a good selection of locally produced craft beer.

ORGANIC PRODUCE

There is an agro-ecological market, the **Feria Agroecológica La Carolina** (Pasaje Rumipamba *y* Av. Shyris, tel. 98/063-0519, Facebook @carolina.feria.71, 8am-2pm Sun.) every Sunday next to the botanical garden in Parque La Carolina. A few blocks north of the park, **Mega Organik** (Av. Río Coca E 6-90 *y* Isla Genovesa, tel. 2/243-6864, http://megaorganik.com, 9:30am-5:30pm Mon.-Sat., 10am-2:30pm Sun.) stocks fruit, vegetables, eggs, and chicken, alongside coconut oil, *guayusa* tea, *kombucha* tea, and natural toiletry products. Home deliveries are available every Wednesday. East of Carolina Park, **Wayruro Orgánico** (Juan de Dios Martínez N35-120 *y* Portugal, tel. 2/224-4855, Facebook @wayruro.organico, 10am-6pm Tues.-Sat.) sells organic Ecuadorian products that contribute to the sustainable development of communities. West of La Mariscal, near the Santa Clara Market, is **Camari** (Marchena Oe-2 38 *y* Versalles, tel. 2/254-9407, www.camari.org, 8am-6pm Mon.-Fri., 8:30am-4:30pm Sat.), a fair trade store with a wide range of products, listed in their online catalog.

MARKETS

Markets are great places to pick up fresh fruit and vegetables (including many never-seen-before varieties), flowers, meat, and other items, with the income going straight to local people. Every produce market has a food court, where you can sample cheap, typical Ecuadorian dishes alongside the locals. Quito's best markets include New Town's **Mercado Santa Clara** (Antonio de Ulloa, near the Central University, 7am-5pm Mon.-Fri., 8am-2pm Sat.-Sun.); **Mercado Iñaquito** (Iñaquito Bajo, 6am-5pm daily), located north of Carolina Park; and, a few blocks from Plaza Grande in Old Town, **Mercado Central** (Av. Pichincha, 6am-5pm daily).

You will find large supermarkets, either **Supermaxi, Megamaxi,** or **Mi Comisariato,** at all the major malls.

Accommodations

Quito has an enormous range of hostels and hotels, from bargain basement to lavish luxury. Most are found in New Town, although Old Town has a growing number of good options, many in renovated colonial mansions. There are several accommodations near the airport in Tababela.

OLD TOWN
UNDER $10

There are few budget options in Old Town, but **Hostal Sucre** (Bolívar 615 y Cuenca, tel. 2/295-4025, Facebook @hostel.sucre, $5-7 pp) bucks the trend. It's astonishing that such a cheap place is right on Plaza San Francisco with views of the square (it's worth paying the extra dollar for a room with a window). Rooms are basic, all bathrooms are shared, and there is no breakfast, but guests can use the communal kitchen. The hostel entrance is not easy to find; look for a double wooden door with a square hole and stairs leading up to the second floor.

$10-25

Quito Family & Youth Hostel (Galápagos y Benalcázar, tel. 99/549-8055, Facebook @Quito Family & Youth Hostel, $12 s, $13 d) is up a steep hill in a residential apartment block, but it's a good option for the price and location near the basilica. All bathrooms are shared and there is a communal kitchen. Breakfast is available at additional cost. Book in advance as it gets busy.

There are several hostels in the La Tola neighborhood on a steep hill to the east of Avenida Pichincha. If

walking from Old Town, take Manabí rather than Esmeraldas, as the latter is the red-light district. **Colonial House** (Olmedo y Los Ríos, tel. 2/316-1810, www.colonialhousequito.com, $10 dorm, $25 s/d) is a spacious, friendly, colorful place with a big garden and communal area with pool and foosball. Spanish and salsa classes and tours are available. Breakfast costs $3.50. Family-owned ✪ **Huasi Lodge** (Olmedo y Los Ríos, tel. 2/316-1644, www.huasilodge.com, $10 dorm, $25 s, $40 d, including breakfast) is an absolute gem. Situated in a historical house with wooden floors and a courtyard, the rooms are large, bright, stylish, and spotlessly clean. Service is top-notch. Rooms are cheaper without breakfast or with shared bathroom.

$25-50

Also in the La Tola neighborhood is family-owned ✪ **Community Hostel** (Pedro Fermín Cevallos y Olmedo, tel. 95/904-9658, www.communityhostel.com, $10 dorm, $30 s/d). Immaculate, modern, and stylish, the hostel has wooden floors throughout, and the famously comfortable beds are made by a local artisan carpenter. Dorms have double-width bunk beds and plenty of showers. Staff are English-speaking trained chefs and food is a focus. Gourmet breakfast is available at additional cost. Communal dinners are offered nightly with vegetarian and vegan options. The hostel offers a free walking tour, free yoga on the rooftop terrace, and daily evening activities. It's a great place to meet fellow travelers. Ten percent of the proceeds support local community efforts in education. There are sister hotels in Alausí and Baños.

Bright, stylish, and friendly, **Minka Hostal** (Matovelle *entre* Venezuela *y* Vargas, tel. 98/024-3729, www.minkahostel.com, $9-11.50 dorm, $30 s/d) is an excellent option near the basilica. Services include a free walking tour, daily activities, a tour agency, Spanish classes, a pool table, and a communal kitchen. The hostel makes efforts to compost organic waste and supports the Camino a Casa Foundation, which rescues and seeks homes for stray dogs. Reception is on the second floor. A good breakfast is available at additional cost.

A former colonial home, the **Hotel San Francisco de Quito** (Sucre *y* Guayaquil, tel. 2/228-7758, www.sanfranciscodequito.com.ec, $46 s, $73 d) is a wonderful upper midrange option, with a fountain and ferns filling the courtyard and a rooftop patio with great views.

$50-100

All the Old Town hotels listed in the categories below include breakfast in the price, unless stated otherwise.

The **Hotel Boutique Plaza Sucre** (Sucre *entre* Guayaquil *y* Flores, tel. 2/295-4926, www.hotelplazasucre.com, $57 s, $65 d) has a lovely courtyard lobby. Rooms are clean and spacious. The included buffet breakfast is good, with views overlooking the Panecillo.

✪ **Portal de Cantuña** (Bolívar *y* Cuenca, tel. 2/228-2276, www.portaldecantunaquito.com, $79 s, $79 d) is an absolute gem. The lovingly restored 200-year-old convent tucked away on a side street, run by the same family that has owned it for generations, is an oasis of calm. The service is friendly and top-notch. Solar panels provide some of the hotel's energy. There is a restaurant, and tours can be arranged.

A former family home dating back to 1705, **El Relicario del Carmen** (Venezuela *y* Olmedo, tel. 2/228-9120, www.hotelrelicariodelcarmen.com, $86 s, $112 d) has been meticulously renovated and turned into an 18-room hotel. The abundant artwork, handmade furniture, and stained-glass windows are particular highlights.

$100-200

Patio Andaluz (García Moreno *y* Olmedo, tel. 2/228-0830, www.hotelpatioandaluz.com, $200 s/d) is a restored 16th-century colonial home. Rooms are luxurious and service is excellent. The hotel is part of the Rainforest Alliance's Sustainable Tourism Program, audited in areas such as clean technologies, waste management and recycling, carbon offsets, biodiversity conservation, cultural preservation, and gender equality.

✪ **Carlota** (Benalcázar *y* Mejía, tel. 2/380-1410, www.carlota.ec/en, $200 s, $250 d) is a stylish 12-room boutique hotel in the renovated home of the owner's grandmother. Facilities include a bistro and a rooftop bar overlooking Old Town. Rates include a one-way transfer to or from the airport. Carlota is the first hotel in Ecuador to be LEED Certified (Leadership in Energy & Environmental Design) by the U.S. Green Building Council, with all operations and services Green Globe certified. Their sustainable and environmentally responsible practices include solar panels; gray water re-usage with an advanced water filtration system; biodegradable toiletry products; high efficiency water and lighting fixtures; use of recycled and upcycled materials in construction and finishes; and an urban garden growing organic ingredients for the menu.

NEW TOWN
UNDER $10

Those looking for rock-bottom dorm prices will find a couple of options in New Town, though it's worth bearing in mind that you get what you pay for. If you have the few extra dollars for one of the pod hostels, it's worth the extra investment. **Hostel Luz Robles** (Calle General Robles *y* Juan León Mera, tel. 2/255-5604, cdc_2466@ outlook.com, $6 dorm, $10 s, $18 d) is shabby with a shared kitchen. **Hostal New Bask** (Lizardo García *y* Diego de Almagro, tel. 2/256-7153, www.ne-whostalbask.com, $6 dorm, $16-20 s/d) has a café and shared kitchen.

$10-25

✪ **Mogens Pod Hostel**, (9 de Octubre *y* Luis Cordero, tel. 2/601-6913, www. mogenspodhostel.com, $10 s, $25 d) is a budget traveler's dream. Opened in 2016, the hostel is stylish, modern, and immaculately clean. Rather than standard bunk beds in the dormitories, there are 2-6 "pods" (single or double), each with curtains, electrical sockets, a reading lamp, and a locker. The hostel has an excellent 24-hour café with vegetarian options, a bakery, a bar, laundry, and parking. The beds are comfortable, the Wi-Fi is good, the showers have great pressure, and the bilingual staff are friendly and helpful.

Another excellent hostel with pod beds is **El Patio** (Luis Cordero *y* Reina Victoria, tel. 2/252-6342, www.elpa-tiohostels.com, $12 pp). Run by two friendly local sisters who converted their family home into the hostel, El Patio has 12 pods in dormitories and three double rooms ($25). The pods are wide enough to comfortably sleep couples. The hostel is bright, modern, colorful, and welcoming. There is a rooftop food garden, and the hostel recycles, composts, and uses biodegradable cleaning products. Yoga classes are offered several times a week. On the edge of La Mariscal, it's quieter than many other New Town hostels. Emphasis is on community; it's a great place to meet other travelers.

$25-50

All hotels in this category and up include breakfast in the price unless otherwise indicated.

Sakti (Jerónimo Carrión *y* Amazonas, tel. 2/252-0466, www. sakti-quito.com, $22-28 s, $45-60 d) is a newly renovated, family-run B&B with an excellent vegetarian restaurant attached.

A few blocks uphill from La Mariscal in the quiet, bohemian neighborhood of La Floresta is **Aleida's Hostal** (Andalucia *y* Francisco Salazar, tel. 2/223-4570, www.aleidashostal.com.ec, $33 s, 45 d), a friendly family-run guesthouse with large guest rooms. The owner, Elena, is a wonderful host.

Bright, modern, and spotlessly clean with friendly service, **Cayman Hotel** (Juan Rodríguez *y* Reina Victoria, tel. 2/256-7616, www.hotel-caymanquito.com, $39 s, $61 d) has 11 rooms, a huge fireplace, a lush garden, and a terrace. The hotel is certified by the Ministry of the Environment, audited in its energy- and water-saving measures, waste disposal, and use of biodegradable products.

$50-100

Casa Joaquín Boutique Hotel (Joaquín Pinto *y* Juan León Mera, tel. 2/222-4791, www.hotelcasajoaquin.

com, $85 s, $110 d) features 13 stylish, spotless rooms in a restored colonial house with a rooftop terrace and bar. Service is top-notch.

The bright and clean **Hostal de La Rábida** (La Rábida 227 y Santa María, tel. 2/222-2169, www.hostalrabida. com, $61 s, $61-95 d) has 11 rooms, an immaculate white interior, and dark wood floors. Amenities include a fireplace in the living room and a peaceful garden. The vegetables for the restaurant are grown organically in a greenhouse. A pet-friendly room is available.

OVER $100

Boutique hotel ✪ **Cultura Manor** (Jorge Washington y Ulpiano Páez, tel. 2/222-4271, www.culturamanor. com, $250 s/d) is the spectacular result of a seven-year project to restore a colonial mansion with exquisite attention to detail. Each room is uniquely decorated with frescoes inspired by Renaissance masters. Some have private balconies. The excellent restaurant has vegetarian and vegan options. Every Thursday evening, a different Latin American writer joins the guests for dinner after making an appearance at the Centro Cultural Benjamín Carrión across the street. Cultura Manor is part of a group of luxury eco-hotels, haciendas, lodges, and yachts across Ecuador. The hotel re-uses gray water; harvests and uses rainwater; grows organic produce for the restaurant in an on-site greenhouse; and is in the process of building 14 off-the-grid rooms.

La Coupole (Vicente Ramón Roca y Reina Victoria, tel. 2/515-4960, info@hotellacoupole.com, $112 s/d) is a renovated family mansion from 1800 with distinctive Moorish blue tiled cupolas. The interior is light and airy with wooden floors. Each room has a balcony. Service is friendly.

✪ **Anahi Boutique Hotel** (Tamayo y Wilson, tel. 2/250-1421, www.ana-hihotelquito.com/en, $130 s/d) has 16 uniquely decorated, elegantly themed suites within a restored colonial mansion. Price includes buffet breakfast and access to the Jacuzzi. Staff are friendly and attentive. The hotel is LGBTQ friendly and certified by the Rainforest Alliance and the International Ecotourism Society. The hotel is part of a group that works with a Kichwa community and has invested to protect 280 hectares (690 acres) of Ecuadorian Amazon.

CLOSE TO THE AIRPORT

All hotels in this category include private bathroom and breakfast. All offer airport transfers for $8-10 each way.

$25-50

Hostal El Parque (29 de Abril Oe1-125 y 24 de Septiembre, Tababela, tel. 2/239-1280 or 99/272-0615, www. hostalelparqueaeropuerto.com, $25 s, $40 d) uses solar power for the hot water and lights. All rooms have satellite TV and overlook the attractive gardens, which feature avocado, lime, and orange trees. Nonalcoholic drinks are complimentary, and there is a free airline ticket printing service. **Hotel-Residential El Viajero** (Nicolas Baquero S1-125 y 29 de Abril, Tababela, tel. 2/359-9054 or 98/440-3800, hotelviajero-quito@hotmail. com, $25 s, $40 d) offers clean, basic rooms and friendly service.

Set in beautiful gardens with views of Cotopaxi and Cayambe, ✪ **Zaysant Ecolodge** (Calle Manuel Burbano, Puembo, tel. 98/248-7487, https://zaysant.com, $45 s, $90 d, including breakfast) is owned by a welcoming local family. Just 15 minutes from the airport, it's a peaceful spot. Built with local materials, the rooms are comfortable and stylish. There is a small gym and a spa with Turkish bath, sauna, and massages. Organic gardens supply the kitchen, where decent pasta dishes are rustled up.

$100-200

Owned by an Ecuadorian family, ✪ **Hacienda La Jimenita** (Barrio Andrango via Pifo, Pifo, tel. 2/38-0253 or 99/875-0972, www.jimenita.com, $99 s, $130 d) is an absolute gem and well worth a visit in its own right. The hacienda sits on a 7.3-hectare (18-acre) eco-reserve with beautiful gardens and plenty of places to sit and enjoy the mountain scenery. Sunsets are spectacular, as are the early morning views of Cotopaxi. Guests can explore ancient Inca trails and a mysterious 300-meter (980-ft) archaeological tunnel, the origins of which are unknown. All food served in the restaurant is GMO free, organic, and grown either on-site or by local families as part of a fair trade program. Meals can be enjoyed outside with the hummingbirds or inside by a cozy fire. The menu includes vegetarian and vegan options. Half of all income from the hacienda goes to the sustainable protection of 30 hectares (74 acres) of local forest and 700 hectares (1,730 acres) of primary forest in Santa Clara in the province of Pastaza. The owners work with the local community to provide sustainable sources of income, offering training in hospitality, language, organic agriculture, construction, nutrition, water conservation, and alternative energies.

Hacienda La Jimenita

Accommodations are luxurious and the service is bilingual and friendly.

OUTSIDE TOWN
$50-100
San Jorge Eco-lodge Quito (km 4 Vía Cotocollao-Nono, tel. 2/224-7549, http://sanjorgeecolodges.com, $77 s, $85 d) is an 18th-century Spanish hacienda 30 minutes from central Quito. Set on an 80-hectare (200-acre) bird reserve in one of the last remnants of pristine Andean forest around the city, the house was once owned by former Ecuadorian president Eloy Alfaro. There are beautiful gardens, a lake, a spring-fed swimming pool, and wonderful views from 3,000 meters (9,800 ft) up in the Pichincha foothills. You can get here by taxi or arrange transport with the lodge. San Jorge is part of a group of eight private reserves and four ecolodges in birding hot spots around the country, including the Tandayapa Cloud Forest Reserve and Mindo.

LONGER STAYS
Most hotels will arrange a discount for stays of a few weeks or more. **St. Gallen Haus** (Guanguiltagua N37-04 y Diego Noboa, tel. 2/225-3699, www.stgallenhaus.com) specializes in longer-term rentals and is in the scenic El Batan neighborhood, north of New Town and away from the fray. The modern complex has a wide variety of accommodations, ranging from a single room with shared bathroom ($88 weekly/$280 monthly) to a double room with private bathroom ($189 weekly/$450 monthly) and an apartment with three bedrooms ($440 weekly/$1,000 monthly).

For a more authentic cultural experience and a chance to practice your Spanish, consider a **homestay** with a local family for $17-25 per day, including some meals. It is often just as affordable as a budget hotel. Check with Spanish schools for their recommendations as they often have a list of families they trust with their students.

Information and Services

VISITOR INFORMATION
There are state **tourist offices** (www.quito-turismo.gob.ec) in various locations around the city, where English-speaking staff can provide information, maps, and brochures. The walking map, with themed historical and cultural routes, is excellent. The main office, **El Quinde Visitors Center,** on the corner of the Plaza Grande (Palacio Municipal, Venezuela y Espejo, tel. 2/257-2445, 9am-6pm Mon.-Fri., 9am-8pm Sat., 10am-5pm Sun.) also has public restrooms, lockers, free Internet, a bookstore, a café, a chocolate store, and a handicrafts store. There are other offices in La Mariscal (Galería Ecuador, Reina Victoria y Lizardo García, tel. 2/223-9469, www.galeriaecuador.com, 9am-9pm Mon.-Sat., 10am-8pm Sun.), the Mariscal Sucre International Airport (tel. 2/255-1566), and at Quitumbe bus terminal (Av. Cóndor Ñan y Av. Mariscal Sucre, tel. 2/382-4815, 8:30am-5:30pm daily).

The tourist office works with the Tourism Unit of the Metropolitan Police to provide two **guided tours** of Old Town: *patrimonio*, focusing on religious art and history (2 hours, $17), and *fachadas* (facades, 1.5 hours, $8.50).

VISAS

For anything visa related, head to the **Ministerio de Relaciones Exteriores** (Carrión E1-76 at 10 de Agosto, tel. 2/299-3200, 8:30am-5pm Mon.-Fri.). See the *Essentials* chapter for more information about visas.

EMBASSIES AND CONSULATES

Several nations have embassies or consulates in Quito, including: **Canada** (Av. Amazonas 3729 *y* Unión Nacional de Periodistas, tel. 2/245-5499, 9am-noon Mon.-Fri., www.canadainternational.gc.ca, Australians also welcome; the Australian consulate is in Guayaquil), **United Kingdom** (Ed. Citiplaza, 14th Fl., Naciones Unidas *y* República de El Salvador, tel. 2/297-0800, www.gov.uk, 9am-11am Mon.-Fri.), and the **United States** (Av. Avigiras *y* Av. Eloy Alfaro, tel. 2/398-5000, https://ec.usembassy.gov, 8am-12:30pm and 1:30pm-5pm Mon.-Fri.). For details of other embassies and consulates, see www.embassypages.com.

MAPS

The **Instituto Geográfico Militar** (IGM, Seniergues *y* Gral. Telmo Paz *y* Miño, Sector El Dorado, tel. 2/397-5100, www.igm.gob.ec, 7:30am-4pm Mon.-Thurs., 7am-3pm Fri., 10am-3pm Sat.-Sun.) provides general tourist maps of Ecuador, as well as topographical maps for hiking. Maps can be requested in person at the office (visitors must surrender their passport at the gate) or online (see *Servicios* on the IGM website).

The main state tourism office on the corner of the Plaza Grande (Palacio Municipal, Venezuela *y* Espejo, tel. 2/257-2445, 9am-6pm Mon.-Fri., 9am-8pm Sat., 10am-5pm Sun.) can supply maps with themed routes for self-guided walking tours.

POST OFFICES AND COURIERS

Quito's main **post office (Correos del Ecuador)** is in New Town (Eloy Alfaro 354 *y* 9 de Octubre, tel. 2/256-1962, 8am-6pm Mon.-Fri., 9am-1pm Sat.), including the Express Mail Service (tracked national and international deliveries). There are several branch offices, including in the commercial center at the Palacio Arzobispal on the Plaza Grande (tel. 2/295-9875, 8am-1pm and 2pm-5pm Mon.-Fri.).

For national courier deliveries, **Servientrega** has several offices in Quito, including New Town (Av. Amazonas N24-31 *y* Pinto, tel. 2/254-0372, 9am-1pm and 2pm-6pm Mon.-Fri.) and Old Town (Plaza del Teatro, tel. 2/295-5860, 9am-1pm and 2pm-5:30pm Mon.-Fri.). If you're sending something important, urgent or internationally, using **DHL** is the best option. There are several offices throughout the city, including on Eloy Alfaro *y* Avenida de Los Juncos (8am-6pm Mon.-Fri.) and Colón 1333 at Foch (8:15am-7pm Mon.-Fri., 9am-5pm Sat.).

MONEY

BANKS AND ATMS

Bank branches and ATMs are located all over the city. Most reliable for foreign cards are **Banco Pichincha** (www.pichincha.com), **Banco Bolivariano** (www.bolivariano.com), and **Banco Internacional** (www.bancointernacional.com.ec).

For locations, see the bank websites or Google Maps.

EXCHANGE HOUSES

Since the introduction of the U.S. dollar, exchanging other currencies has become more difficult, and many exchange houses have closed, though there is one at the airport.

HEALTH
HOSPITALS AND CLINICS

A centrally located public hospital is **Hospital Carlos Andrade Marín** (Av. 18 de Septiembre *y* Ayacucho, tel. 2/256-4939, emergency tel. 2/256-2206, http://hcam.iess.gob.ec/).

Private hospitals are likely to have shorter waiting times and a higher level of care, especially for more complicated medical issues. **Hospital Metropolitano** (Av. Mariana de Jesús *y* Nicolás Arteta, tel. 2/399-8000, http://hospitalmetropolitano.org) is the best hospital in Quito, priced accordingly. The emergency room is on the east side of the building. The American-run **Hospital Voz Andes** (Villalengua 267 *y* 10 de Agosto, tel. 2/397-1000, http://hospitalvozandes.com) is cheaper and receives the most business from Quito's foreign residents. It's described as fast, competent, and inexpensive, with an emergency room and outpatient services. To get there, take the trolley bus north along 10 de Agosto just past Naciones Unidas.

Medicentro (Veracruz N35-100 *y* Av. República, tel. 2/394-9490, www.medicentro.ec) has a laboratory that can perform analysis for internal parasites, plus blood and urine tests. **Clínica de la Mujer** (Amazonas N39-216 *y* Gaspar de Villarroel, tel. 2/245-8000, www.clinicadelamujer.com.ec) is a 24-hour women's health clinic.

OTHER SERVICES
LAUNDRY

Laundries (*lavanderías*) are not hard to find, especially in La Mariscal (head for Wilson, Pinto, and Foch). Some places offer collection and delivery to nearby accommodations. Dry cleaners (*lavado en seco* or *lavaseco*) also exist. Both **Clean & Clean** (www.cleanclean.com.ec) and **La Química** (www.laquimica.ec) have several locations around the city.

SPANISH LESSONS

Quito is an especially good place to learn Spanish because the people tend to speak clear, fairly textbook Spanish. Dozens of schools offer intensive Spanish instruction, and it's worth your while to shop around for one that fits your needs. Tuition usually includes 2-6 hours of instruction per day, either in groups ($5.50-6.50 per hour) or one-on-one ($7-13). Four hours daily are usually plenty. An initial registration fee may be required ($20-35), and discounts are often possible for long-term commitments. Make sure to get a receipt when you pay, and check to see if any extras are not included in the hourly rate.

Many schools offer extras such as sports facilities and activities such as cooking, dancing, cultural experiences, and group trips. Some will house you in private or shared accommodations (prices vary) or arrange for a homestay with a local family (typically $20-25 per day for full board, $17-20 for board plus 2 meals per day). Don't sign any long-term arrangements until you're sure of both the school and the family.

The following schools have received many positive reviews:

- **Yanapuma Spanish School**

(Guayaquil N9-59 *y* Oriente, tel. 2/228-0843, www.yanapumaspan-ish.org) is part of a nonprofit organization that promotes sustainable development in indigenous and marginalized communities.

- **Simon Bolivar Spanish School** (Mariscal Foch E9-20 *y* Av. 6 de Diciembre, tel. 2/254-4558, www.simon-bolivar.com)

- **Ailola Quito Spanish School** (Guayaquil N9-77 *y* Oriente, tel. 2/228-5657, www.ailolaquito.com)

- **Cristóbal Colón Spanish School** (Colón 2088 *y* Versalles, tel./fax 2/250-6508, www.colons-panishschool.com) is the most

economical for one-on-one classes at $7 per hour.

- **Guayasamín Spanish School** (Calama E8-54 *cerca* 6 de Diciembre, tel. 2/254-4210, www.guayasamin-school.com)

- **Instituto Superior de Español** (Guayaquil N9-77 *y* Oriente, tel. 2/228-5657, www.superiorspanish-school.com)

- **La Lengua** (Av. Cristóbal Colón E6-12 *y* Rábida, Building Ave María, tel. 2/250-1271, www.la-lengua.com)

- **South American Language Center** (Amazonas N26-59 *y* Santa María, tel. 99/520-2158, http://span-ishschoolsouthamerican.com)

Getting There and Around

GETTING THERE AND AWAY

AIR

The award-winning **Mariscal Sucre International Airport** (tel. 2/395-4200, www.aeropuertoquito.aero) opened in February 2013, replacing the old airport of the same name. The impressive new facility serves all airlines flying in and out of Quito and is located in the suburb of Tababela, 12 kilometers (7.5 mi) east of the city center.

Airport services include tourist information, a post office, restaurants, a money exchange, luggage storage, ATMs, telephone and Internet booths, airport shuttles, car rental, duty-free shops, Wi-Fi, a children's area, and a VIP lounge (domestic $19, international $31). Personalized arrival and departure assistance can be arranged at the collection desks located on Level 1 of the Passenger Terminal, next to

the Administration entry door and the Amazonia Café. Customer Services can be contacted at supervisor.sac@quiport.com or tel. 99/831-4152. **The Quito Airport Center** (http://qui-toairportcenter.com), across the road from the airport's main exit, has restaurants, a pharmacy, ATMs, and a room where you can rest between flights. You can buy an Ecuadorian SIM card at the Claro center.

The following airlines serve Quito to/from domestic destinations: **TAME** (tel. 2/396-6300, www.tame.com.ec), **Avianca** (tel. 2/294-3100, www.avi-anca.com), and **LATAM** (tel. 2/299-2300, www.latam.com). Good deals (e.g., $60 return tickets) are sometimes available on domestic flights if you book online, in advance, and can be flexible with your dates and departure times.

The following airlines serve Quito to/from international destinations:

AeroMexico (tel. 3/332-212, www. aeromexico.com, to/from Mexico City); AirEuropa (www.aireuropa. com, to/from Madrid); **American Airlines** (tel. 2/299-5000, www. aa.com, to/from Dallas and Miami); Avianca (tel. 2/294-3100, www.avianca.com, to/from San Salvador, Bogota, and Lima); Condor (www. condor.com, to/from Munich, Frankfurt, and Dusseldorf); **Copa Airlines** (tel. 2/394-6680, www.copaair.com, to/from Panama); **Delta Airlines** (tel. 2/333-1691, ext. 92, www.delta.com, to/from Atlanta); Iberia (tel. 2/256-6121, www.iberia.com, to/from Madrid); JetBlue (U.S. tel. 801/449-2525, www.jetblue. com, to/from Fort Lauderdale); **KLM** (tel. 2/298-6820, www.klm.com.ec, to/from Amsterdam); **LATAM** (tel. 2/299-2300, www.latam.com, to/from Lima); **TAME** (tel. 2/396-6300, www. tame.com.ec, to/from Bogota, Cali, Caracas, Lima, Fort Lauderdale, and New York); United (tel. 2/255-7290, www.united.com, to/from Houston); and Wingo (1800/400-423, www. wingo.com, to/from Bogota).

GETTING TO AND FROM THE AIRPORT

Aeroservicios (tel. 2/604-3500, www. aeroservicios.com.ec) offers an airport shuttle running between the new airport and the Parque Bicentenario (the site of the old airport) in the north of Quito for $8. The buses depart every half hour (every hour in off-peak times), and the journey takes around 45 minutes. From the city center to the airport, buses run 3:30am-11pm Monday-Friday, 4am-9:30pm Saturday, 4am-11:30pm Sunday. From the airport to the city center, buses run 4:30am-11pm Monday-Friday, 5am-10:30pm Saturday, 5am-11:30pm

Sunday). Passengers are allowed one bag up to 50 pounds (23 kg) and a small carry-on bag. A $2 fee is charged for each additional bag. Tickets can be bought online or at the departure points with cash or credit card.

Cheaper and just as quick are the **public transportation buses** that run between the airport and three of Quito's bus terminals for $2. Buses to Quitumbe run every 15 minutes (5:40am-9pm daily), and the journey takes an hour. Buses to Río Coco run every 20 minutes (6:20am-10pm daily), and the journey takes 40 minutes. Buses to Carcelén run every 30 minutes (6:20am-8pm daily), and the journey takes an hour.

In the airport, there is a **taxi** desk next to the car rental booths. Taxis to and from the airport have set rates, mostly between $22 and $33, though the fare may be as high as $47.50 for some peripheral areas. The normal rate for either La Mariscal or Old Town is $26. **Car rental** is available with Thrifty, Hertz, Avis, Budget, and Localiza.

INTERNATIONAL BUSES

See the *Essentials* chapter for information on international buses to/from Quito.

NATIONAL BUSES

Quito has three major bus terminals. The biggest, **Quitumbe,** in the far south of the city, mostly serves long-distance routes traveling west, east, and south. The other interprovincial terminal, **Carcelén,** in the north of Quito, historically served northern destinations, though it also has buses to the coast (Manta and Salinas) and the Oriente (Coca, Tena, Puyo), among other destinations. The other northern terminal, **Ofelia,** is only for county buses (including Mindo and Otavalo). The trolley bus serves all three terminals. A shuttle bus service connects the Ofelia and Carcelén terminals. From the city center, a taxi to the Carcelén or Ofelia bus terminal might cost $5; to Quitumbe it's $8.

RENTAL CARS AND MOTORCYCLES

Few visitors rent vehicles in Ecuador (see the *Getting Around* section of the *Essentials* chapter for more information). If you do decide to hire a car, several major rental companies operate in Quito, including **Avis** (at the airport, tel. 2/281-8160, www.avis.com.ec); **Thrifty** (at the airport, tel. 2/222-8688, www.thrifty.com.ec); **Budget** (at the airport, tel. 2/281-8040, Av. Eloy Alfaro S40-153 *y* José Queri, tel. 2/224-4095, www.budget-ec.com); and **Hertz** (at the airport, tel. 2/281-8410, and via Inka's Rent A Car, República del Salvador 35-126 *y* Suecia, tel. 2/333-3207, www.hertz.com).

For motorcycles, U.S.-owned **Ecuador Freedom Bike Rentals** (Finlandia *y* Suecia, tel. 98/176-2340, www.freedombikerental.com, 10am-6pm daily) offers various options for exploring the country on their fleet of high-end motorcycles and scooters. These include guided tours and self-guided GPS tours through the Andes, the coast, and the jungle using relatively unknown routes.

TRAINS

These days Ecuador's railway, **Tren Ecuador** (tel. 1800/873-637, http://trenecuador.com/en) operates as a scenic tourist attraction, rather than a functional means of transport. Quito's historic **Chimbacalle train station** (Sincholagua *y* Maldonado) is a few kilometers south of Old Town and can

be accessed easily on the trolley bus. Three round-trip services are available. Quito to El Boliche to Machachi to Quito (8:30am-5:30pm Fri.-Sun., $53) is a day trip. Quito to Ambato to Quito (departs once a month, see website for dates, $63 single, $100 round-trip) takes one day each way. Tickets can be bought online, by phone, or at El Quinde Visitors Center on Plaza Grande.

GETTING AROUND

LOCAL BUSES

Local bus routes are rather complicated, so it's best to stick to simple, short journeys along the major roads, especially Amazonas and 10 de Agosto. It's a good idea to ask a local person at the bus stop which bus number goes to your destination. For more complex journeys, you're better off taking the trolley systems or a taxi.

Any of 10 de Agosto's major crossroads, including Patria, Orellana, and Naciones Unidas, are good places to find a bus heading south to Old Town or north as far as the turn to Mitad del Mundo. "La Y," the meeting of 10 de Agosto with América and De la Prensa, is a major bus intersection. Have the fare ($0.25) ready and take care with your belongings.

TROLLEY SYSTEMS

Quito's network of three electric trolley buses is the best of its kind in Ecuador; it is cheap, clean, fast, and well-organized. The trolleys have their own lane, so they can be much faster than traveling by car, especially in heavy traffic. Flat fare for all services is $0.25, payable at machines on entry. There are manned kiosks at every station to give change. Trolleys arrive every 5-10 minutes.

BUSES FROM QUITO TERMINALS

FROM QUITUMBE

Alausí	$7	6 hours
Ambato	$4	3 hours
Baños	$4.25	3.5 hours
Coca	$12.50	9 hours
Cuenca	$12	9 hours
Esmeraldas	$10	7 hours
Guayaquil	$10	9 hours
Latacunga	$2.35	1.5 hours
Manta	$11	8 hours
Puerto López	$14	10 hours
Puyo	$7	5 hours
Riobamba	$5	4 hours
Santa Elena	$13	10 hours
Tena	$7.5	5 hours
Tulcán	$6	5 hours

FROM CARCELÉN

Baños	$4.25	3.5 hours
Cuenca	$13	10 hours
Esmeraldas	$8	7 hours
Guayaquil	$10	9 hours
Los Bancos	$3	2 hours (indirect to Mindo)
Manta	$13.20	8 hours
Otavalo	$2.70	2 hours
Riobamba	$5	4.5 hours
Santa Elena	$13	10 hours
Tulcán	$5	5 hours

FROM OFELIA

Mindo (direct)	$3.10	2.5 hours
Mitad del Mundo	$0.40	1.5 hours (via the Metrobus line)
Otavalo	$2.50	2 hours

There are a few downsides. Pickpockets are rife, so stay alert, strap your bag to the front of your body, and keep valuables well hidden. At peak times, the buses can be full, and it may sometimes be necessary to wait until the next one comes, as it's simply impossible to squeeze on. There are route maps at all the trolley stations, though not all the buses have them onboard and some don't announce the next stop. It helps to take a digital photo of the trolley map for reference and to keep count of the number of stops. The central stops are shown on the maps in this chapter. Your fellow passengers will be happy to help if you're not sure where to get off. If you miss your stop, it's usually not far until the next one. Don't be put off; if you master the trolley system, you will save an enormous amount of money compared to using taxis and will have the satisfaction of being one of the few foreigners to be traveling like a local.

El Trolébus runs north-south from Carcelén station to the Quitumbe station. En route it passes Estación Norte (La Y) and the major tourist areas (Mariscal, Parque Ejido, Plaza del Teatro, and Plaza Chica (the stop for Plaza Grande). The main Trolébus thoroughfare is the 10 de Agosto.

The **Ecovia** is similar, but without

the overhead wires. It also runs north-south, from Río Coca terminal to Quitumbe terminal. Notable stops are the Casa de Cultura and the Naciones Unidas (for the Olympic Stadium). The third line, **Sur Occidental,** runs between Quitumbe terminal and Ofelia terminal.

Note that different trolley numbers service different sections of each line. This isn't clear from the maps at the stations and can cause confusion, but makes more sense if you look at the online map: www.trolebus.gob.ec. For example, on the Trolébus line, C1 buses run from El Recreo to Estación Norte, whereas C5 buses run from Ejido to Carcelén. Ask at the change kiosk at the station if you are unsure which bus number to take. Different buses have different operating hours, so check the website if you need to travel early, late, or on a Sunday.

METRO

At the time of writing, the **Quito Metro** (www.metrodequito.gob.ec) was under construction and is projected to be operational by July 2019 (delays not withstanding). Extending from Quitumbe in the south to El Labrador in the north, the line's 15 stations will include San Francisco, La Alameda, El Ejido, Universidad Central, La Carolina, and Iñaquito.

TAXIS

Taxi meters in Quito start at $0.50, with a $1.45 minimum charge ($1.75 after 7pm). Rides within and between Old Town and New Town shouldn't be more than $3 during the day or $4 in heavy traffic. Prices increase at night but shouldn't be more than double. From the city center, a taxi to the Carcelén or Ofelia bus terminal might cost $5; to Quitumbe $8.

Quito (especially La Mariscal) is one of the worst places in the country for "express kidnappings," where criminal taxi drivers relieve passengers of their valuables and PIN numbers. Victims are usually released unharmed, but these incidents are terrifying and can turn violent. See the Crime section of the *Essentials* chapter for more information on how to travel safely by taxi in the city.

The surest way to avoid this kind of crime is to ask your hotel, restaurant, or bar to call you a radio (pre-booked) taxi, rather than flagging one down on the street, especially at night. If you have a phone, save the number of a reliable taxi firm and call one yourself. In Quito, recommended companies are **Quito Sur** (tel. 99/501-1230) or **Taxi Amigo** (tel. 2/222-2222 or 2/222-2220). Both are reliable and available at any hour.

BICYCLES

The **Quito Bike Rental Network** (tel. 98/401-4852, Facebook @ QuitoBikeRentalNetwork) has 3 locations: Dulce Albahaca (Juan León Mera *y* Wilson); El Cafecito (Reina Victoria *y* Cordero); and Lord Guau (Cumbayá, one block from the Chaquiñan entrance).

Vicinity of Quito

CALDERÓN

Nine kilometers (5.6 mi) from Quito's northern suburbs, this small town is famous for its artisans, who make varnished figures out of a type of bread dough called *masapan*. This craft originated with the creation of bread babies for the annual Day of the Dead in November. Craftspeople in Calderón gradually developed more elaborate and lasting figures, adding salt, carpenter's glue, and aniline dyes. In stores all over town, tiny indigenous dolls called *cholas* stand in formation next to brightly painted parrots, llamas, fish, and flowers. They make unusual, inexpensive gifts and are popular as Christmas ornaments. Buses for Calderón leave regularly from the Ofelia terminal.

LA MITAD DEL MUNDO

The main reason to come to the Middle of the World complex is to stand with a foot in each hemisphere. **La Mitad del Mundo** (tel. 2/239-4803, 9am-6pm daily, www.mitaddelmundo. com, $7.50) lies just beyond the village of **Pomasqui,** 14 kilometers (8.7 mi) north of the city. The centerpiece is a 30-meter-high (98-ft-high) monument topped by a brass globe; a bright red line bisecting it provides the backdrop for the obligatory photo. However—whisper it quietly—the real equator is actually a few hundred meters away. Inside the monument are interactive, equator-themed **science exhibits** and an **ethnographic museum** with displays on Ecuador's diverse indigenous

boulevard leading to La Mitad del Mundo

Vicinity of Quito

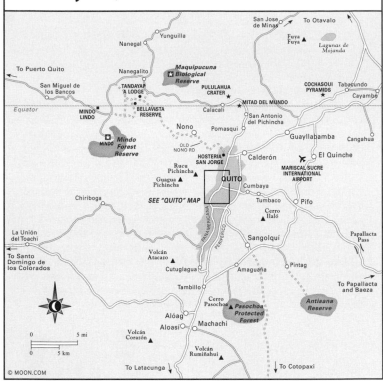

© MOON.COM

cultures. Tours are available in English and Spanish.

The rest of the complex has an assortment of attractions and feels somewhat like a theme park. The **France building** tells the story of the expedition to plot the equator in the mid-18th century. The **Fundación Quito Colonial** features an intricate model of colonial Quito that took almost seven years to build. There are several restaurants and craft shops. At the weekends and public holidays, the central square hosts music and dance performances.

To get to the Mitad del Mundo, take the Metrobus on Avenida América to the Ofelia terminal and catch the connecting Mitad del Mundo bus, or join a tour organized by a hotel or tour operator in Quito. The **Quito Tour Bus** (tel. 2/245-8010, www.quitotourbus.com) organizes a daily tour leaving Quito at noon ($30).

MUSEO DE SITIO INTIÑAN

Located about 300 meters (980 ft) east of the Mitad del Mundo complex on the real equatorial line, the **Museo de Sitio Intiñan** (tel. 2/239-5122, www.museointinan.com.ec/en, 9:30am-5pm daily, $4) features displays on local plants and indigenous cultures. Visitors are able to participate in equator-themed experiments: flushing water in opposite directions on either side of the line; walking along the line and feeling the strong gravitational pull; and the nearly impossible task of balancing an egg on the equator (you get a certificate if you can do it).

MUSEO TEMPLO DEL SOL PINTOR ORTEGA MAILA

Past the Museo de Sitio Intiñan, toward Calacalí by the Mirador Pululahua, is the **Museo Templo del Sol Pintor Ortega Maila** (Calle Eduardo Kingman y Av. Manuel Córdova Galarza, tel. 98/484-1851, Facebook @PintorOrtegaMaila, 9am-6pm daily). The studio and art gallery of the artist Ortega Maila was designed to replicate an Inca temple. If you're lucky, the artist might be there working.

PULULAHUA CRATER AND GEOBOTANICAL RESERVE

About 6 kilometers (3.7 mi) north of Mitad del Mundo, the 3,200-hectare (7,900-acre) **Pululahua Reserve** ($5 pp) sits inside one of the largest inhabited volcanic craters in the world. The volcano bubbled with lava thousands of years ago, but these days the main activity is that of the hundred farming families who reside in the flat, fertile bottom.

Buses and taxis take the road from the base of Mitad del Mundo's pedestrian avenue toward the village of Calacalí. Ask to be let off just after the gas station in Caspigasi, where a dirt lane leaves the road to the right and climbs 1.2 kilometers (0.7 mi) to the lip of the crater at the Ventanilla viewpoint; this becomes a path that continues down into the crater. It's a 90-minute hike to the bottom and back. Alternatively, to go directly to Pululahua from Quito, there are buses from the Ofelia terminal.

With an office inside the Mitad del Mundo complex, **Calimatours** (tel. 2/239-4796, www.mitaddelmundotour.com) offers bilingual tours to Pululahua ($8, 1.5 hours).

Located in the crater, **Pululahua Hostal** (tel. 99/946-6636, www.pululahuahostal.com, $20-40 s, $30-50 d) is an eco-hostel and restaurant that serves food largely grown on its organic farm. Lunch and dinner (soup, main course, salad, dessert, and coffee) both cost $12. The hostel has a variety of rooms and bamboo cabins, two with their own wood-burning stove. It generates its own power with a combination of solar, wind, and biogas. The water for showers and the Jacuzzi is heated by a thermo-solar system. Guided or self-guided tours on foot, bike, or horseback are available on several trails within the reserve, where there is good birding. The hostel accepts volunteers.

THE PICHINCHAS

Towering over Quito, the twin peaks for which the province was named dominate the city's history as well as its landscape. It was on the flanks of these volcanoes that Ecuador won its independence in 1822. Both are named Pichincha, which is thought to come from indigenous words meaning "the weeper of good water." **Rucu** (Elder) is actually shorter (4,700 m/15,420 ft) and nearer to the city, while **Guagua** (Baby) stands 4,794 meters (15,728 ft) high and has always been the more active of the two. After erupting in 1660, Guagua sat quietly until October 1999, when it blew out a huge mushroom cloud that blotted out the sun over Quito for a day and covered the capital in ash.

MEASURING THE EARTH

By 1735, most people agreed that the world was round, but another question remained: *How* round was it? **Isaac Newton** had theorized that the rotation of the earth caused it to bulge outward slightly in the middle and flatten at the poles, while others disagreed. With explorers setting out frequently to the far corners of the globe, it became increasingly important to determine how much, if any, the earth bulged in the middle, since even a few degrees of error on navigational charts could send ships hundreds of kilometers in the wrong direction.

To resolve the debate, the **French Academy of Sciences** organized two **expeditions**: one to **Lapland,** as close to the Arctic pole as possible; the other to **Ecuador** on the equator. Each party was tasked with measuring one degree of latitude, about 110 kilometers (68 mi), in its respective region. If the length of the degree at the equator proved longer than the degree near the Arctic, then the earth bulged. If they were the same length, it didn't.

The **expedition to Ecuador,** which was then part of the Spanish territory of Upper Peru, was led by academy members **Louis Godin, Pierre Bouguer,** and **Charles Marie de La Condamine.** They were accompanied by seven other Frenchmen, including a doctor-botanist, a surgeon, a naval engineer, and a draftsman, and two Spaniards. In 1736, the party sailed into Ecuador's port of Manta and then traveled to Quito, where Ecuadorian mapmaker and mathematician Pedro Vicente Maldonado joined the expedition.

The party decided to take the measurements in the flat plains near Yaruquí, 19 kilometers (12 mi) northeast of Quito. As the work progressed, troubles mounted. Unused to the elevation and the cold, the Europeans began to fall ill and suffered their first death—the nephew of the academy's treasurer, one of the youngest team members. As they continued to wander the plains with their strange instruments, local residents grew suspicious. Rumors began circulating that they had come to dig up and steal buried treasure, maybe even Inca gold. The situation became so tense that La Condamine was forced to travel to Lima to obtain official papers from the viceroy to support their

---

Climbing Rucu is easier and more accessible, requiring no special equipment. Unfortunately, the trail has been plagued by robberies. The opening of the TelefériQo (cable car) has led to increased security, especially on weekends, but it is wise to inquire locally about the current situation. It is highly recommended to hire a local guide from the **Ecuadorian Association of Mountain Guides** (tel. 2/254-0599, www.aseguim.org). To make the hike, take the TelefériQo to Cruz Loma and allow 5 hours for the round-trip. Start early and wear suitable footwear and warm clothes. Bring a waterproof jacket, water, and energy snacks; the weather can change suddenly and it's a demanding hike at high altitude.

Private transportation—preferably a four-wheel-drive vehicle—is essential to reach Guagua. The starting point is the village of **Lloa,** southwest of Quito. A dirt road leaves the main plaza and heads up the valley between the Pichinchas, ending in a shelter maintained by the national civil defense directorate. Park here, pay the entry fee ($1), which goes toward the guardian's salary, and don't leave anything of value in the car. A three-hour hike will take you to the summit, where the west-facing crater is pocked by smoking fumaroles, active domes, and collapsed craters. Hire a guide through the **Ecuadorian Association of Mountain Guides** (tel. 2/254-0599, www.aseguim.org) or go with a climbing-tour operator, such as **Andean Face** (www.andeanface.com, tel. 2/245-6135).

story. By 1739, the goal of determining the true shape of the earth was in sight. Then disastrous news arrived from the academy: The verdict was already in. The Lapland expedition had succeeded in determining that the earth was flattened at the poles.

As La Condamine tried to keep the Ecuadorian expedition from disintegrating, more bad luck struck. The party surgeon, Juan Seniergues, was stabbed to death in a dispute over a woman, forcing the rest of the group to seek refuge in a monastery. In the confusion, the botanist, Joseph de Jussieu, lost his entire collection of plants, representing five years' work; the loss eventually cost him his sanity as well. The draftsman was then killed in a fall from a church steeple near Riobamba.

Finally, in March 1743, the remaining scientists made the last measurements, confirming the Lapland expedition's findings and, in the process, laying the foundation for the entire modern metric system. Upon completion of their task, most of the party went back to Europe. French cartographer Jean Godin des Odonais stayed on in what is now Ecuador, settling in Riobamba after marrying a local woman. In 1749, after a visit to French Guiana, he was barred from re-entering the country, thus becoming separated from his wife, Isabel. They were to be reunited two decades later, in 1770, after she became famous for being the only survivor of a 42-person, 4,800-kilometer (3,000-mi) expedition through the Amazon Basin to look for him.

La Condamine, accompanied by Maldonado, also completed an epic Amazon journey, traveling by raft for four months to reach the Atlantic Ocean. From there, the pair sailed to Paris, where they brought the first samples of rubber seen in Europe and were welcomed as heroes. Maldonado died of measles in 1748, while La Condamine enjoyed the high life in Paris until his death in 1774.

In 1936, on the 200th anniversary of the earth measurers' arrival in Ecuador, the Ecuadorian government built a stone pyramid on the equator in their honor. This pyramid was eventually replaced by the **30-meter-tall (100-ft-tall) monument** that stands today at **Mitad del Mundo.** Busts along the path leading to the monument commemorate the 10 Frenchmen, two Spaniards, and one Ecuadorian who risked their lives—and sanity—for science.

TOP EXPERIENCE

✪ MINDO

Set in a tranquil valley northwest of Quito, Mindo is known for the astonishing biodiversity of its surrounding cloud forest. Since being recognized as South America's first Important Bird Area by Birdlife International in 1997, this small peaceful town has gradually blossomed into a world-class birding and ecotourism destination. There are over 500 bird species here, many of them endemic, including antpittas, toucans, and the famous Andean cock-of-the-rock. In fact, Mindo has won the international Christmas Bird Count six times, meaning that more bird species were counted here in a 24-hour period than in any other location in the world. Even non-birders will love watching countless jewel-bright hummingbirds flit around the feeders that many hotels and restaurants have in their gardens.

Aside from birds, the 19,200-hectare (47,400-acre) **Mindo-Nambillo Protected Forest** is home to 250 species of butterfly, 80 species of orchid, and a great variety of reptiles and amphibians, including tree frogs and glass frogs. Mammal species, harder to spot, include armadillos, anteaters, monkeys, ocelots, sloths, and deer. It's relatively easy to explore parts of the forest alone, but for a more informative experience, particularly for bird-watchers, it's recommended to hire a local guide. Adventure seekers will enjoy zip-lining through the forest canopy,

Mindo

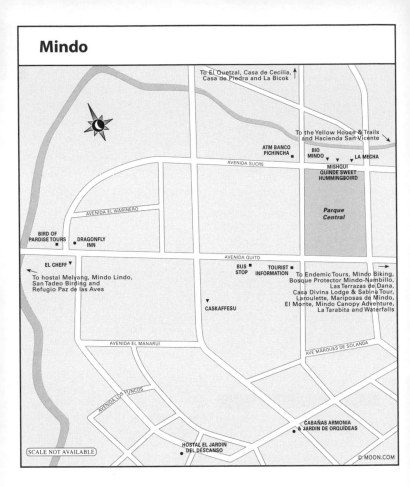

To El Quetzal, Casa de Cecilia, Casa de Piedra and La Bicok

To the Yellow House & Trails and Hacienda San Vicente

ATM BANCO PICHINCHA

BIO MINDO ▼ ▼ LA MECHA

MISHQUI QUINDE SWEET HUMMINGBOIRD

AVENIDA SUCRE

AVENIDA EL WARINERO

Parque Central

BIRD OF PARDISE TOURS ■ DRAGONFLY INN

EL CHEFF ▼

To hostal Melyang, Mindo Lindo, San Tadeo Birding and Refugio Paz de las Aves

AVENIDA QUITO

BUS ■ TOURIST ■ STOP INFORMATION

To Endemic Tours, Mindo Biking, Bosque Protector Mindo-Nambillo, Las Terrazas de Dana, Casa Divina Lodge & Sabina Tour, Laroulette, Mariposas de Mindo, El Monte, Mindo Canopy Adventure, La Tarabita and Waterfalls

▼ CASKAFFESU

AVENIDA EL MANARUI

AVE MARQUES DE SOLANDA

AVENIDA LOS YUNCOS

CABAÑAS ARMONIA & JARDIN DE ORQUÍDEAS

HOSTAL EL JARDIN DEL DESCANSO

SCALE NOT AVAILABLE

© MOON.COM

tubing down the pristine rivers, hiking to waterfalls, or exploring the area on two wheels.

The daytime temperature in Mindo can reach 26°C (79°F), with nighttime lows of 10°C (50°F). Mornings tend to be clear and sunny, the afternoons cloudy or rainy. It's wetter from January to May, though rain is common year-round. Mindo fills up on the weekend with day-trippers from Quito, so consider coming during the week for a quieter experience.

RECREATION AND TOURS
Wildlife

While Mindo is not difficult to navigate, many businesses don't have addresses. At the center of the village is the Parque Central, where a taxi rank, two ATMs, and a pharmacy can be found. **Bird of Paradise Tours** (http://mindobirdparadisetours.com) has put together an excellent map of Mindo's main attractions, available in many of the tourist establishments and downloadable on their website.

Mindo is filled with knowledgeable **bird-watching guides.** Dawn is the best time to go. The most popular trip is to see the spectacular mating display of the brilliant crimson-colored Andean cock-of-the-rock ($10 pp plus $25 for transport). For other tours, most guides charge small groups $60 for a half day and $100 for a full day. Three highly recommended English-speaking guides, all Mindo locals, are Julia Patiño (tel. 98/616-2816, juliaguideofbirds@gmail.com), Danny Jumbo (tel. 99/328-0769, mindobirding@gmail.com), and Irman Arias (www.mindobirdguide.com).

For customized, private bird-watching and nature tours in and around Mindo, contact **SabinaTour** (tel. 98/659-4965, U.S. tel. 650/855-4077, www.mindosabinatour.com). Co-founded by Mindeño Efrain Toapanta, the company has unrivaled knowledge of the area and is at the forefront of local conservation efforts. All the SabinaTour guides are bilingual and native to the region.

The Yellow House & Trails / Hacienda San Vicente (no address, located near the south end of the main park, tel. 2/217-0124, www.ecuadormindobirds.com) is a privately owned 200-hectare (500-acre) forest reserve at the north end of Mindo. It has a main trail and five side trails, for which maps are provided. Trail 3 leads to a viewing platform from where you can see the entire Mindo valley. Aside from birds, butterflies, and orchids, lucky visitors might glimpse armadillos, porcupines, and monkeys. There is a $6 entrance fee for day visitors, which includes juice from fruit grown at the hacienda.

A German-Ecuadorian couple owns a section of 7 hectares (17 acres)

Andean green hummingbird in Mindo

of land 7 kilometers (4.3 mi) uphill from Mindo called **Mindo Lindo** (tel. 99/807-5177, www.mindolindo.de/en), which offers easy access to the cloud forest. The couple have been involved in the conservation of Mindo for many years, working in the areas of forest conservation, environmental education, reforestation, and scientific research. They charge $5 per person to use the trails and $30 per person for accommodations.

Near Mindo Lindo is **San Tadeo Birding** (6am-6pm daily, tel. 98/089-9882, Rolando-garcia62@hotmail.com, $5), a beautiful spot for stationary birding, ideal for those who want to see birds without having to hike. The first garden, with comfortable seats where hot drinks are served, is for viewing birds that feed on bananas. The second garden is for hummingbirds and has an incredible view of Mindo nestled in the valley below. Even if you're not into birding, it's a charming and peaceful place to visit. The friendly owner, Rolando, is a knowledgeable bird guide who speaks a little English. He organizes trips to see the cock-of-the-rock mating display ($10). A one-way taxi from Mindo to San Tadeo costs $5. The taxi can wait for you, or Rolando will call you a taxi for the return journey.

Past San Tadeo, 20 kilometers (12.4 mi) northeast of Mindo, is another highly recommended birding spot. Established and run by a local family, **Refugio Paz de las Aves** (between Nanegalito and Mindo at km 66, tel. 2/211-6124, www.refugiopazdelasaves.com) is a fairly pricey option, but birders report that it is well worth it. There are two day tours on offer: a one-hour visit to see the cock-of-the-rock ($10) or a three- to four-hour tour ($35), which includes the cock-of-the-rock display,

observation of antpittas and other birds at the feeding area, and a good breakfast. A two-day, one-night tour is also available. Longer stays are possible at the lodge. Mindo taxi drivers charge $20 for round-trip transport to the cock-of-the-rock tour and $30 for the full tour, including waiting time.

For a stationary birding spot in Mindo itself, head to **Hostal El Jardín del Descanso** (tel. 99/482-9587, http://mindoeldescanso.com, entrance to the garden 6:30am-5:30pm daily, $4), by the southwest corner of the sports courts. The hostel's back garden is filled with hummingbirds flitting around the many feeders. Toucans, armadillos, and monkeys are also occasionally spotted. There is seating on the covered patio, where food and drinks are available.

By the southeast corner of the sports courts, **Cabañas Armonía & Jardín de Orquídeas** (Lluvia de Oro y Sixto Durán Ballén, tel. 2/217-0131, www.birdingmindo.com, $3) is a friendly, family-run hostel that allows visitors into the orchid garden, which features 250 species, as well as bromeliads and hummingbirds. The garden was established by the father 25 years ago, and a member of the family will give a tour (English available).

If you are in Mindo in mid-December, you can register with the Mindo Guide Association to participate in the **Christmas Bird Count** (tel. 98/634-0341, www.mindoguides.com, $10 pp), an international competition that counts the number of bird species spotted in a 24-hour period. Mindo has won the global title six times, and it's a big community event. No knowledge of bird-watching is necessary, as you will be assigned to a group with an expert leader. The fee includes a boxed lunch.

chrysalises waiting to hatch at Mariposas de Mindo

Southeast of town is the best access point into the **Bosque Protector Mindo-Nambillo** cloud forest. The main road coming out of this side of town runs parallel to the Río Mindo before splitting. Take the left fork to reach the largest butterfly farm in Ecuador, **Mariposas de Mindo** (Vía al Mariposario, tel. 99/920-2124, www.mariposasdemindo.com, 9am-4pm daily, $7.50). Among the 25 species is the iridescent Peleides blue morpho, with a 20-centimeter (7.9-in) wingspan. There is a very brief talk in English or Spanish explaining the four-stage life cycle from eggs to caterpillars to pupae to butterfly, then visitors are free to enjoy the garden. The best time to visit is between 10am and noon, to see the butterflies hatching, with the owner on hand to give a helping hand to any that are struggling. The pupae are quite beautiful, some like gold earrings. All the species are local, and some are released daily into the wild as part of a conservation program, simply by opening the door. A restaurant overlooks tropical gardens full of birds (vegetarian options are available). The staff are friendly and helpful.

Chocolate Tours

Two blocks north of the park is **El Quetzal** (9 de Octubre, tel. 2/217-0034, www.elquetzaldemindo.com), an organic, fair trade, bean-to-bar chocolate factory offering one-hour tours in English or Spanish (10am-5pm daily, $10). The tour includes a tasting of the factory's seven chocolate varieties, a cup of cacao tea, and a truly delicious brownie. The onsite shop sells a wide range of chocolate products. An additional tour, The Legend of Chocolate (6pm daily, book in advance, $10) allows visitors to participate in making a chocolate drink from a 5,000-year-old recipe, accompanied by live drumming. El Quetzal also has a hotel and restaurant.

Adventure Sports

The right fork of the main road (away from the butterfly farm) leads to the canopy tour. **Mindo Canopy Adventure** (km 2.5 Vía las Cascadas, tel. 98/542-8758, www.mindocanopy. com, 9:30am-4:15pm daily, $20) has 13 zip lines and a 40-meter (130-ft) Tarzan swing, suitable for adults and children over 6 years old. The company's safety record is excellent and there are guides to assist throughout. A coffee tour is also available.

About 1 kilometer (0.6 mi) up the hill from Mindo Canopy Adventure is a more relaxed way to travel across the treetops. **La Tarabita** (tel. 99/949-5044, Facebook @MindoTarabita, $5) is a cable car that cruises 150 meters (500 feet) above a river basin. On the far side trails lead to several **waterfalls.** Although the paths are not well marked, you're unlikely to get lost because the route is circular. The entire loop takes 2-3 hours and gets muddy in places. A basic level of fitness is required. Wear hiking boots and bring waterproof clothing, food, and water, as there is nowhere to buy anything. There is another waterfall on the opposite side, **Tambillo** (entrance $5 pp), where you can swim or slide downstream. It's about an hour's walk uphill from Mindo to reach La Tarabita and the entrance to the waterfalls, so consider taking a taxi for $7.

Another fun activity is **tubing**— tumbling down the river rapids in an inflatable tube. This can be arranged with any of the agencies in Mindo ($10 pp) or directly with the **Mindo Tubing Association** (tel. 99/544-9292 or 98/733-3813).

A highly recommended tour operator for a wide range of Mindo tours and activities, including hiking, zip-lining, tubing, horseback riding, and canyoneering, is **SabinaTour** (tel. 98/659-4965, U.S. tel. 650/855-4077, www.mindosabinatour.com). SabinaTour offers a high standard of English-speaking customer service and is at the forefront of local conservation efforts.

Take any road out of town to discover the incredible scenery of the cloud forest on two wheels. **Endemic Tours** (Av. Quito y Gallo de la Peña, tel. 2/217-0265) rents bicycles for 90 minutes ($5), four hours ($10), and all day ($15). If you're not too confident about striking out on your own, **Mindo Biking** (Vicente Aguirre y Av. Quito, tel. 2/217-0350, www.mindo-biking.com) offers English-speaking bike tours led by local guides.

Bucketpass (www.bucketpass. com) offers discounted rates on Mindo activities. You can choose four of the following activities for $38 (a discount of $12): chocolate tour, butterfly house, zip-lining, cable car with waterfall tour, biking.

FOOD

Mindo might be small, but there are some great restaurants to choose from. Most people will find something to their taste on Gourmet Avenue, off the main road near the park, where three of Mindo's best restaurants are clustered. ✪ **Bio Mindo** (tel. 98/372-4955, $3-10) serves nutritious soups, salads, burgers, steaks, and ceviches, made with flair and freshly prepared from scratch. Veggies and non-veggies are equally well catered to, and the service is excellent. Next door, **Mishqui Quinde / Sweet Hummingbird** (tel. 98/489-9234, Facebook @MishquiMindo, 10am-5pm Wed.-Mon.) is a vegetarian restaurant specializing in quinoa burgers and quinoa desserts with fruit and home-made ice cream. Even non-veggies give it rave reviews. Across the road is Italian restaurant **La Mecha** (tel. 98/057-4817, Facebook @restauranteit.lamecha, noon-8pm Mon.-Wed., noon-10pm Thurs., noon-11:15pm Fri., noon-2am Sat., noon-5pm Sun.), which serves pizza and pasta freshly made to order. The eggplant and vegetable pizza is the house specialty.

On the main road, carnivores will appreciate **El Cheff** (Av. Quito, tel. 2/217-0478, 9am-8pm daily, $4-10), where the set lunch is great value at $3.50 and the specialty is steak. On a side street off the main road, opposite the church, is **Caskaffesu** (Sixto Durán Ballén *y* Quito, tel. 2/217-0100), which serves chili con carne (or *sin carne* for the veggies, $7.50), coffee from their own plantation, and desserts. There is live music (Tues.-Sat., $3 cover) and a bar. Two blocks north of the park is **El Quetzal** (9 de Octubre, tel. 2/217-0034, www.elquetzaldemindo.com, 8am-9pm daily), offering a fusion of Ecuadorian and North American cuisine made from fresh, local ingredients, some grown in the restaurant's two-acre organic garden. The restaurant specializes in chocolate dishes and cocktails. The brownie is squidgy heaven.

Just before the butterfly farm, Swiss/Ecuadorian-owned **La Roulotte** (Vía al Mariposario km 2, tel. 99/014-2921, www.hosterialaroulottemindo.com) serves cheese fondue, *rösti* (potato fritters), and wood-fired pizza in a large, airy dining area. A small organic vegetable garden provides the salad. The butterfly farm, **Mariposas de Mindo** (Vía al Mariposario, tel. 99/920-2124, www.mariposasdemindo.com, 9am-4pm daily, $7.50-18), has a restaurant with an extensive menu and lots of vegetarian options. Open after 4pm for reservations.

ACCOMMODATIONS
Under $10
On the northwest edge of town on the main road is **Hostal Melyang** (Vía a Mindo *y* Bijao, tel. 99/388-8125, Facebook @Hostal.Melyang. Mindo, $6 dorm, $10 s, $16 d), the lowest-priced place in town. It's basic but the service is friendly. Dorms are single sex with three bunk beds in each. All private rooms have private bathrooms and hot water. There is a shared kitchen and a common area on the third floor with a nice view.

$10-25
On the northern edge of town, **Casa de Cecilia** (north of 9 de Octubre, tel. 2/217-0243, $10 dorm, $11-25 pp private room) is a decent budget option with rooms in rustic cabins on the edge of a rushing stream. Breakfast is available at extra cost. Casa de Cecilia works with the nature reserve Mindo Lindo.

Cabañas Armonía & Jardín de Orquídeas (Lluvia de Oro *y* Sixto Durán Ballén, tel. 2/217-0131, www.birdingmindo.com, $12.50-25 pp, including breakfast) is run by a local family. Comfortable, clean rooms and cabins are available with shared or private bathrooms. What sets the hostel apart is the friendly service and the beautiful orchid garden, which hostel guests can access for free. Breakfast is served in the garden by the hummingbird feeders.

Nearby **Hostal El Jardín del Descanso** (tel. 99/482-9587, rodny_garrido@hotmail.com, Facebook @ Hostal El Descanso, $15 dorm, $22 pp private room, including breakfast) has a garden full of hummingbirds.

The Yellow House & Trails / Hacienda San Vicente (no address, located near the south end of the main park, tel. 2/217-0124, www.ecuadormindobirds.com, $20 pp without breakfast, $25 pp with breakfast) is a privately owned reserve at the north end of Mindo. The lodge is family-owned and run by three sisters, who are very kind hosts. Breakfast is made with organic produce from the hacienda (including the coffee) and nearby farms. Guests have free access to the six walking trails, which costs $6 for nonguests.

On a quiet street on the other side of the stream to Casa de Cecilia, ✪ **Casa de Piedra** (Calle Julio Goethche, Barrio Magdalena, tel. 2/217-0436, www.casadelpiedramindo.com, $15 dorm, from $25 pp s/d) is an absolute gem and excellent value. Set in large gardens, the rooms are very stylish and the service is exceptionally friendly and helpful. A wide range of accommodation options are available, from a mixed dorm to a three-bedroom apartment. It has a restaurant, games room, and an outdoor pool. Massage and bike hire are available. Pet friendly.

$25-50

All the rates in this category and up include breakfast.

On the main road as you arrive in town, **The Dragonfly Inn** (Av. Quito y Río Canchupí, tel. 2/217-0319, $30 s, $50 d) is a popular midrange choice. Rooms are wooden, each with a balcony and hammock. A good but pricey restaurant with fresh, often organic ingredients overlooks the river (vegetarian options available). On the main road, it's not the most peaceful spot, but it's a good option for those who like to be near all the amenities of town.

At **El Quetzal** (9 de Octubre, tel. 2/217-0034, www.elquetzaldemindo.com, $35 s, $68 d), each room features a balcony with a hammock and includes a tour of the chocolate factory. The staff speak English.

At the north end of town, tucked away on a side street just past Casa de Piedra, **La Bicok** (tel. 99/942-1945, $9 camping, $45 s, $70 d) was designed by a bioclimatic architect to have a low environmental impact. The construction is 100 percent natural materials, there is a gray water system to reduce water consumption, and the restaurant serves local organic produce (for guests only, upon request). The rooms are stylish and excellent value. One room has a wheelchair-accessible shower. There is a swimming pool with sun loungers. A fire is lit every night for guests.

Part of the butterfly farm, ✪ **Hostería Mariposas de Mindo** (Vía al Mariposario, tel. 99/920-2124, www.mariposasdemindo.com, $43 pp) has eight attractive wood-paneled cabins set in tropical gardens. Staff are helpful and friendly. Guests have free, unlimited access to the butterfly garden ($7.50 for nonguests). There is a good on-site restaurant.

$50-75

Halfway to the butterfly farm is the Swiss/Ecuadorian-owned **La Roulotte** (Vía al Mariposario km 2, tel. 99/014-2921, www.hosterialaroulottemindo.com, $50 s, $75 d). Five charming gypsy wagons (two with wood-burning stoves) serve as sleeping accommodations surrounding an expansive central restaurant that doubles as a bird-watching station. Toucans and hummingbirds are frequent visitors. It's a quiet, peaceful spot. Additional amenities and services are quirky: an impressive bamboo maze and a *petanque* court. There is a small organic vegetable garden and a filtration system for the output from the toilets, which fertilizes the massive stands of bamboo.

$100-200

Just outside town to the east are three excellent ecolodges that deserve special mention. All include breakfast.

Las Terrazas de Dana (Vía a Las Cascadas, km 1.2, tel. 98/409-9146, www.lasterrazasdedana.com, $130 s, $140 d) offers six immaculate modern cabins, each with a two-person hot tub and private terrace with spectacular views. All three meals can be brought to your room and enjoyed on the terrace, surrounded by butterflies and hummingbirds attracted to the specially chosen flowering plants. You can also book an in-room massage with organic Ecuadorian chocolate and coffee products. The lodge's owner, David, and all the staff go out of their way to make sure their guests have a wonderful stay. The lodge was the first in Mindo to receive an Environmental Certificate from the provincial government. The sister tour company, Dana Tours, offers local birding and adventure trips and Galápagos cruises.

Next to Terrazas de Dana, ✪ **Casa Divina Lodge** (tel. 98/659-4965, www.mindocasadivina.com, $145 s, $250 d) is owned and managed by Mindo local Efrain Toapanta and his Californian wife, Molly Brown. With a warm, welcoming main lodge and hospitality to match, Casa Divina is set in bird-filled gardens on 2.7 hectares (6.7 acres) of cloud forest. The property features two self-guided forest trails and a bird observation deck. The four thoughtfully appointed wooden guest cabins, each with a private balcony and hammock, were hand-built by Efrain, along with most of the furniture. Efrain was instrumental in establishing Mindo as an ecotourism destination from the very beginning, over 30 years ago. He and Molly have purchased a 100-hectare (250-acre) protected reserve and are at the forefront of local conservation efforts. The lodge is an internationally certified community-based green business, built and operated for minimum environmental impact. The restaurant uses locally produced, organic ingredients. All the staff, guides, and drivers are local. Molly and Efrain also own SabinaTour, an excellent tour operator for a wide range of Mindo tours and activities (www.mindosabinatour.com).

To really get away from it all, head to **El Monte Sustainable Lodge** (tel. 99/308-4675, www.ecuadorcloudforest.com, $140 pp, reservation only), just past the butterfly farm. The entrance to the lodge is via a hand-pulled cable car over a rushing river. Upon arrival, either telephone or shout loudly and someone will appear to pull you across. It's a fun and novel experience that only serves to heighten the feeling of isolation, as does the lack of Internet (although Wi-Fi connection is available in the office upon request). The six guest cabins and large, open-sided central lodge are a perfect mix of rustic and luxury. Guests eat a delicious candlelit dinner together in the evenings, with vegetarians beautifully catered for. Rates include all meals and a Spanish-speaking naturalist guide. Solar panels and a micro-hydro system generate part of the electricity; an organic garden supplies some of the fruit and vegetables for the restaurant;

and there is a biological sewage system. To facilitate cloud forest research, El Monte founded the Mindo Biological Station, which protects 6,500 hectares (16,100 acres) of land within the Mindo-Nambillo Protected Forest.

INFORMATION
There's a **Centro de Información** on Avenida Quito near the plaza.

GETTING THERE
The road from Quito to Mindo runs west from Mitad del Mundo. The direct service by **Cooperativa Flor del Valle** takes around 2.5 hours and leaves from the Ofelia terminal. Note that the buses leave from a separate concourse just outside the main terminal. Exit the terminal just left of the row of snack stalls and cross the road to find it. Buses leave Monday-Friday at 8:30am, 9am, 11am, 1pm, and 4pm; Saturday at 7:40am, 8:20am, 9:20am, 11am, 1pm, 2pm, and 4pm; and Sunday at 7:40am, 8:20am, 9:20am, 11am, 1pm, 2pm, and 5pm. Coming back from Mindo, direct buses to Quito leave from the town center Monday-Friday at 6:30am, 11am, 1:45pm, 3:30pm, and 5pm; on Saturday at 6:30am, 11am, 1pm, 2pm, 4pm, and 5pm; and Sunday at 6:30am, 11am, 1pm, 2pm, 4pm, and 5pm. For up-to-date bus schedules check www.lasterrazasdedana.com/the-lodge/how-to-get-the-lodge.

If you miss the bus from Ofelia, head for the Carcelén terminal and take the first bus to Los Bancos, which leaves you on the main road at the top of the hill above Mindo, where you can catch a taxi (around $3). Leaving Mindo, take a taxi to the main road and flag down any Quito-bound bus.

✪ MAQUIPUCUNA BIOLOGICAL RESERVE

Just two hours north of Quito, the **Maquipucuna Reserve & Bear Lodge** (tel. 99/421-8033, www.maquipucuna.org, $95-208 s, $185-337 d) protects over 6,000 hectares (14,800 acres) of pristine rainforest in the heart of the Chocó Andean Corridor, one of the earth's top five biodiversity hot spots. The reserve's wide range of eco-zones between 900 and 2,785 meters (3,000-9,000 ft) has led to an astonishing diversity of flora and fauna. A whopping 25 percent of Ecuador's bird species and 10 percent of its mammal species call Maquipucuna home, among them the reserve's most famous resident, the Andean or spectacled bear. In fact, this is the best place in the world to see these shy endangered creatures, which come to the forest to feed on a type of wild avocado that is only abundant at Maquipucuna. As well as watching bears, visitors can go on guided walks, explore self-guided trails, bird-watch, go on night hikes, and bathe in waterfalls and swimming holes. A less vigorous activity is harvesting and processing cacao and then enjoying a chocolate massage with the results!

Maquipucuna is managed by Rebeca and Rodrigo Ontaneda, the Ecuadorian couple who first established the area as a reserve in 1988. Both speak English and are on hand to share their fascinating stories and knowledge with visitors. Accommodation prices include three meals (vegetarians catered for) and daily guided walks with a bilingual guide. Camping is also available. The reserve accepts volunteers. Note that the bears are not present year-round and their annual migration to the

THE ANDEAN BEAR

If you spend any time in the center of Quito, you will probably see a government poster campaign promoting the city as the Tierra de Osos, or Land of Bears (www.quitotierradeosos.org). The bears in the posters are Andean bears, which are in danger of extinction due to hunting and habitat loss.

The only bear species in South America, it is also known as the "spectacled bear" for the markings on its face, which are unique to each individual. The males are larger than the females, reaching 1.8 meters (5.9 ft) in height and 175 kilograms (385 lb) in weight. Despite their size, the bears are 90 percent vegetarian, which is fortunate because they can run at up to 50 kph (30 mph). These clever, arboreal animals build platforms and nests in trees for eating and sleep-

a spectacled bear in the Maquipucuna Biological Reserve

ing. They are so shy and secretive that little is known about their habits. In fact, they are so good at hiding that it can hard to spot one up a tree, even if you know it is there.

The story of how these elusive creatures were adopted as mascots of the city is a fascinating one. It started in 1985 when an Ecuadorian couple, Rebeca Justicia and Rodrigo Ontaneda, first decided to protect a section of cloud forest north of Quito. After establishing the 6,500-hectare (16,100-acre) Maquipucuna Reserve in 1988, the couple spent the following decades restoring degraded pasturelands and working with local communities and the government to protect the surrounding forests. Their work was instrumental in creating a safe haven for at least 60 Andean bears, dozens of which congregate annually to feed on their favorite fruit—the small, wild avocados that are now only abundant on the northern end of the reserve. Maquipucuna is now the best place in the world to see the Andean bear in the wild.

After three decades of conservation work, the government of Quito declared Maquipucuna and the surrounding area a protected bear corridor, preserving a total area of 65,000 hectares (161,000 acres). In July 2018, it was declared a UNESCO Biosphere Reserve.

The ecotourism opportunities presented by the congregation of Andean bears may be the key to finding sustainable economic alternatives to destructive logging and mining practices. Thus, the couple's efforts are not about saving just bears, but the Ecuadorian cloud forest itself, one of the earth's top five biodiversity hot spots, and all the species that call it home. For more information, see www.maquipucuna.org.

reserve can happen anytime between July and February. Check the reserve's Facebook page for updates. Also be aware that afternoons at Maquipucuna tend to be rainy.

To get to the reserve, take a bus from Quito's Ofelia station to Nanegalito, the nearest village to Maquipucuna. From there, hire a taxi to the reserve ($15). The reserve can arrange transport from the airport ($142 for 2 people) or from Quito ($87 for 2 people). A taxi from Mindo to the reserve should be around $35.

YUNGUILLA

An hour north of Quito, **Yunguilla** (tel. 98/021-5476, www.yunguilla.org.ec) is a cloud forest reserve of 2,600 hectares (6,400 acres) that borders Maquipucuna to the west. Until the late 1990s, the 60 families that inhabit the reserve were forced to traffic moonshine and fell their forests for charcoal production to make ends meet. When the Maquipucuna Foundation realized the extent of the threat posed by their neighbors' unsustainable land-use practices, they assisted the Yunguilla community to find alternative sources of income. Funds were raised for the purchase of the Tahuallullo farm, which has a central building that serves as a hostel and the headquarters of a community enterprise that produces orchids, handicrafts, and organic cheeses and jams. Other projects included reforestation, soil conservation, and the creation of organic gardens. Now completely financially independent and flourishing, Yunguilla is a shining example of eco- and community tourism. Visitors can sleep and eat at the lodge or with local families, all of whom have guest rooms in their homes. To get to Yunguilla, take a bus to Calacali from the Ofelia terminal, then take a taxi or pickup truck from Calacali's central park ($4).

PASOCHOA PROTECTED FOREST

The most untouched stretch of forest close to Quito is the **Pasochoa Protected Forest** (open daily, $5 pp), 30 kilometers (19 mi) southeast of the city. The reserve ranges 2,700-4,200 meters (8,900-13,800 ft) in elevation, the highest point being Cerro Pasochoa, an extinct volcano. The forest and *páramo* ecosystems are home to 126 species of birds, including many hummingbirds and a family of condors.

Loop paths of varying lengths and difficulty lead higher and higher into the hills, ranging from 30 minutes to eight hours in duration. A guide and a good level of fitness are required for the longer hikes. It's possible to climb to the lip of Cerro Pasochoa's blasted volcanic crater in six hours. Take food, water, and waterproof clothes. Campsites and a few dorm rooms with showers and cooking facilities are available near the bottom.

From Quito, take a bus marked Playón from the south end of the Plaza La Marín below Old Town to the village of Amaguaña (30-40 minutes, $0.60). Hire a taxi or pickup ($5-8) from the village plaza to the turnoff for the reserve. From there, a dirt road leads 7 kilometers (4.3 mi) up a rough, cobbled road to the reserve. Ask the driver to come back for you, or take a phone and call a taxi for the return journey. Some tour operators in Quito offer day trips to hike Cerro Pasochoa, including **Gulliver's** (tel. 2/252-8030, www.gulliver.com.ec).

EXCURSIONS

For a whistle-stop tour of Ecuador that includes the Sierra, volcanic landscape, and an indigenous community, expand your visit to Quito with these nearby excursions.

Otavalo is a good base for exploring the northern Sierra region; the textile market and town itself can be seen in a day. South of Quito, the central sierra region is home to Machachi and the Cotopaxi National Park. Hike, bike, or horseback ride through the park or climb the country's most beautiful volcano. West of Quito, Santo Domingo serves as an access point for one of Ecuador's indigenous Tsáchila communities. Stay in a traditional cabin and spend time learning about ancestral ceremonies.

HIGHLIGHTS

✪ **OTAVALO'S TEXTILE MARKET:** Even non-shoppers will enjoy browsing the incredible range of textiles and handicrafts at Otavalo's Saturday market—or just soaking in the festival atmosphere (page 88).

✪ **COTOPAXI NATIONAL PARK:** Llamas graze and wild horses gallop on grasslands strewn with wildflowers, overlooked by the picture-perfect cone of the country's most beautiful volcano (page 110).

✪ **CHIGÜILPE:** This indigenous Tsáchila community near Santo Domingo holds ancestral healing ceremonies in a candlelit underground chamber and has a tree especially for hugging (page 117).

Quito to Otavalo

LAS TOLAS DE COCHASQUÍ

On the road from Quito to Otavalo, west of Cayambe, are the ruins of 15 flat-topped pre-Inca pyramids and 21 burial mounds. At 3,100 meters (10,170 ft) elevation, **Cochasquí** (tel. 2/399-4524, 8am-4pm daily, $3) is one of Ecuador's most important archaeological sites, built by the Cara and/or Caranqui people between AD 950 and the Spanish conquest in the 1530s.

Cochasquí is thought to have been a military, ceremonial, and astronomical center. Excavations have revealed what appears to be a calendar atop one pyramid, with stones casting shadows to indicate the solstices and the best times to plant and harvest. Festivals are still held here at the solstices and equinoxes. The site's setting is dramatic, with spectacular views over Quito, Cotopaxi, the Ilinizas mountains, and Antisana on clear days.

Visitors must be accompanied by a guide, and a tour is included in the ticket price (English-speaking available), which is payable at the clearly marked entrance. As well as a scale model of the site, there are small archaeological and ethnographic museums, and replicas of traditional buildings with medicinal gardens. Local cuisine is available at a small restaurant. **Camping Cochasquí** (tel. 99/491-9008, campingcochasqui@pichincha.gob.ec) offers cabins ($10 pp), rented tents ($10 for 2 people), and camping spaces ($3 pp).

GETTING THERE

Take a bus from Quito's Ofelia terminal to the small village of Malchingui with a bus company of the same name (approx. 1 hour). In Malchingui, take another bus headed for Cayambe and ask the driver to let you off after 6 kilometers (3.7 mi) at Cochasquí ($0.50), or hire a *camioneta* ($3-5 one way). *Camionetas* can also be hired in Tabacundo or Cayambe ($15 one way). Ask the staff at Cochasquí to call a driver for your return journey.

CAYAMBE-COCA ECOLOGICAL RESERVE

Home to the snowcapped volcano Cayambe and the headwaters of the Coca River, the 4,000 square kilometers (1,500 sq mi) of the **Cayambe-Coca Ecological Reserve** (http://areasprotegidas.ambiente.gob.ec) range in elevation from 600 to 5,790 meters (2,000-19,000 ft). Encompassing windswept *páramo*, Amazon rainforest, and everything in between, the park boasts some 900 species of birds, from condors to toucans and macaws. Among the 200 mammal species are spectacled bear, mountain tapir, howler monkey, and spider monkey.

The reserve spans four provinces, divided according to altitude. The parts of the park that fall within Pichincha and Imbabura are known as the *zona alta,* or high zone; those within Napo and Sucumbíos are the *zona baja,* or low zone. The key attractions of the high zone are the **Oyacachi hot springs** and the **Cayambe volcano.**

OYACACHI

The Kichwa community of **Oyacachi** (tel. 6/238-6019 or 95/891-8101, http://oyacachi.org) is known for the wood-carving skills of its inhabitants and its **hot springs** (8am-5pm daily, $5), which are popular with locals on weekends and less busy on midweek days. Accommodations are available at the **Cabañas Oyacachi** (tel. 99/370-0529, www.cabanasoyacachi.com, $15 pp, including breakfast). As well as taking visitors on hikes and horseback rides to nearby rivers and waterfalls, local guides offer a strenuous but spectacular two- to three-day trek from Oyacachi to El Chaco in the Amazon. The best season for this adventure is November to February; it may be too rainy the rest of the year, but ask locally for current conditions. Local guides can be found at the information office next to the entrance to the hot springs. For an English- and French-speaking guide, contact Ivan Suarez (tel. 99/993-3148, http://www.all-about-ecuador.com).

VOLCÁN CAYAMBE

The summit of Ecuador's third-tallest peak (5,790 m/18,996 ft) is not only the highest point in the world on the equator, but also the coldest—and the only place where temperature and latitude reach zero simultaneously. Suitable for advanced climbers only, **Cayambe** is a seven-hour climb from the refuge to the summit, and there are many obstacles—an ever-changing network of crevasses, unusually high winds, strong snowstorms, and occasional avalanches. At 4,600 meters (15,090 ft), the **Bergé-Oleas-Ruales refuge,** named for three mountaineers killed in an avalanche in 1974, offers a mattress, dinner, and breakfast ($32 pp, bring your own sleeping bag). See the **Ecuadorian Association of Mountain Guides** (tel. 2/254-0599, https://aseguim.org/miembros) to find a guide, or contact **Andean Face** (www.andeanface.com) in Quito. In Otavalo, all the tour operators listed offer the climb, including a night at the refuge (approx. $280).

GETTING THERE

The Cayambe-Coca reserve is accessed via the town of Cayambe. To get there, take a bus with **Flor de Valle** (http://coopflordelvalle.com) from Quito's Ofelia terminal (1.5 hours). From Otavalo, there are frequent buses to Cayambe.

Buses from Cayambe to Oyacachi take 1.5 hours, leaving Cayambe at 8am and 3pm, returning at 10am and 5pm. A *camioneta* to Oyacachi from Cayambe costs $35 one way. To drive to Oyacachi, you'll need four-wheel drive. Take the road from Cayambe to Cangahua and drive for 40 kilometers (25 mi) until you reach a checkpoint, from where Oyacachi is another 15 minutes.

A *camioneta* to the Bergé-Oleas-Ruales refuge from Cayambe is $35 one way (1 hour). To drive there from Cayambe, take the Juan Montalvo-El Hato-PieMonte road in a four-wheel-drive vehicle.

OTAVALO

Otavalo is one of the oldest towns in Imbabura Province and was a market town long before the Incas arrived. Today, the textile market is the biggest in Ecuador and one of the most renowned in South America. Textile and handicrafts stalls are a permanent fixture in the Plaza de Ponchos, but the biggest day is Saturday, when the streets near the square are pedestrianized to make room for the additional vendors who flock into town and there is a festival atmosphere.

The town has a dramatic setting, nestled at 2,530 meters (8,300 ft) in the verdant Valle del Amanecer (Valley of the Sunrise) between two dormant volcanoes: Cotacachi to the northwest and Imbabura to the east. There is great hiking around several stunning lakes and waterfalls close to town, and adventure sports such as climbing, rafting, and biking in the surrounding mountains and rivers. Traditional crafts are still practiced in the neighboring indigenous villages, where there are several community tourism projects.

On the whole, the streets of Otavalo are safe, even at night. Sadly, however, the large number of visitors has led to occasional robberies, and there are bag-slashers and pickpockets in the crowded Saturday market. Take care with your belongings on the bus between Otavalo and Quito. When exploring the area's trails and more remote locations, it's best not to go alone, as robberies of lone hikers are not unheard of.

ORIENTATION

Otavalo is easy to navigate, with most hotels, restaurants, and amenities near the two main squares, Plaza de Ponchos (to the northeast of the center) and Parque Simón Bolívar (less than a kilometer to the southwest). The main avenue between the two squares is Antonio José de Sucre. The Pan-American Highway skirts the town to the west.

SIGHTS

TOP EXPERIENCE

✪ Textile Market

The town's biggest draw is the Saturday **textile market** (7am-6pm). By 9am, the Plaza de Ponchos is packed with a brightly colored, murmuring throng of vendors and visitors haggling over every imaginable type of textile and craft. Although there is a wide range of goods available throughout the week, the largest market is on Saturday, and it's worth a visit even if you don't intend to buy anything. Wednesday is the second-biggest day.

Traditional wares include wool and alpaca sweaters, blankets, wall hangings, and ponchos; embroidered shirts; and long cloth strips called *fajas,* used by Sierra Kichwas to tie back their hair.

Otavalo

To Museo Otavalango
and Quiroga

To Peguche
and Ibarra

HOSPITAL SAN LUIS
DE OTAVALO

Bus
Terminal

COLLAHUAZO

PANAMERICANA

PEÑA LA
JAMPA

SUCRE

BOLÍVAR

ORDOÑEZ

ATAHUALPA

To Cascadas
de Peguche

31 DE OCTUBRE

CASA LATITUD
POSADA DEL QUINDE

RICAURTE

RUNA
TUPARI

BANCO PICHINCHA

Quito

ALY SAMAYLLA

TOURIST OFFICE

To El Lechero
and Parque
Condor

EGAS

TEXTILE MARKET

MACHANA

Plaza de
Ponchos

QUIROGA

HOSTAL ARAUCO

CAVA CARAN

THE DELI

SALINAS

CISNEROS

JARAMILLO

BOCA

CISNEROS

SEE
DETAIL

MORALES

Yana Yacu
Public Pools

Animal
Market

COLON

CALDERON

MUNDO ANDINO
SPANISH SCHOOL

HOTEL EL
INDIO INN

FLYING DONKEY

HOTEL CORAZA

Plaza
González
Suárez

IGLESIA
EL JORDAN

ALTA ANDINA

DOÑA ESTHER HOSTAL &
RESTAURANT ÁRBOL
DE MONTALVO

FOOD MARKET

TRAIN STATION

MERCADO
24 DE MAYO

Parque
Bolívar

QUINO RESTAURANT
"SABOR Y ARTE"

PANAMERICANA

BANCO PACÍFICO

SANTA
FE

RIVIERA SUCRE

To Laguna
San Pablo

GARCIA

OTAVALO
LEARNING &
ADVENTURE

MORENO

PALACIO
MUNICIPAL

BANCO DE
PICHINCHA

PIEDRAHITA

OLMEDO

ROCA

IGLESIA
SAN
FRANCISCO

MEJÍA

ROCAFUERTE

To Police Station
and Mojanda

MORA

PANAMERICANA

BOLÍVAR

ATAHUALPA

CEMENTERIO
INDIGENA

To Cayambe
and Quito

0   250 yds

0   250 m

© MOON.COM

CAFÉ
SHANANDOA

SALINAS

JARAMILLO

EQUATORFACE

SUCRE

GALERÍA DE
ARTE QUIPUS

INCAZEN
TEA HOUSE

THE RED PUB

MORALES

PEÑA
AMAUTA

ECOMONTES

ANTARA

COLON

LA CASA
DE INTAG

WEAVING THE HISTORY OF THE KICHWAS OF OTAVALO

Alongside Otavalo's white and mestizo residents, more than 40,000 indigenous Otavalos of Kichwa nationality live in the town and surrounding villages. Thanks to their famous weaving skills, the Kichwas of Otavalo are a special case among indigenous groups; their unusual financial success and cultural stability allow them to travel internationally and educate their children abroad while still keeping a firm hold on their traditions at home.

When the Incans arrived, the Otavalos had already been using the backstrap weaving loom for centuries. The Incas, appreciating the fine work, collected the weavings as tributes. Specially chosen women dedicated their lives to creating fine textiles, some of which were burned in ritual offerings to the sun. After the Spanish conquest, exploitation of the local craftspeople pervaded, and they were forced to work in sweatshops, or *obrajes*, in terrible conditions. In the 19th century, mass production switched to factories, where the oppression continued. In the early 20th century, Otavalo's weavers caught the world's attention with a popular and inexpensive imitation of cashmere, a fine woven cloth from Asia, but their virtual slavery continued until the Agrarian Reform Law of 1964. This law granted indigenous people land and control over their choice of work, enabling them to weave in their own homes on a self-employed basis.

Although traditional weaving is still practiced in a few of the surrounding villages, these days most Otavalos have adapted their processes to keep up with the global economy, using electric machines or cheaper material bought in other countries. Others work as merchants or in the tourism industry. The Kichwas of Otavalo own most of the businesses in the town, as well as many stores throughout Ecuador and in other countries in South America. They travel extensively abroad in the Americas, Europe, and Asia to sell their products.

While some Otavalos still wear the traditional poncho, particularly on special occasions, others prefer western clothes. However they dress, the Otavalos of Kichwa take great pride in their cultural identity, and the election of Otavalo's first indigenous mayor in 2000 reflects the strength of their presence in the region.

There is a wide range of hats, from felt to Panama to woolly with bobbles; lots of jewelry made from beads, *tagua* nut, and silver; and handbags of every variety. Other items include paintings, wooden ornaments, hand-painted wooden plates and dishes, musical instruments, dream catchers, leather goods, fake shrunken heads, and spices.

While there are some true treasures to be found in the market, as the city has become more of a tourist attraction, some of the goods have started to be mass-produced in nearby factories; many are actually made in China or Peru. Some blankets and ponchos are advertised as "alpaca" but may be synthetic. Unless you're a textile expert, there is really no way to know what you're buying. A good general rule is, if you like it, buy it, regardless of its claimed origin or pedigree. The only items likely to be handmade locally are the traditional wall hangings, or *tapices*, which have pre-Columbian geometric motifs or depict a row of indigenous people in hats, seen from behind (these figures are known as the *chismosas* or "the gossipers"). *Tapices* are still made in the surrounding villages using traditional methods.

For the Saturday market, it's best to spend Friday night in town, but make a reservation because hotels fill up fast. Alternatively, get a Saturday morning bus from Quito. Bargaining is expected, even in the textiles and handicrafts stores in town. Foreigners are naturally offered rather inflated prices, so haggle away, but don't be too pushy; if you get 30 percent off the starting price, you're doing well. Linger toward the end of the day for the best deals.

Parque Bolívar

The most attractive and historic part of Otavalo is at the south end of town. **Parque Bolívar** is dominated by the statue of Inca general Rumiñahui, who valiantly resisted the Spanish invaders and remains a symbol of indigenous resistance. The park often hosts events and live music on weekends. On the west side of the park is the main church, **San Luis,** built in the late 19th century with a single octagonal tower. Two blocks southeast on Calderón and Roca is a more attractive church, **El Jordán,** which has impressively carved wooden doors.

Museo Otavalango

It's worth making the trip a couple of kilometers northwest of town to visit the **Museo Otavalango** (Antigua Fábrica San Pedro, Pedro Perez, Vía Antigua a Quiroga, tel. 6/290-3879, https://otavalango.wordpress.com, 9am–5pm Mon.-Sat., free). The museum was once the home of Ecuador's first president, José Féliz Valdivieso, before being converted into the northern Sierra's first factory in 1858, where indigenous Otavalos were forced to work in slave-like conditions. Although working life improved, the factory continued to operate until the late 1990s before closing its doors. Years later, an ex-worker at the factory, René Zambrano, visited his former workplace to find it derelict. He and his wife, Ludmilla, organized a group of ex-factory workers to raise the funds needed to buy the site and turn it into a museum, which opened in 2011. As well as housing exhibits on the history of the factory, the museum is a living community space, dedicated

colorful indigenous wood carvings for sale at the Saturday textile market

to the preservation of Kichwa culture, encouraging local youngsters to maintain their ancestral traditions. A visit here is not a highly polished experience, but that is its charm; you may have to wander around a bit before finding someone to show you around. Call ahead of time to make a reservation for a tour in English or to request special demonstrations of traditional weaving, music, and dance.

Cementerio Indígena

On Mondays and Thursdays between 7am and 10am, many indigenous Otavalos gather to pay their respects to the dead at the **Cementerio Indígena,** which is just across the Pan-American Highway south of town. They bring the favorite dishes of the deceased, socialize, and share food with one another. It is perfectly acceptable for non-indigenous people to visit the cemetery, but be respectful; don't go in a big group or take photos near visiting families. The best day to visit is November 2, the Day of the Dead.

Mirador El Lechero

Four kilometers (2.5 mi) outside town, the **Mirador El Lechero** is a hill offering 360-degree views of Otavalo, Laguna de San Pablo, and Imbabura. The mirador's name, which means "the milkman," comes from a tree with milky white sap that is renowned for its healing powers. The tree has been used as a ceremony site for shamanic rituals and, along with 12 others planted in the area over a century ago, is where the umbilical cords of newly born babies were buried to connect local communities with the land. The mirador is a one-hour uphill walk from Otavalo. Head southeast out of town on Piedrahita and follow the signs as the road quickly steepens into

a series of switchbacks. Alternatively, take a taxi from Otavalo for $3.5-4 (one way). Ask the driver to wait, or make the return journey on foot.

Parque Cóndor

Parque Cóndor (tel. 98/431-1769, www.parquecondor.com, 9:30am-5pm Wed.-Sun., $4.75), 2.5 kilometers (1.6 mi) north of the mirador, is a sanctuary for condors, hawks, eagles, owls, and other birds of prey, which are well cared for after being rescued or donated. There are shows at 11:30am and 3:30pm (in Spanish), where visitors can see the birds flying up close. The center has a strong focus on environmental education. Walk there via El Lechero, or take a $4 taxi from Otavalo. Ask the driver to come back at an allotted time (2 hours is plenty, including the show).

ENTERTAINMENT AND EVENTS
Nightlife

Nightlife is low-key in Otavalo during the week but gets going on weekends, particularly Saturdays. Recommended bars include ✪ **Cava Caran** (Modesto Jaramillo *y* Salinas, tel. 99/189-7959, Facebook @CavaCaran, 5pm-midnight Tues.-Fri., 10am-midnight Sat.), a basement bar on Plaza de Ponchos serving locally brewed craft beer and whisky made with a still that belonged to the friendly owner's grandfather. The food menu includes burgers, burritos, pizzas, and sandwiches, with veggie options available. Also right on the plaza, **Machana** (Sucre, tel. 99/258-5316, Facebook @Machana Lounge) is a café, bar, live music venue, and gallery that is hopping with an arty, alternative crowd on weekends. Another option is **The Red Pub** (Morales *y* Sucre, tel.

barn owls at Parque Cóndor

98/762-7666, Facebook @TheRedPub, 3pm-midnight Sun.-Wed., 3pm-3am Thurs.-Sat.). Despite its name, it's frequented by as many locals as gringos. It has an alternative vibe and plays rock music.

For dancing, try **Peña Amauta** (Morales 5-11 *y* Modesto Jaramillo, tel. 2/924-435, Facebook @amautabar, 8pm-3am Fri.-Sat.), an intimate spot with live traditional Andean music every Friday and Saturday at 10pm; or **La Jampa** (31 de Octubre *y* Panamericana Norte, tel. 99/818-8976, Facebook @lajampa, 9pm-2am Fri.-Sat.), which has live music every Saturday, often folkloric or salsa. Three dance floors play a mix of dance, salsa, *reggaetón,* merengue, and rumba.

Festivals

These festivals can fall on different days from year to year, so check with the tourist office on the Plaza de Ponchos (http://otavalo.travel) for specific dates.

Pawkar Raymi (Blossoming Festival) is the Quechua equivalent of Carnival, usually held in February, to celebrate the fertility of the earth. Celebrations last for 11 days and include fireworks, parades, musical events, an indigenous football competition, and various rituals involving water and flowers.

The **Fiesta del Coraza,** a local festival dating back to the early 18th century, is celebrated in and around Laguna San Pablo between June 9 and 15. Two personages on horseback appear during the event: the *coraza,* his skin painted white to represent the Spanish and his face covered in silver chains to symbolize greed; and the *pendonero,* who represents resistance to the Spanish invasion, dressed as a warrior waving a blood-red flag. Another highlight of the festival is a race on the lake between floating horses made of reeds.

Inti Raymi (Quechua for Sun Festival) is the Inca festival of the northern solstice and the most important Andean celebration. Every indigenous group has its own specific dates and traditions for Inti Raymi, but the main event starts on June 21 and continues for several days. In the Otavalo area, people gather to bathe in sacred rivers and waterfalls on June 22 to eliminate negative energies accumulated during the previous year, to purify themselves and kick off the festivities. The Peguche waterfall is the best spot to participate in this cleansing ritual, known as Armay Chishi. Throughout the celebrations, there is live music and dancing in the Plaza de Ponchos as well as the streets and houses of the surrounding villages.

The **Yamor** festival, held from the end of August until the first week of September, dates back to pre-Incan times and centers around a drink, a type of *chicha*, which is made from seven varieties of corn and represents the unity of the people, coming together like grains of corn. This is a local festival that originated in the village of Monserrat, home to the Virgin of Monserrat, the patron saint of Otavalo. The festival includes parades, musical events, and a swimming competition in the Laguna San Pablo.

RECREATION AND TOURS
Hiking
The **Mirador El Lechero** and **Parque Cóndor** make a good combined hike from Otavalo. It's also possible to add the waterfalls and town of **Peguche** for a total 10-kilometer (6.2-mi) walk, which will take most of a day. The path is signposted. There are cafés at the Condor Park and in Peguche, but take plenty of water, snacks, and sunblock. There may be some unfriendly dogs en route to Peguche, so it's a good idea to carry a stick. The tourist office on the Plaza de Ponchos has hiking maps,

which are also available on their website: http://otavalo.travel/en/.

Tour Operators
Although many of the areas around Otavalo can be explored independently, several agencies in town organize English-speaking tours. Most offer day trips to see weavers and other artisans in the surrounding villages ($50 pp); hikes around Cuicocha ($40 pp); trips to Lagunas de Mojanda and Fuya Fuya ($40 pp); and ascents of the region's peaks. See their websites for the full range of tours.

The most ecologically minded tour agency in Otavalo is **All About EQ** (tel. 99/993-3148, www.all-about-ecuador.com), owned by friendly Otavaleño Ivan Suarez, who speaks fluent English and French. As well as all the usual local activities, Ivan is a skilled mountain guide for the whole northern Sierra region. He has a special interest in community tourism and offers a spectacular multi-day trekking and/or horseback-riding adventure, starting in the remote mountain village of Piñan and ending in Intag.

Runa Tupari (Calle Sucre *y* Quiroga, tel. 6/292-2320, www.runatupari.com) provides the most authentic indigenous experiences. The company can set up homestays ($35 pp including meals and transportation) with 25 families in five nearby small communities. Also available is a shamanic medicine tour ($55 pp), horseback-riding in Cotacachi-Cayapas National Park ($45 pp), and a downhill bike ride into the Intag Valley ($85 pp).

Half a block from Plaza de Ponchos, locally owned **EquatorFace** (Sucre *entre* Salinas *y* Morales, tel. 6/292-2665, www.equatorface.com) is a new, friendly, and professional outfit. As

THE LANGUAGE OF THE INCAS

Indigenous peoples in the Sierra speak various dialects of Kichwa that are very different from those spoken by the Kichwas in the Amazon. The language evolved from Quechua, which pre-dates the Incas and was enforced by them as the official tongue of the empire. Many Kichwa words are commonly used in English, including "condor," "jerky," "llama," "puma," and "quinine." South American Spanish is also full of Kichwa words, including *"papa"* (potato), *"choclo"* (corn), *"chompa"* (sweater), and, more amusingly, *"chuchaqui"* (hangover). Some other basic phrases are:

- *Ama shua, ama llulla, ama killa*—Don't steal, don't lie, don't be lazy

- *Napaykuna*—Greetings

- *Alli puncha*—Good morning

- *Alli chishi*—Good afternoon

- *Alli tuta*—Good evening

- *Yupaychani*—Thank you/Thanks for everything

- *Alli shamushka*—You are welcome

- *Ima shinalla?/allillachu kanki?*—How are you?

- *Allilla, kan ka?*—Fine, and you?

- *Ima shuti kanki?*—What's your name?

- *Ñuka_____shutimi kani*—My name is_____.

- *Maymanta shamunki?*—Where are you from?

- *Ñukaka _____ mantami kani*—I am from _____.

- *Rikunakushun*—See you later

- *Kayakama*—See you tomorrow

- *Tayta*—Sir, gentleman

- *Mama*—Madam, lady

- *Mashi*—Friend

- *-pay* (verb suffix)—Please

- *Mikupay*—Eat, please

- *Shamupay*—Come on, please

- *Apapay*—Bring it, please

- *Imamanta*—Why?

well as all the local activities, a variety of national tours are offered, up to 15 days in length.

Another reputable agency in town is family-run **Ecomontes Tour** (Sucre y Morales, tel. 6/292-6244, http://otavaloguide.com), where the friendly staff specialize in adventure tours (climbing, mountain biking, rafting, kayaking). Mountain-bike rental is also available.

Tren Ecuador offers a scenic round-trip train ride ($39) is available from Otavalo to the Afro-Ecuadorian community of Salinas, leaving on Fridays, Saturdays, Sundays, and public holidays at 8am and getting back into Otavalo at 5:55pm. During the stop in Salinas, visitors can learn about Afro-Ecuadorian history and culture, and sample the cuisine. See http://trenecuador.com for more information.

SHOPPING

In addition to the market, throughout Otavalo are stores where you can browse huge selections of woven goods and other textile products such as clothes, bags, and hammocks. **La Casa de Intag** (Colón y Sucre, tel. 6/292-0608, Facebook @LaCasadeIntag) is a café and fair trade store opened by grassroots organizations in the Intag region, offering local organic coffee and honey, bags and handicrafts made from cloud forest sisal, and handmade aloe toiletry products. Proceeds go toward local communities and environmental conservation.

Sisa Morales (Facebook @coloressisa) is an Otavalo Kichwa fashion designer who makes beautiful, hand-embroidered traditional indigenous clothing with a contemporary twist. She employs local single mothers as embroiderers. **Alta Andina** (www.

Near Otavalo there are many opportunities to experience traditional Andean music and gastronomy.

TOURISM MICRO-ENTERPRISES

The following projects have been set up by local people to share their traditions with visitors. Supporting them is an excellent way to boost the local economy and help keep ancestral customs alive. Most are not of sufficient size to have someone manning the operation at all times, so it's necessary to make reservations a few days in advance. Be aware that almost no English is spoken in rural communities. The tourist office on the corner of the Plaza de Ponchos has more information about these micro-enterprises on its website under Tourism Projects (http://otavalo.travel). They can also help to set up visits and advise on transport.

- **Sumak Pacha** (turismopijal@hotmail.com or sumakpacha@hotmail.com, tel. 6/261-8150 or 99/758-7263): The Community Tourism Center in the village of Kayambi offers family homestays and activities including organic agriculture, music, dance, traditional cuisine, hikes, and horseback riding. Location: Pijal community, San Pablo Lake parish, $6 taxi from Otavalo.

- **Asociacíon Pachamama** (pachamama@hotmail.com, tel. 98/253-0105 or 98/501-0112) offers talks on Andean cosmovision and medicinal plants, traditional energy cleansing and purification rituals ($6), traditional gastronomy (tortillas made with quinoa, amaranth leaves, nettle, beets, Swiss chard, and *zambo* squash), pomades of medicinal plants, totems against bad energy, and embroidery. Location: Angla community, $6-8 taxi from Otavalo or $4 from Laguna San Pablo.

- **Totora Sisa** (www.totorasisa.blogspot.com, totorasisa@yahoo.coman) is an association of communities near the Laguna San Pablo that make mats, furniture, and decorative items from reeds that grow in the lake. The workshop is open to the public and they give demonstrations. Location: San Rafael, Laguna San Pablo, $0.30 by bus from Otavalo or $3 by taxi.

- **Inka Tambo** (inkatamboecuador@gmail.com, tel. 6/269-0798 or 99/362-2058) offers indigenous plant-based medicine, organic agriculture, traditional gastronomy, and handicrafts. Location: Peguche, $0.30 by bus or $3 by taxi from Otavalo.

- **Jatary** (asojatary@outlook.com, tel. 98/911-2465 or 6/269-0512) is an association of Kichwa female entrepreneurs that promote *"sumak kawsay"* (good living in harmony with nature and community). They provide lodging, local gastronomy, hiking, and textile demonstrations. Location: Peguche, $0.30 by bus or $3 by taxi from Otavalo.

- **Kawsaymi** (www.kawsaymi.com, kawsaymi@gmail.com, tel. 98/768-4914) is a Kichwa family offering Andean cooking classes, local gastronomy, homestays, music, dance, and long-term volunteering. *"Kawsaymi"* means "our daily living" in Kichwa. Location: Parroquia San José de Quichinche, Comunidad Kichwa Panecillo, Vía Andaviejo; $0.30 by bus from Otavalo to Panecillo, or $3 by taxi.

- **Ayllukunapak** (Facebook @ayllukunapak, tel. 93/916-1458 or 99/298-2433) is an agro-ecological association that holds a twice-weekly organic farmers market (7am-2pm Wed. and Sat.). The community also offers a homestay package ($100 pp), where guests help to harvest the ingredients for traditional meals, which are then cooked together with the hosts, accompanied by an Andean band. Location: San Vicente de Cotama, $0.30 on the bus heading to Los Lagos or $2 by taxi.

altaandina.com), based at the train station on Calle Guayaquil with a stall at the Saturday market, offers lovingly handcrafted leather products, including bags, belts, and wallets, that are made to order and come with a lifetime guarantee. All materials are ethically sourced. **Antara** (Morales *y* Sucre, tel. 6/292-6107, Facebook @ casamusicalantara) sells handmade Andean musical instruments, such as guitars, flutes, and panpipes. For work by local artists, try the **Galería de Arte Quipus** (Sucre *y* Morales), which specializes in oil paintings and watercolors. At the west end of town on Morales, just before the Panamericana, the **Municipal Market 24 de Mayo** is the best place to pick up fresh produce.

FOOD

On the south side of the Plaza de Ponchos, the legendary **Café Shenandoah** (Salinas 5-15, 11am-9pm daily, $2-3) has been serving home-made fruit pies for decades. Choose from 10 flavors, including lemon, passion fruit, and blackberry. One block from the market, ✪ **IncaZen Tea House & Gallery** (Sucre y Morales, Facebook @incazentea, 11am-8pm Thurs.-Sun., noon-2pm Mon.) offers Ecuadorian teas, *kombucha*, cocktails, cupcakes, and vegan food. The friendly Californian owner supports local producers and artists. ✪ **La Casa de Intag** (Colón y Sucre, tel. 6/292-0608, Facebook @LaCasadeIntag) is a café and fair trade store opened by grassroots organizations in the biodiverse Intag region, serving great organic coffee, fried yucca, pancakes, breakfasts, and sandwiches.

The best place to sample Andean cuisine alongside local people is the **Municipal Market 24 de Mayo,** at the west end of town on Morales, just before the Panamericana. The food court on the upper floor serves local specialties, including *hornado* (slow roasted pork), *llapingachos* (potato patties), and *mote con fritado* (hominy with fried pork). A good place for Ecuadorian seafood dishes is **Quino Restaurant Sabor y Arte** (Roca near Montalvo, tel. 6/292-4994, 10am-11pm daily, $6-13).

A couple of places offer a mix of national and international dishes. Half a block from Parque Bolívar, Dutch-owned **Restaurant Árbol de Montalvo** (Montalvo y Roca, inside Hostal Doña Esther, tel. 6/292-0739, www.otavalohotel.com, 6pm-9pm Tues.-Thurs., 7am-10pm Fri.-Sun., $8-11) offers typical Ecuadorian specialties such as *cazuela* (a fish and shrimp dish with plantain and peanuts) alongside its famous wood-fired pizza. ✪ **The Deli** (Quiroga y Bolívar, tel. 6/292-1558, www.delicaferestaurant.com, 10am-8pm Mon.-Sat., $5-8) is a cozy little gem of a café a block from the market. The menu includes *mote con fritado* (hominy with fried pork), *humitas* (ground corn mashed with cheese, onion, garlic, eggs, and cream and steamed in corn leaves), Tex-Mex, pasta, and pizza, with vegetarian options.

ACCOMMODATIONS

Otavalo has lots of locally owned budget and midrange accommodations, with some top-end haciendas outside town. During the week there is usually plenty of availability, but the best hotels fill up fast on Friday and Saturday nights, so consider booking ahead.

$10-25

Right on the Plaza de Ponchos, **Hostal Aly Samaylla** (Quiroga y Modesto Jaramillo, tel. 6/292-6865, $10 s, $15 d) is one of the cheapest options. Simple rooms with private bathrooms, hot water, Wi-Fi, and cable TV overlook the market.

Slightly to the west of the town center near the Mercado 24 Mayo, ✪ **Hostal Arauco** (Calle Miguel Egas y Calle Salinas, tel. 99/911-5019, Facebook @arauco.hs, $15 s, $20-40 d) offers amazing value. Light, airy, and stylish, the individually decorated guest rooms are immaculate and quiet at night. Beds are comfortable and the showers are excellent.

Many of the best accommodations

are located toward Parque Bolívar. **Hostal Flying Donkey** (Abdón Calderón *y* Simón Bolívar, tel. 6/292-8122, Facebook @flyingdonkeyotavalo, $9.50 dorm, $12-17 pp private room) is a friendly, family-run hostel with clean rooms, a shared kitchen, fast Wi-Fi, and a terrace with wonderful views. Mountain bike hire is available. The rooms at nearby **Hotel Coraza** (Calderón *y* Sucre, tel. 6/292-1225, https://hotelcoraza.wixsite.com/otavalo, $18.50 pp, including breakfast) are very clean and comfortable. **Hostal Santa Fe** (Roca *y* García Moreno, tel. 6/292-3640, www.hotelsantafeotavalo.com, $16 pp or $19 pp including breakfast) is warm and inviting, with excellent service and a good restaurant.

Over $25

The renovated colonial **Doña Esther** (Montalvo 444 *y* Bolívar, tel. 6/292-0739, www.otavalohotel.com, $45 s, $65 d, including breakfast) is the best value in this range, with 12 attractive rooms around a central, plant-filled courtyard and a great restaurant. The Dutch couple who owns it are welcoming hosts, happy to share information about the area.

The ✪ **Hotel Riviera Sucre** (Moreno *y* Roca, tel. 6/292-0241, $25 s, $40 d) is an excellent option, with a courtyard, flower-filled garden, lounge area, and spacious, colorful rooms. Breakfast is available for $2.50-4.

The **Hotel El Indio Inn** (Bolívar *y* Abdón Calderón, tel. 6/292-0325, www.hotelelindioinn.com, $43 s, $64 d, including breakfast) has comfortable guest rooms arranged around two inner courtyards. Service is friendly and helpful. Massages are available ($40/hour).

For longer stays and group bookings, email Maggie Reniers (maggie@latitudefoundation.org), owner of the beautiful **Casa Latitud** (previously Posada del Quinde, Av. Quito *y* Miguel Egas, tel. 6/292-0750, www.casalatitud.org). Home to Fundación Latitud, the hotel shares space with Maggie's scholarship program, local acupuncture clinic, and English-language school, all nonprofit ventures. Availability can be limited when groups are lodging.

INFORMATION AND SERVICES

The **tourist office** (Quiroga *y* Jaramillo, tel. 6/292-7230, http://otavalo.travel, 8am-5:30pm Mon.-Fri., 8am-5pm Sat.) is at the corner of Plaza de Ponchos. It has helpful English-speaking staff, good maps on attractions and hikes, and free storage lockers. The website, available in English, is a good source of information and downloadable maps.

Banco Pichincha has ATMs near Plaza de Ponchos and Simón Bolívar Park. The local **hospital** (tel. 6/292-0444) is northeast of town on Sucre, and the **police station** (tel. 101) is at the southwest edge of town on the Panamericana.

Spanish Lessons

Mundo Andino Spanish School (Bolívar *y* Abdón Calderón, 3rd floor, tel. 6/292-1864, www.mandinospanishschool.com) and **Otavalo Learning & Adventure** (García Moreno *y* Atahualpa, tel. 99/700-8542) are recommended.

GETTING THERE AND AROUND

There are frequent buses (2 hours, $2.50) to/from Quito's Carcelén terminal with Cooperativa Otavalo (tel. 6/292-0405 Facebook @cooperativatransotavalo) and Cooperativa Los Lagos (tel. 6/292-0382).

Otavalo's **bus terminal** (Atahualpa and Ordoñez) is on the northeast corner of town, where you can catch buses to Quito, Ibarra (40 minutes, $0.55), Cayambe, Cotacachi, and local villages such as Ilumán and Peguche.

Taxis charge $1.25 for short journeys around town and $3 for attractions on the edge of town (e.g., Peguche waterfall and El Lechero).

LAGUNA DE SAN PABLO

The nearest lake to Otavalo is the huge **Laguna de San Pablo** that you pass on the way from Quito. At the foot of **Volcán Imbabura,** it's a pleasant spot with impressive views of the volcano. Although the area around the lake is increasingly developed, the small shoreline villages still specialize in making traditional woven reed mats (see *Tourism Micro-Enterprises* in the Otavalo section). The road surrounding the lake makes a nice hike (3-4 hours) or bike ride.

The southwestern side of the lake is less developed than the north side, with less infrastructure and more greenery. Just off the Panamericana, near the community of San Rafael, there is a floating dock, the **Muelle Flotante Cachiviro,** with expansive views and a community tourism project which takes visitors around the lake by boat (8am-5pm, $20 for a 30-minute boat ride, 2 person minimum). The turnoff for dock is clearly signposted on the highway, from where it's a short drive or walk. On this side of the lake is the **Hostería Puertolago** (tel. 6/263-5400, www.puertolago.com, $65-135 s, $80-135 d), which has individual cabins with

fireplaces set in beautiful grounds. The restaurant (7:30am-9pm Mon.-Thurs., 7:30am-9:30pm Fri.-Sun.) serves good quality national and international dishes with all vegetables grown in the organic gardens.

The northeastern side of the lake is very popular with local families on weekends. The **Parque Acuático Araque** (tel. 98/728-8158 Facebook @parqueacuaticoaraque) is a community tourism project offering boat trips, horseback riding and local cuisine. Nearby, the comfortable **Hostería Cabañas del Lago** (tel. 6/291-8108, www.cabanasdellago.com.ec, $115-160 s/d), has cabins with fireplaces and a lakeside restaurant (8am-10:30am and noon-8pm daily) serving Ecuadorian food with a contemporary twist.

A taxi from Otavalo to the lake costs $3. The 4-kilometer (2.5-mi) hike from Otavalo takes about an hour, or go via El Lechero and Parque Cóndor for a longer walk. For the south side of the lake, take any bus heading to Quito and ask the driver to let you off. For the north side, take the bus heading to Araque.

Ecuadorian-owned **My Sachaji** (tel. 9/845-65012, www.mysachaji.com, $290-380 pp, including breakfast) is a luxury hotel and wellness retreat a few kilometers east of the lake. Rooms with views of the lake or volcano are designed for ultimate coziness, with fireplaces, thermal windows, blackout curtains, and a poncho to wear. Various treatments and therapies are available and the staff includes a shaman, a yoga teacher, a massage therapist, and an indigenous traditional medicine practitioner. Among the facilities are a hydro-massage pool, a polar plunge pool and a trampoline. The hotel was built using sustainable

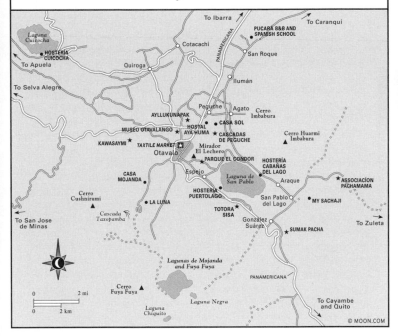

Otavalo and Vicinity

© MOON.COM

and environmentally-friendly methods, including bricks made from earth excavated on-site, and used tires as below-floor insulation. Green roofs reduce CO2 emissions and solar panels are installed above the rooms. For each wooden door, a tree of the same species was planted on site. Water for bathing is sun-heated and comes from rainwater and nearby waterfalls. Organic gardens supply fruit, vegetables and herbs for the restaurant. The hotel is LGBTQ friendly.

LAGUNAS DE MOJANDA AND FUYA FUYA

South of Otavalo, the cobbled Vía a Lagos de Mojanda winds up into the *páramo* to three beautiful lagoons in the shadow of dark, jagged mountains. The **Laguna Grande** (also known as Caricocha), **Laguna Negra** (Huarmicocha), and **Laguna Chiquita** (Yanacocha) are 3,700 meters (12,100 ft) above sea level. At 2 kilometers (1.2 mi) wide, Laguna Grande is the biggest, with a dirt road extending part of the way around it to simple cabins, accessible by four-wheel drive or on foot, where it is possible to stay ($20) or camp ($2, bring your own tent). Only breakfast is available, so bring food with you. Be aware that the *páramo* is very cold at night, with sudden rains. An overnight stay is especially recommended on clear, full moon nights, when the sky is spectacularly reflected in the lake's surface. Trails also lead east and south from Laguna Grande to the two smaller lakes.

The peak of **Fuya Fuya** (4,262 m/13,983 ft), the highest point to the west, is a popular climb as acclimatization practice for higher peaks. Paths lead up the mountainside from Laguna Grande and can be climbed without a guide for a four-hour round-trip.

The lakes are 15 kilometers (9.3 mi) from Otavalo, a 30-minute taxi ride ($15 each way). To have a quick look around and take some photos, ask the taxi driver to wait. If you are planning on hiking for a few hours, arrange a pickup time. For a more informed experience, go with a tour agency from Otavalo ($40 pp).

Until the new highway was built in 1900, the road to the lakes was the main thoroughfare from Otavalo to Quito for people on their way to the capital to sell goods. Since the trek took 2-3 days, there were a couple of simple lodgings en route for travelers to sleep. Legend has it that the owners of one such place, the Remache family, used to kidnap and kill some of their guests and serve them up as *fritada* to other unsuspecting customers. Once a year, on the last Saturday of October, the municipal government organizes a walk to commemorate the old road and the people who used it. It's a popular event, leaving from the Parque Bolívar in Otavalo at 4am. Participants are transported to a spot 52 kilometers (32 mi) up the Vía a Lagos de Mojanda and return to Otavalo on foot, via the lakes. To join the walk, register with the tourist office in Otavalo (Quiroga y Jaramillo, tel. 6/292-7230, http://otavalo.travel) a couple of days in advance.

Casa Mojanda

Four kilometers (2.5 mi) from Otavalo on the road to the Mojanda lakes, the American/Ecuadorian-owned ✪ **Casa Mojanda** (tel. 6/304-9253 or 98/033-5108, www.casamojanda. com, $116-122 s, $134-146 d, including breakfast) is an organic farm and lodge, constructed for minimal environmental impact using rammed earth adobe. The hotel clings to the edge of a valley with wonderful views of Volcán Cotacachi. The airy, whitewashed main lodge is full of fascinating artifacts, including pre-Columbian pottery found on the grounds and a stringed musical instrument made from an armadillo. Eight guest cabins are dotted around the grounds, alongside a library and an outdoor wood-fired hot tub. There is also a replica of a traditional mud dwelling that is used for shamanic treatments (available upon request). Ask for a tour of the extensive organic gardens, which supply the restaurant using biodynamic and permaculture principles. Any ingredients that don't come from the garden are sourced from local cooperatives utilizing fair trade principles. Lunch and dinner are available upon request; the latter is served family-style next to a cozy fire. Casa Mojanda was instrumental in developing a plan to secure protected status for the Mojanda lakes and grasslands and is involved in a program to sterilize local dogs. The lodge employs local people, and service is absolutely top-notch.

La Luna

A kilometer (0.6 mi) farther up the road from Casa Mojanda is English/Ecuadorian-owned ✪ **La Luna Mountain Lodge** (tel. 99/315-6082, www.lalunaecuador.info, camping $8, dorm $14 pp, $22-30 s, $38-47 d), an excellent option for travelers of all budgets. Rooms are rustic and charming, with fresh flowers, hammocks, and wonderful views. Some have their own fireplace. Breakfast is included in

Volcán Cotacachi seen from Casa Mojanda

the small restaurant, which also offers lunch and dinner, with plenty of vegetarian options. A small organic garden partially supplies the restaurant.

Casa Mojanda and La Luna are a 90-minute walk or $4-5 taxi ride from Otavalo. Buses operated by Cooperativa Imbaburapak leave the terminal every 40 minutes ($0.40) and go as far as La Luna before turning around.

Cascada de Taxopamba

A kilometer (0.6 mi) farther up the road from La Luna is the trailhead for the **Cascada Taxopamba,** a 40-meter (130-ft) waterfall fed by Laguna Mojanda. Almost as beautiful as Cascada Peguche, Taxopamba has far fewer visitors; it feels like a hidden treasure, and you may well have it to yourself. It's a scenic 15-minute walk from the road; avoid getting lost by staying on the path, and don't go through any gates. There are a couple of unfriendly dogs en route, so be ready to pick up a stick.

PEGUCHE

A small indigenous village near Otavalo, Peguche is renowned for its artisan wares, particularly weavings and musical instruments, with various workshops around town. For fine tapestries, visit either **José Ruiz Perugachi** or **José Cotacachi. Artesanía El Gran Condor** on the central plaza (tel. 6/269-0161, www. artesaniaelgrancondor.com) is another good textile workshop. A couple of blocks north of the plaza, **Ñanda Mañachi** (tel. 6/269-0076, open daily) makes a variety of traditional instruments, including *flautas* (reed flutes) and *rondadores* (Andean panpipes). See *Tourism Micro-Enterprises* in the *Otavalo* section for other local ventures.

Cascadas de Peguche

Surrounded by lush, green vegetation, the **Peguche waterfall** plunges 30 meters (100 ft) into a large pool, before the waters continue down the valley into Laguna de San Pablo. The

THE SHAMANS OF ILUMÁN

Ilumán shamans work with candles and medicinal plants.

Ilumán is known for its *curanderos* or *yachaks* (native healers or shamans), who have passed down natural remedies and spiritual cures through the generations for centuries, treating everything from back problems to cancer. Most older people in the region have sought their services at one time or another, though the younger generation often prefers Western medicine.

The shamans, who usually wear white to represent purification, work with a blend of indigenous and Christian rituals and herbal medicines. In a traditional cleansing session, invocations in Kichwa to Mama Cotacachi and Taita Imbabura are sent up alongside prayers in Spanish to the Virgin Mary and the saints. Diagnoses are made by passing a guinea pig or candle over the patient, then watching for the reaction in the animal or flame. The shaman will then recommend a cure for any ailment discovered, which may take the form of prayers or medicinal herbs like wild fuchsia, nettle, and red and white carnation petals.

Even for those who speak some Spanish, a visit to an Ilumán shaman can be a bewildering and intense experience, as they often don't explain what they are doing or why. Patients may get whipped with plants and will very likely be covered in spittle.

There are about 30 shamans in the **Asociacíon de Yachaks de Ilumán** (tel. 96/967-3924), which is recognized by the Public Health Ministry. A cleansing ritual may cost $20-40. Alternatively, a recommended shaman is Yuru Parayaku, who speaks a little English and is in Natabuela, between Ilumán and Ibarra (tel. 99/945-1682).

entrance is 1.5 kilometers (0.9 mi) south of Peguche, where there is a small visitors center (8:30am-5pm daily). There is no entrance fee, but you are asked to give a small donation, which goes toward the upkeep of the forest. From the center, it's a short, pleasant walk through the trees to the waterfall.

The *cascadas* are perfectly safe if you arrive via the main entrance and stick to the main paths leading to the biggest waterfall and the mirador. There is a secondary fall, higher up, where occasional robberies have been reported, so it's advisable to go with a guide or a group.

Rustic but charming wooden cabins are available for rent in a forest clearing ($5 pp) near the visitors center. They have electricity and access to toilets and a barbecue area, but nothing else. Bring an inflatable mattress if you don't want to sleep on the floor, plus a sleeping bag. Food is available in the village. Camping is available for $1 (bring your own tent).

A taxi from Otavalo to Peguche or the waterfall costs $3. There are buses from the Otavalo terminal to the village of Peguche or Las Cascadas, and it's a short walk between the two. To make the 45-minute hike from Otavalo, follow the railroad tracks north out of town at Quito and Guayaquil. Follow the road right when it leaves the tracks at the police station, and look for the sign at the waterfall entrance. Keep heading north to reach the village.

Food and Accommodations

Peguche offers a few options for those who want to stay outside of Otavalo but close to town. Just up the hill from the entrance to the waterfall is **La Casa Sol** (tel. 6/269-0500, www.lacasasol.com, $49 s, $59 d, including breakfast). Eight cozy, colorful rooms and two suites were built using traditional materials and methods. Each is equipped with a private bathroom, a fireplace, and a balcony with great views over Peguche and the Otavalo Valley. The restaurant is good and the staff are friendly.

Straddling the railroad tracks farther into town is **Hostal Aya Huma** (tel. 6/269-0333, www.ayahuma.com, $23 s, $37 d), which has fireplaces, hammocks, and a beautiful garden. There is live Andean music most Saturday nights. Among the many services offered are Spanish classes, massage, reiki, and personal coaching (in English). There is a sweat lodge on the first Saturday of every month, and various ceremonies and shamanic

the Peguche waterfall

rituals are also available. Staff can help organize hikes, bike trips, horseback riding, and tours to several villages. The restaurant, open for breakfast and dinner, offers vegetarian options. The hostel is pet-friendly and camping is available. To get there, follow the signs through town, or ask directions.

Central Sierra

South of Quito, the central highlands contain Ecuador's most dramatic Andean scenery and its legendary volcanoes, among them picture-perfect Cotopaxi.

Latacunga is the best access point for Cotopaxi, with Machachi an alternative.

MACHACHI

Located in the Valley of the Nine Volcanoes, **Machachi** (elevation 2,950 m/9,680 ft) is a small town an hour south of Quito along the Panamericana. There isn't much to see in the town itself, but, surrounded by majestic peaks, it's a good base for popular climbs, including Cotopaxi, Rumiñahui, the Ilinizas, and Corazón, and for accessing Cotopaxi National Park as a day trip.

This is agricultural country, known for being home to the Andean cowboy, or *chagra*. These skilled horsemen still ride the highlands dressed in poncho, chaps, scarf, and hat, rounding up bulls and driving them into corrals for branding and vaccinating.

SIGHTS

Machachi's central plaza is flanked by an ornate painted **church,** the **Teatro Municipal,** and the **tourist office** (9am-1pm and 2pm-5pm Mon.-Fri.), which can provide maps and information on exploring the surrounding area on horse, foot, and bike. On Sundays, Machachi hosts one of the region's largest **markets,** with people flocking from the surrounding rural communities to sell their fruit, vegetables, eggs, cheeses, and yogurts.

The town comes alive on the third Saturday of July for the **Processional Parade of the Chagra,** where 2,000 cowboys ride through the streets with bands and dancers.

Outside Machachi, 8 kilometers (5 mi) to the southwest is **Bee Farm Shunku** (Rieles del Tren, La Moya, tel. 98/461-7156, www.beefarmecuador.com), a working bee farm that offers tours on weekends with apiculture activities ($25, including breakfast or lunch, reserve one day ahead), honey and pollen products, and honey massages. Intensive, 48-hour apiculture workshops are also available.

FOOD AND ACCOMMODATIONS

The **Central Market** (Amazonas *y* Cordero, 7am-7pm daily) is the place to sample local dishes. ✪ **Steak House El Rincón del Valle** (Av. Amazonas *y* Kennedy, tel. 2/231-5908, Facebook @steakvalle) is one of the best restaurants in town and can put together a surprisingly good vegetarian plate. South of town on the Panamericana, **El Café de la Vaca** (Panamericana Sur km 41, 0.5 km/0.3 mi *al norte del* Peaje, tel. 2/231-5012, www.elcafedelavaca.com, 8am-5:30pm daily, $7-16) offers traditional Ecuadorian dishes, with vegetarian options. All to-go packaging is biodegradable, made from sugarcane, and the restaurant doesn't use straws.

By far the best place to stay is ✪ **Casa Sakiwa** (Los Quishuares y Los Mortiños, tel. 99/266-8619, www.casasakiwa.com, $27.50 s, $40 d, including breakfast). The 20 rooms are clean, modern, and comfortable, with excellent Wi-Fi, breakfast, and hot water, but what really sets the hotel apart is the local family that owns it, who are outstandingly kind, efficient, and helpful. They are an excellent source of information about activities in the area and can book guides and tours, with the most popular being to Cotopaxi National Park.

A full-day **basic tour** ($120 pp for 1 person, $50 pp for 4 people) includes transport from the hotel, a visit to the Limpiopungo Lake, and a walk to the refuge at 4,800 meters (15,750 ft) elevation, from the car park at 4,500 meters (14,750 ft). If conditions are good, it may also be possible to walk beyond the refuge to the glaciers at 5,000 meters (16,400 ft). Another tour includes the same elements but with horseback riding with a local cowboy to the base of Rumiñahui ($140 for 1 person, $180 for 2 people, $220 for 3 people, including lunch). A third option is a tour with Biking Dutchman, where participants descend from the Cotopaxi refuge by bike ($65 pp including lunch). A full-day tour from the hotel to the Quilotoa Lake costs $90-120 per person. It's also possible to book transport and guides for climbing any of the surrounding peaks, including the Ilinizas. The family is equally happy to provide details on how to explore the area independently. Casa Sakiwa gets busy, so it's advisable to book

accommodations and tours ahead of time, especially in high season (late May to mid-September).

If Casa Sakiwa is full, a decent alternative is **Hostería Chiguac** (Calle Los Caras y Cristóbal Colón, tel. 2/231-0396, www.hosteriachiguac.com, $16.50 pp, including breakfast).

GETTING THERE AND AROUND

From Quito, the **Cooperatives Carlos Brito** (tel. 2/231-5192) and **Mejía** (tel. 2/231-5014) operate direct buses from Quitumbe and Trebol (near Old Town) 5am-9pm weekdays and until 6:30pm on weekends ($0.75, 55 minutes). Alternatively, any bus running north or south along the Panamericana can drop you on the western edge of Machachi, leaving a 1-kilometer (0.6-mi) walk or taxi ride into the center. Buses back to Quito leave Machachi from two blocks west of the plaza.

ILINIZA ECOLOGICAL RESERVE

The 149,900-hectare (370,400-acre) **Iliniza Ecological Reserve** (http://areasprotegidas.ambiente.gob.ec) encompasses an incredible variety of ecosystems, from Andean *páramo* to subtropical forests. Established in 1996, the reserve spans the provinces of Cotopaxi, Los Ríos, Pichincha, and Santo Domingo de los Tsáchilas and is home to pumas, Andean bears, and highland wolves. Its main attractions are **Laguna Quilotoa,** the twin peaks of **Iliniza Norte** and **Iliniza Sur,** the **Corazón volcano,** the **Cunucyacu waterfall,** and **Sacharuna thermal waters.**

Climbing the Ilinizas

According to indigenous tradition, **Iliniza Norte** (5,126 m/16,818 ft, also known as **Tioniza**) and **Iliniza Sur** (5,263 m/17,267 ft), the country's eighth and sixth highest peaks, respectively, were once young lovers. Tioniza, the beautiful daughter of the Zarabullo tribe's chief, fled with her forbidden love from the enemy Insilivies tribe to live in hiding on the *páramo*. When her father discovered their whereabouts, he sent his sorcerers after the couple, and they were turned into mountains.

Iliniza Norte is known for being less difficult to climb and, in good conditions, can be tackled by anyone with decent hiking and scrambling skills. In snow/ice conditions, however, it can be challenging, even for experienced climbers. While it is not compulsory to climb with an accredited guide, it is highly recommended, as is wearing a helmet. Iliniza Sur has permanent snow cover, as it receives greater humidity from clouds coming

in from the coast. Climbers must be accompanied by an accredited, specialized guide and be registered in the Biodiversity Information System (SIB), which was introduced in 2015 to log the identities of all climbers on glaciated mountains. Any reputable agency will take care of this formality.

The Ilinizas are accessed via the village of **El Chaupi,** 15 kilometers (9.3 mi) south of Machachi. Buses leave Machachi every half hour from outside the TIA supermarket (45 minutes) by the Central Market. From El Chaupi, it's 9 kilometers (5.6 mi) to the Ilinizas parking lot, **La Virgen,** at 3,900 meters (12,800 ft), where camping is available (bring everything with you). From La Virgen, it's a three-hour signposted hike to the **Nuevos Horizontes refuge** (tel. 98/133-3483, www.ilinizasclimbing.com, $15 pp) at 4,700 meters (15,420 ft). Built right on the saddle between the two peaks, it's well located

Iliniza Sur and Iliniza Norte

for climbing either. Facilities include bunk beds and mattresses (bring your own sleeping bag), a kitchen, living room, fireplace, electricity, outdoor toilets, and running water. Meals are available for $7.50. For a $5 fee (per tent) campers are allowed to use the refuge's facilities.

In El Chaupi, head to the **Refugio Los Ilinizas Office** (tel. 98/133-3483, www.ilinizasclimbing.com), at the north side of the park, to organize two-day climbs of Iliniza Sur ($150 pp) or Iliniza Norte ($120 pp); a one-day climb of Norte ($80); transport to La Virgen ($15); horseback riding ($35/day); and horses to carry luggage. The office is managed by the same people as the Nuevos Horizontes refuge. The telephone number stated is for Fernando Isa, who speaks English. A good place to stay in El Chaupi is **La Llovizna Lodge** (tel. 9/969-9068, https://lalloviznalodge.weebly.com, $12-19 pp), just past the church, which has warm bedrooms, fireplaces, and a shared kitchen. The owner, Vladimir Gallo, can arrange guided hikes, climbs, and horses.

Climbing Volcán Corazón

A short distance west of Machachi across the Panamericana sits this extinct volcano, first climbed in 1738 by Charles Marie de La Condamine while on a break from measuring the planet. At 4,788 meters (15,709 ft), **Corazón** is a challenging day climb, consisting mostly of uphill hiking through grassy fields, with some moderate but exposed rock scrambling for the last 500 meters (1,640 ft). There are two ways to summit Corazón. Starting from Andes Alpes hostel in El Chaupi, it's a tough 8- to 10-hour round-trip hike. The alternative is to get a *camioneta* to the entrance of the reserve, from where it is a 4- to 6-hour round-trip hike. There is minimal signage. For peace of mind, go with a guide.

Recommended agencies for climbing the Ilinizas or Corazón are **Ecuador Eco Adventure** (tel. 99/831-1282, www.ecuadorecoadventures.com) and **Ilinizas Climbing** (tel. 2/367-4125, https://ilinizasclimbing.com).

Cunucyacu and Sacharuna

Adjoining the Iliniza Ecological Reserve on the slopes of Iliniza Sur a 500-hectare (1,235-acre) section of privately owned, pristine *páramo*. It has three stellar attractions: a millennial **polylepis forest,** the **Cunucyacu waterfall,** and the **Sacharuna hot springs.**

Covered in lichen and moss, the ancient trees of the polylepis forest are worthy of Tolkien. Nearby, the crystalline waters of the Sacharuna hot springs are steaming as they rush out from fern-covered rocks into a natural pool, perfect for bathing at 27°C (81°F). The hot spring feeds the Cunucyacu waterfall, which has cut a deep gully into the rocks, coloring them gold with minerals.

The family that has owned this land for generations has recently converted part of their home into a guest lodge, ✪ **Sacharuna Lodge** (tel. 99/247-0691, Facebook @Casa DeCampo sacharuna Hacienda LaVaqueria, $60 s/d, including breakfast). The lodge offers guided tours of the polylepis forest, waterfalls, and hot springs on foot, horseback, or mountain bike.

With views of Tungurahua, Cotopaxi, and the Ilinizas on clear days, the lodge has four guest bedrooms and a living room with a fireplace. The decor is rustic, stylish, and comfortable, with all furniture made by local artisans. Amenities include Wi-Fi and solar-powered hot water (with gas/electric backup). A biodigester is planned, to cook with gas from animal waste. The hacienda is a working farm, with cattle, organic Andean crops, and beehives. In addition to visiting the forest, waterfall, and hot springs, guests can participate in farming activities; hike to a nearby lake; and enjoy nighttime torch-lit walks and bonfires. Lunch and dinner are available for $5-12, with vegetarian options. The lodge makes tea made from wild herbs as well as jam and wine from native fruits, including the endemic *rundubelines*.

To get to the Sacharuna Lodge, take a bus from Latacunga to Pastocalle (40-50 minutes), then hire a *camioneta* ($5), or contact the owner, David Larrea (tel. 99/247-0691) to request a map or help with transport.

TOP EXPERIENCE

✪ COTOPAXI NATIONAL PARK

Spanning the provinces of Cotopaxi, Napo, and Pichincha, Ecuador's top mainland national park is second only to the Galápagos in the annual number of visitors, and it's easy to see why. Just 50 kilometers (31 mi) south of Quito, 32,255 hectares (79,700 acres) of *páramo* enclose one of the most beautiful volcanoes in the Americas, with its picture-perfect cone and permanent mantle of snow. Llamas graze and wild horses gallop on grasslands strewn with wildflowers, including clouds of purple lupines. Higher up, the landscape is barren and lunar, a stark canvas from which to marvel at the colossus that is **Volcán Cotopaxi,** whose name means "Neck of the Moon."

At 5,897 meters (19,347 ft), this is Ecuador's second tallest peak after Chimborazo, and one of the world's highest active volcanoes. It's often shrouded in cloud, but the weather is ever-shifting and, when Cotopaxi does choose to show her face, it's an awe-inspiring sight. July to September tends to be the clearest time of year to visit but can be windy. Since the beginning of the Spanish conquest, Cotopaxi has presented five major eruptive periods: 1532-1534, 1742-1744, 1766-1768, 1853-1854, and 1877-1880. Most recently, it rumbled into life in April 2015 by emitting a 10-kilometer (6.2-mi) ash plume, culminating in an eruption in August 2015 that caused earth tremors in the nearby towns. Gas and steam were released over the next several weeks, along with thousands of tons of ash that covered the surrounding countryside and even reached Quito.

There are several ways to explore **Cotopaxi National Park** (tel. 3/305-3596, http://areasprotegidas.ambiente. gob.ec, Facebook @Parque Nacional Cotopaxi, free). Entrance is permitted 8am-3pm daily, although visitors can remain within the park until 6pm. ID is required to enter. If you have your own four-wheel-drive vehicle, you can drive around the signposted tracks that lead to the various attractions. From the main entrance (**Control Sur**), the road through the park curves in a semicircle north around Volcán Cotopaxi. As it heads northeast, 10 kilometers (6.2 mi) from the entrance is a small **museum** (8am-3pm daily, free) with an exhibition on the geology, history, flora, and fauna of the park.

Shortly beyond the museum, there's a path leading to **Laguna Limpiopungo,** a shallow lake at 3,800 meters (12,470 ft) elevation whose

COTOPAXI'S DARK SECRET

Once upon a time, an old woman called María Juana Veracruz sought a wealthy wife for her son. Upon finding a suitable candidate, the marriage was quickly arranged, but the woman and her son mysteriously disappeared during the celebrations, and the bride was not seen again. A few months later in a different village, the residents were invited to celebrate the nuptials of the same young man whose mother had, it seems, found an even wealthier wife for her offspring. Once again, however, the duo fled following the ceremony. Upon the man's third wedding, the local *yachaks* (shamans, or wise men) went looking for the suspicious pair before the wedding feast and discovered a horrifying sight: María Juana Veracruz chopping up her son's new bride and cooking the pieces in a cauldron. In unison, the *yachaks* cast a spell on the old woman—"If you cook a woman in a cauldron, you shall be a cauldron!"—and they turned her into a vessel of such boiling fury that even to this day, she hurls torrential rain and freezing temperatures on everyone around her. Though most refer to her as Cotopaxi, older residents can still be heard entreating with her, "Mama Juana, please don't be angry!" "Mama Juana, we'll be good!" "Mama Juana, please don't destroy our crops!"

This story was compiled over three years by a young Latacungan historian, Carlos Sandoval, who collected oral testimonies from several older residents in various parts of the province, who all told the same dark tale.

reeds provide a habitat for several species of birds. The volcano is sometimes spectacularly reflected in the lake's surface. From the lake there is a signposted 90-minute easy **hike** past a **natural spring** and a **viewing point** to the **Control Norte,** as well as two circular **cycle routes,** one to the natural spring (3 hours), the other to the **Santo Domingo Lake** (4-5 hours). A trail leads around the lake to the northwest for access to **Rumiñahui.**

Shortly beyond that trail, another track heads 9 kilometers (5.6 mi) south to the parking lot for the **José Rivas Refuge** (tel. 3/223-3129 or 98/790-8704, Facebook @refugiocotopaxi-joseribas) at 4,800 meters (15,750 ft), which is open to climbers and non-climbers alike. Although the walk from the parking lot to the refuge is only 1 kilometer (0.6 mi), it takes most people 45 minutes to an hour, due to the altitude and level of difficulty. It's a steep walk on rocky paths surrounded by snow. If conditions are good, it's possible to walk beyond the refuge for another hour to the glaciers at 5,000 meters (16,400 ft). If you're planning on doing the walk, bring water, snacks (especially chocolate, which is an excellent source of energy at high altitude), sunglasses, warm clothes, and sunblock. Built in 1971 and remodeled in 2009, the refuge is warm and welcoming, with hot drinks and food available. Be aware that prices are high because all supplies are carried in on foot. A hot chocolate costs $2 (worth it after the walk) and a corn cob with cheese is $5.

On the eastern edge of the park, 15 kilometers (9.3 mi) beyond the lake, are the oval ruins of **El Salitre,** formerly an Inca *pucara* (fortress), abandoned soon after the arrival of the Spanish.

TOURS AND GUIDES

Those without their own transport can take a tour offered by the local guides who wait with trucks by the two main access points to the park. The standard three-hour tour ($50 1 person, may be negotiable to $40; $25 pp for 2 people; and $20 pp for 3 people) includes three stops: the museum; the refuge parking lot (your guide might accompany you while you walk to the refuge or glacier and back, or may wait with the car); and the Limpiopungo Lake. Just driving around the park is an experience, especially when the volcano shows its face, and the guides are happy to stop for you to take photos. Be aware that they speak little English.

For a tour that includes transport to and from the park, or additional activities such as downhill mountain biking or horseback riding, go with an organized tour. From Machachi, the best option is **Casa Sakiwa** (tel. 99/266-8619, www.casasakiwa.com), which offers the same standard tour plus return transport from Machachi ($120 pp for 1 person, $50 pp for 4 people). Another option includes the same elements but with horseback riding with a local cowboy to the base of Rumiñahui ($140 for 1 person, $180 for 2 people, $220 for 3 people, including lunch). **Biking Dutchman** (http://www.bikingdutchman.com) in Quito offers a tour of the park plus a downhill bike ride from the refuge, which can be booked directly with them or via Casa Sakiwa in Machachi ($65 pp including lunch and transport from Quito or Machachi).

In Latacunga, **Cotopaxi Travel** (Guayaquil 6-4 y Sánchez de Orellana, tel. 98/133-3483, www.cotopaxi-travel.com); **Neiges** (Sánchez de Orellana 17-38 & Guayaquil, tel. 3/281-1199 or 99/826-5567, http://neigestours.wixsite.com/neiges); and **Greivag Turismo** (Plaza Comercial Santo Domingo, Calles Guayaquil y Sánchez de Orellana, tel. 3/281-0510 or 99/864-7308, www.greivagturismo.com) all offer the standard tour, with transport and lunch, for $35-100 per person, depending on the number of people.

CLIMBING VOLCÁN COTOPAXI

Cotopaxi is Ecuador's most popular high-altitude climb because of its relative simplicity. Crevasses are usually large and obvious, making it mostly an uphill slog. However, less than half of those who attempt the summit actually reach it. You need to be in good physical condition, be fully acclimatized, be accompanied by an accredited guide, and have a certain amount of luck with the conditions. Technical equipment is necessary: ice axes, crampons, ropes, marker wands, and crevasse rescue gear.

As with any peak over 5,000 meters (16,400 ft), acclimatization is essential. If you've been staying in Quito at 2,850 meters (9,350 ft), this is unlikely to be sufficient preparation (although you may be lucky). Ideally you should trek and sleep at around 4,000 meters (13,000 ft) for a couple of days or, even better, do a practice climb of a smaller peak such as Iliniza Norte or Rumiñahui before attempting Cotopaxi. All mountaineering tour agencies offer acclimatization climbs.

Although Cotopaxi can be climbed year-round, the best months are usually December and January. The February-April period is often clear and dry as well. August and September are also good but windy.

Most climbers make their bid for the summit from the **José Rivas Refuge** (tel. 3/223-3129 or 98/790-8704, Facebook @refugiocotopaxijoseribas, $32 pp, including breakfast and dinner). The refuge has bunk beds, toilets, running water, a fireplace, a café, and lockers for your gear while you climb. A night's stay is usually included in the price of a tour booked with an agency. Camping outside the refuge is not permitted, and

climbers descending the red sand towards José Rivas Refuge

neither is use of the kitchen. Lunch is available for $7.

Catch a few hours of sleep before starting to climb around midnight or 1am. It takes 6-10 hours to reach the summit from the refuge, and the route contains smoking fumaroles reeking of sulfur. The views over the neighboring volcanoes are spectacular. The summit is actually the northern rim of the crater, which is rounded and measures approximately 480 meters (1,575 ft) wide. The descent takes 3-6 hours.

The park has issued the following requirements for those wishing to summit Cotopaxi. Any reputable agency will fulfill these criteria, so make sure that yours has. A reservation is required at one of the three accommodation options within the park: the José Rivas Refuge, the Hostería Tambopaxi Lodge (www.tambopaxi.com), or La Rinconada Camping Area (tel. 98/424-9333). Those climbing with a tour operator must be registered in the Biodiversity Information System (SIB), which was introduced in 2015 to log the identities of all climbers on glaciated mountains. Climbers must be accompanied by an accredited, specialized guide. Members of mountaineering clubs and qualified individuals must apply for permission to enter the protected area at least 15 days in advance by emailing gregorio.nunez@ambiente.gob.ec. Mountaineering clubs must submit a copy of the membership card of each climber and a certificate to show that the club is legally recognized and registered. Entry to the park for climbers is permitted 8am-5pm daily.

Ecuador Eco Adventure (tel. 99/831-1282, www.ecuadorecoadventure.com, ecuadorecoadventure@gmail.com) in Riobamba offers a four-day Cotopaxi climb including acclimatization hikes (4 days, $495 1 person, $375 pp 2 people), as well as a combined Cotopaxi and Chimborazo climbing tour (5 days, $960 1 person, $750 pp 2 people). Prices include a night in Riobamba the night before departure, all equipment, permits, accommodations, and most meals. In Latacunga, contact **Cotopaxi Travel** (Guayaquil 6-4 y Sánchez de Orellana, tel. 98/133-3483, www.cotopaxi-travel.com).

CLIMBING VOLCÁN RUMIÑAHUI

This peak, 13 kilometers (8 mi) northwest of Cotopaxi, was named after Atahualpa's bravest general, who famously hid the huge Inca ransom after Atahualpa's death and refused to give up its whereabouts when tortured by the Spanish. **Rumiñahui** (4,712 m/15,459 ft), officially dormant but most probably extinct, actually has three peaks. It's a relatively straightforward climb, combining an uphill hike with a bit of scrambling, but because the quality of rock can be poor, a rope and climbing protection are recommended for the more exposed stretches. While it is not compulsory to climb with an accredited guide, it is highly recommended. Contact the same agencies as for the Cotopaxi climb.

The east side of Rumiñahui is reached through Cotopaxi National Park along tracks that skirt Laguna Limpiopungo to the north or south. A path toward the central peak is clearly visible along a well-defined ridge. From the lake to the base is about a two-hour hike, and it's possible to camp along the way. The south peak involves some moderately technical rock climbing (class 5.5). The IGM *Machachi* and *Sincholagua* 1:50,000 maps cover this area.

FOOD AND ACCOMMODATIONS

Located 6 kilometers (3.7 mi) from the main park entrance, **Cuello de Luna** (El Chasqui, Panamericana Sur km 44, tel. 3/330-53898 or 99/970-0330, www.cuellodeluna.com, dorm $20 pp, $54-75 s, $66-94 d, including breakfast) has rooms with private bathrooms and fireplaces. The hotel can arrange transport, tours, and horseback riding.

The only hotel within the national park, with great views of Cotopaxi, is **Tambopaxi** (tel. 2/600-0365, www.tambopaxi.com, camping $16 pp, dorm $20 pp, $91 s, $115 d, including breakfast). Rooms have wood-burning stoves, and there is a decent restaurant using organic ingredients with vegetarian options. Horseback riding and hiking tours are available. The hotel is certified by Smart Voyager, a UNESCO- recognized program for environmental sustainability.

Four kilometers (2.5 mi) from the northern entrance of the park is **Hacienda El Porvenir** (tel. 2/600-9533, www.tierradelvolcan.com, $43-113 s, $54-170 d, including breakfast). Accommodation ranges from thatched huts with shared bathrooms to suites. Tours are offered on foot, mountain bike, and horseback. Camping is available for $6 per person (not including breakfast). The hacienda was a finalist for Ecuador's Leading Green Hotel in the 2017 World Travel Awards.

Off the beaten path is the ✪ **Secret Garden Cotopaxi** (tel. 9/357-2714, www.secretgardencotopaxi.com, dorm $40 pp, $60-80 s, $80-125 d), sister hotel of the backpacker favorite in Quito. This ecolodge is set in the foothills of Pasochoa, near the village of Pedregal, overlooking the national park. Rooms range from mixed dorms to hobbit houses and private cabins. Rates include three meals, snacks, drinks, a tour to a waterfall, and use of the Jacuzzi. Daily shuttles

($5) are available from Quito (2 hours) and Machachi (1 hour), as are treks and trips to the nearby peaks.

GETTING THERE AND AROUND

There are two ways to enter the park. The South Entrance or **Control Sur** is the main gate, located 25 minutes south of Machachi along the Panamericana. The North Entrance or **Control Norte,** accessed via the village of El Pedregal to the north of the park, is lesser used, but the route is more scenic. Those planning on arranging a tour with a local guide upon arrival at the park are advised to use the main entrance, especially if hoping to meet fellow travelers to share the cost.

To get to the South Entrance from Quito, take a bus from the Quitumbe terminal heading to Latacunga (or any destination south of the park along the Panamericana) and ask the driver to let you off at the park, after about a 90-minute drive. From any destination south of the park, flag down any bus heading north to Quito along the Panamericana and ask the driver to let you off.

To get to the South Entrance from Machachi, head to the Panamericana on foot, by taxi, or by bus (it's 1 km/0.6 mi from the town center), then flag down any bus going south. Ask the driver to let you off at the park ($0.75).

Local guides with *camionetas* wait at the Panamericana offering tours of the park and transport to the South Entrance, which is another 10 minutes' drive.

To get to the North Entrance, first take a bus to Machachi. From Quito, the **Cooperatives Carlos Brito** (tel. 2/231-5192) and **Mejía** (tel. 2/231-5014) operate buses from Quitumbe and Trebol (near Old Town) 5am-9pm weekdays and until 6:30pm on weekends ($0.75, 55 minutes). Alternatively, any bus running south or north along the Panamericana can drop you at the entrance to Machachi, marked by a statue of a rider on a horse, leaving a 1-kilometer (0.6-mi) walk/taxi into town. A block north of the main square in Machachi, take a bus to Pedregal with **Transportes Machachenas.** Buses leave at 7am, 11am, and 4pm and take 45 minutes. Alternatively, take a *camioneta* from Machachi to El Pedregal ($15) or onwards into the park. Guides wait in El Pedregal to offer tours of the park and transport to the entrance, which is another 25 minutes' drive.

Santo Domingo and Vicinity

Ecuador's fourth-largest city, Santo Domingo (pop. 300,000), is far from being its fourth most appealing. Hot, noisy, and polluted, it's a useful transportation hub, but there is little of interest in the city itself. However, less than 20 minutes to the south is an indigenous village of Tsáchila people with a community tourism project offering a fascinating insight into their rich culture and ancient medicines. It was the Tsáchila that gave the town its full name, Santo Domingo de Los Colorados ("Santo Domingo of the Colored Ones") because of their use of red achiote hair paste.

FOOD AND ACCOMMODATIONS

For those passing through Santo Domingo, there is a food court in the bus terminal offering basic local fare at economic prices. For a bit more variety, try the row of eateries across the road from the terminal, where there are a number of Chinese restaurants. **Restaurant Chef Sheratun** ($4-5) has a small selection of vegetarian pasta and rice dishes. If an overnight stay is necessary, **Santander Don Garcia** (Av. Esmeraldas y Av. de los Colonos, Redondel Sueno del Bolívar, tel. 99/834-9284 or 2/379-1059, $10 s/d) is a kilometer north of the terminal, tucked a block off the main road. It's great value, offering friendly service and clean rooms with private bathrooms, hot water, and TV. Most taxi drivers don't know it, but keep an eye out for the sign on the main road, or tell the driver "*ingresando por la ferretería Don Cabrera una cuadra margen derecho.*"

In the Santo Domingo city center, there are plenty of basic restaurants along 29 de Mayo serving set lunches and dinners. For something a bit better, head to **La Tonga** inside **Gran Hotel Santo Domingo** (Calle Río Toachi y Galápagos, tel. 2/276-7948, https://grandhotelsantodomingo. com, 7am-10:30pm daily, $8-18), which has vegetarian, international, and local specialties. The hotel also has a spa and offers decent accommodations ($80 s, $115 d, including breakfast). **Eco Spa** (Vía a Quito km 5.5, tel. 2/377-0438, Facebook @eco. spa.5, $50 s/d) is 12 kilometers (7.5 mi) east of the city center ($5 taxi), but it's worth it for the excellent massages (1 hour for $20) and friendly service. There is a pool and it gets busy with local families on weekends, so go midweek for a peaceful experience.

GETTING THERE AND AROUND

Santo Domingo's **bus terminal** is 2 kilometers (1.2 mi) north of the center. To get to the center, buses run to and from the bus terminal regularly ($0.30), passing north on Tsáchilas and returning down 29 de Mayo. A taxi costs $1.50.

From Santo Domingo, there are buses every 15 minutes to Quito (3 hours, $4). Transportes Kennedy has several direct buses per day to Mindo (4 hours, $4), more convenient than going via Quito.

✪ CHIGÜILPE

Of the seven Tsáchila communities near Santo Domingo, Chigüilpe is the most organized for tourism. The **Centro Turístico Mushily** (Vía a Quevedo km 7, Comuna Chigüilpe, tel. 98/020-4868 or 99/387-5463, Facebook @Centro Turístico Mushily, 8am-6pm daily, $5) offers excellent guided tours of the village. The undisputed highlight is a visit to the ceremonial site, the domain of the *poné*, which is underground and entered via a tunnel. The Tsáchila believe that the earthen walls allow for greater connection with nature, and it's certainly true that the candlelit chamber possesses a remarkable energy, incredibly strong and, at the same time, deeply peaceful. The walls seem to have absorbed the healing power of the countless ceremonies that have taken place, so that just sitting there for a few minutes can be a moving experience. While in the chamber, the guide demonstrates the instruments used during ceremonies, including the *palo de lluvia* (rain stick), a hollow branch filled with seeds, which sounds like falling rain.

Another highlight of the tour is the ceibo, a deciduous tree whose upper trunk is covered with spikes. The Tsáchila believe that this species is capable of absorbing bad energy, and that the tree is free of spikes on its lower trunk to allow for hugging. When it is saturated with bad energy absorbed from the tree huggers, the ceibo heals itself by shedding its leaves. The tour also includes a demonstration of marimba, a musical style that the Tsáchila share with Afro-Ecuadorian cultures. No reservation is required for the tour, which takes around an hour and a half. English-speaking tours can be arranged with prior notice.

The Tsáchila hold ancestral healing ceremonies in a candlelit underground chamber.

LOS TSÁCHILAS: THE "COLORED ONES" OF SANTO DOMINGO

In 1660, the indigenous Tsáchila people were living in San Miguel de los Bancos near Quito when they were struck with a deadly epidemic of smallpox and yellow fever. During a three-day ayahuasca ceremony, their shamans (known as *ponés*) received visions of their people recovering from the disease by painting themselves with black and red body paint. When they went searching for the paint substance in the forest, one of the Tsáchilas stepped on an achiote fruit and discovered the red paste inside. As per the vision, the people covered their skin with the substance and were indeed healed. To make sure all traces of the diseases were gone, the men cut their long hair and, in tribute to the medicine that had saved their lives, started to color it with achiote paste and style it in the shape of the red fruit. To the Tsáchilas, achiote represents life. They discovered the black body paint in another fruit, the *mali*, which they apply to their arms in stripes to honor the people who lost their lives in the smallpox outbreak and to protect against bad energy.

Following the epidemic, seven families moved from San Miguel de los Bancos to their current location, and the closest city was later named after them, Santo Domingo de Los Colorados (Santo Domingo of the Colored Ones). There are now seven Tsáchila communities living in the area and, in many ways, the people still maintain their ancestral traditions. Education is bilingual, in Spanish and their ancestral language, Tsafiki. The men wear a *mushily*, a cotton doughnut perched on top of their red hair, to symbolize the knowledge of the *poné*, and a black and white skirt in honor of the highly venomous echis snake. Women wear rainbow-colored skirts.

A variety of ancient medicinal techniques are still practiced by the Tsáchila *ponés*. The *poné* will make a diagnosis by passing a candle over the patient's body and watching the flame. Medicinal plants are then prescribed and gathered from the forest. Half the leaves are boiled to make an infusion, which the patient drinks. The rest of the leaves are placed in a hole in the ground along with fire-heated rocks, which are splashed with water to create a medicinal steam bath. The patient sits over the hole, covered in a blanket, to absorb the vapor. The *poné* also channels the energy of the rocks, trees, rivers, and waterfalls to heal patients. Ayahuasca ceremonies are held regularly, during which sacred songs are sung to cleanse a patient's energy, accompanied by traditional instruments.

In other ways, the Tsáchila lifestyle has changed in modern times. As Catholicism was adopted, the women started to wear sequined tops, instead of being naked from the waist up. Renowned for their weaving skills, the Tsáchila historically traded cotton textiles and garments, but the introduction of the modern clothing industry forced them to seek alternative sources of income. Though they still wear traditional woven skirts, most of the cotton bushes have been cleared to make way for yucca, plantain, sugarcane, pineapple, and citrus fruits. Agriculture is now their principal economic activity.

As the city has encroached, the rivers have become so polluted that it is no longer possible for the Tsáchila to drink, bathe, fish, or wash clothes in the water. This is especially tragic for a people whose primary food is fish, and who now have to walk for hours or travel by motorbike to fish in clean water. A people who find sacred energy in the rivers and waterfalls now have to use tanks of city water for bathing and drinking.

Despite these changes, a visit to the Tsáchila community is a fascinating and magical experience. Indeed, every visit helps the people keep their remaining traditions alive.

There is lodging for 15 guests in traditional **cabins** ($10 pp). *Maito*, a traditional dish of fish wrapped in a leaf and cooked over a fire, is available with yucca ($5). Vegetarians can be catered to with prior notice.

The Tsáchila also offer traditional **healing rituals** with the *poné*. A session costs $40 and includes a medicinal steam bath; a bath with flowers, orchids, and floral essences; a massage; an energy cleaning session with

The indigenous Tsáchila rid themselves of bad energy by hugging the ceibo tree.

musical instruments; and a medicinal drink. Be clear about what you want when you book, otherwise you may end up with the "invigorating" treatment; i.e., a cold-water dousing at dawn with wild garlic water, like this author! Healing sessions should be booked at least one day in advance.

Ayahuasca ceremonies are held every Friday, Saturday, and Sunday at 7pm ($25, including breakfast). Participants should arrive at 4pm and expect to stay until the following afternoon at 4pm. Accommodations are either in the guest cabins or camping (bring your own tent).

Ceremonies should be booked at least one day in advance. On the day of the ceremony, participants should eat no solid food, only vegetable soup, to prepare the body for the ayahuasca medicine.

To get to the Centro Turístico Mushily, take an Ejecutrans bus from outside the Santo Domingo bus terminal that goes to Vía a Quevedo ($0.30). Ask to be let out after 7 kilometers (4.3 mi) at Comuna Chigüilpe, from where a *mototaxi* can take you into the community ($1). A taxi from Santo Domingo costs $8-10. Arrange a pickup time with the driver.

BACKGROUND

The Landscape

The old adage "small is beautiful" applies to Ecuador. Few places in the world have such a rich variety of breathtaking landscapes packed into such a diminutive space; in fact, it's the most biodiverse country in the world per unit area. The fourth-smallest country in South America (only Uruguay, the Guyanas, and Suriname are smaller) extends over 283,561 square kilometers

(109,484 sq mi) on the northwestern shoulder of the continent, with Colombia to the north, Peru to the east and south, and the Pacific Ocean to the west. Named for the equator that bisects it, Ecuador is roughly the size of Colorado and slightly bigger than the UK. From the tourist's point of view, its small size is a huge asset. You can get from one end of Ecuador to the other in a day. And what a day it is—moving from Pacific beaches up through misty cloud forests and windswept *páramo* moorlands, past snowy volcanic peaks and down again to the Amazon rainforest.

GEOGRAPHY

The Andes run through the country like a spine. Though these mountains and their foothills fill only about one-quarter of Ecuador's land area, they certainly pack a punch, with 10 peaks over 5,000 meters (16,400 ft) and another dozen over 4,000 meters (13,000 ft). In the southern Sierra, the cordillera is older and less volcanically active, without the soaring mountains that are found in the north. Two parallel mountain ranges run north-south—the Cordillera Occidental (Western Range) and the wider and higher Cordillera Oriental (Eastern Range). Between them is one of the most spectacular drives on the continent: the aptly named Avenue of the Volcanoes, which runs along the Panamericana south of Quito.

The 10 main intermountain basins, called *hoyas*, are where about half of Ecuador's population lives. All the main cities in the Sierra—including Otavalo and Quito—sit at 2,000-3,000 meters (6,500-10,000 ft) above sea level. Above the tree line but below the snow line, at 3,000-5,000 meters (9,800-16,500 ft) above sea level, are the windswept Andean grasslands, or *páramos*, surrounding the icy peaks. Due to high moisture retention in the soil, the *páramos* are the birthplace of several of Ecuador's rivers and a key source of water for much of the country, including major cities such as Quito.

GEOLOGY

It comes as no surprise that a country with an Avenue of Volcanoes has a violent geological heritage. The country sits right on the Pacific Rim of Fire, where two tectonic plates—the Nazca Plate and the American Plate—grind together.

About 65 of Ecuador's peaks began as **volcanoes,** and at least six have been recently active. **Cotopaxi,** one of the world's highest active volcanoes, rumbled into life in April 2015 by emitting a 10-kilometer (6.2-mi) ash plume, culminating in an eruption in August 2015. Tremors were felt in the surrounding towns, and gas and steam were released over the following weeks, along with thousands of tons of ash that covered the surrounding countryside, even reaching Quito.

By far the show-stealer in the past decade has been **Tungurahua** ("throat of fire" in Kichwa), which awoke from an 80-year sleep in 1999, forcing an evacuation of nearby tourist town Baños. Since then, the volcano has remained in an eruptive phase. The 2006 eruptions caused pyroclastic flows on the volcano's western slopes, and ashfall traveled nearly 300 kilometers (185 mi) away. Fortunately Baños lies to the south. Further eruptions occurred in 2010, 2012, 2013, and 2014, when an ash plume reached 10 kilometers (6.2 mi) into the sky. Other recent eruptions include **Reventador,** the aptly named "Exploder," which lived up to its name in 2002, and **Guagua Pichincha,** which showered Quito in ash in 1999. **Sangay** is one of the most active volcanoes on earth, with a constant pool of lava bubbling in its crater.

More destructive than volcanoes in recent decades have been **earthquakes.** On April 16, 2016, an earthquake of 7.8 magnitude struck the province of Manabí. It was the country's largest recorded earthquake since 1979, and tremors were felt as far as Colombia and Peru. At least 676 people were killed and 16,600 were injured.

On a smaller scale but also deadly are **landslides,** usually triggered by heavy rain. Avalanches of melted ice, snow, mud, and rocks can reach 80 kilometers per hour (50 mph) when careening downhill, and there are landslides every year in the Andes and the foothills.

CLIMATE

Ecuador's climate is so varied that it is impossible to make sweeping generalizations. Often the weather varies more with altitude than geography; sometimes you can be sweltering in one place and then freezing less than an hour's drive away. Even without moving an inch, some of the Sierran cities are well known for showing visitors "four seasons in one day." The good news is that there is no bad time to visit Ecuador. If you're coming from colder climes, never underestimate the strength of the equatorial sun; always wear sunscreen, even on a cloudy day.

The Andes climate is often described as ideally "springlike," but this is an oversimplification. You will probably need several blankets overnight and wake up to a chill in the air,

but it can heat up quickly by midday. Daytime temperatures average 15-20°C (59-68°F), occasionally peaking at 25°C (77°F), with nights falling to 7-8°C (45-46°F) but sometimes dropping to 0°C (32°F).

The driest, warmest season is June-September. October and November are cooler, with showers common in the mornings. December-May is the rainy season. Whatever the time of year, the weather can change quickly, so wear layers and always have a sweater and sun cream with you.

ENVIRONMENTAL ISSUES
PROBLEMS

Ecuador has a reputation for being an environmental pioneer, largely due to its 2008 constitution, which was the first in the world to grant legal rights to nature. Sadly, however, the opposite is true. According to Mongabay, Ecuador has the highest deforestation rate and worst environmental record in South America. The discrepancy can partly be explained by the recent Correa government's world-class marketing department and control of the media. For example, while Ecuador was lauded in the international press for its 2015 Guinness World Record-breaking effort to plant 647,250 trees of 200 species in a single day, it was largely unreported that 3 million hectares (7.4 million acres) of largely virgin rainforest were being simultaneously auctioned to oil companies. The sale of the Amazon is just one example of Correa's extractivist policies, which wrought large-scale destruction through oil exploitation and mega-mining, and are currently being ramped up by his successor, Lenín Moreno.

Ecuador is not a safe country for

environmental defenders, who are criminalized, threatened, attacked, and even assassinated for attempting to uphold the rights of nature decreed in the constitution. While the overt incitement to hatred against environmental activists ended when Moreno replaced Correa as president and some imprisoned indigenous leaders were freed, the intimidation and threats continue.

Mega-mining projects for gold and copper pose the biggest threat to ecosystems in the Sierra. There has been gold mining in Ecuador since the arrival of the Incas, but it remained fairly small scale and national until a series of laws opened the gates for transnational mega-mining projects. Following the oil price crash, Correa increasingly turned to minerals to pay for government spending, passing a controversial water rights law in 2014 that prioritized the use of water for mining over human consumption and agriculture and creating a mining ministry in 2015. The value of Ecuador's mining industry is forecast to jump from $1.1 billion in 2017 to $7.9 billion in 2021.

Mining causes contamination and desertification. Obtaining 10 grams (0.35 oz) of gold generates between 20 and 60 tons of waste and uses 7,000 liters (1,850 gallons) of water, which is normally contaminated with cyanide, arsenic, and other heavy metals. Despite 92 percent of local people voting against the Kimsacocha mine in a referendum attended by international observers, the ombudsman's office, and human rights organizations, the project is currently in its exploration phase and already water quality has been affected. Indigenous leaders who oppose the mine have been threatened and criminalized.

SOLUTIONS

With much of the environmental damage enabled by the state, it's not surprising that the best solutions come from grassroots actions. Supporting these efforts is the best way for visitors to help conserve what is left of Ecuador's staggering biodiversity.

The most effective ways to defend threatened ecosystems tend to be community-led and multifaceted, incorporating a variety of strategies, including nonviolent resistance and direct action, legal action, habitat regeneration, and the creation of alternative, sustainable sources of income that reduce dependence on extractivism and destructive agricultural practices.

Since 1995, the communities of the **Intag** region have been engaged in a battle to protect the cloud forest ecosystem from mining. As well as direct actions such as roadblocks, residents have created an alternative development model, including renewable energy from small-scale hydroelectric plants and a diversified, sustainable economy based on ecotourism; small-scale fruit farming; an organic coffee growers association; artisanal natural soaps, shampoos, and creams; and handicrafts made from woven sisal. With the coffee grown in the shade of native trees, the conservation (rather than destruction) of the region's cloud forest is incentivized. A café and store in the tourist hub of **Otavalo** sells Intag's products and raises awareness of their struggle. See www.decoin.org and http://codelcoecuador.com for more information.

Other projects involve the regeneration of damaged ecosystems. One of the most inspiring examples started in 1985 when an Ecuadorian couple, Rebeca Justicia and Rodrigo

Ontaneda, decided to protect and restore an area of degraded cloud forest north of Quito. After establishing the 6,500-hectare (16,100-acre) **Maquipucuna Reserve** (www.maquipucuna.org), they spent three decades reforesting it with native species, including a type of wild avocado—a favorite food for the Andean or spectacled bear, which had all but disappeared from the area. Attracted by the avocados, the bears started coming back. The reserve now provides a safe haven for at least 60 of these endangered mammals and is the best place in the world to see them in the wild. Recognizing the importance of this achievement, the government of Quito declared Maquipucuna and the surrounded area a protected bear corridor, preserving a total area of 65,000 hectares (161,000 acres). In 2018, UNESCO announced the creation of the new **Chocó Andino de Pichincha Biosphere Reserve,** with Maquipucuna at its core—a simply monumental accomplishment.

Ethical Tourism

While irresponsible or mass tourism can cause severe environmental impacts, **ethical tourism** is often the best solution for preserving threatened ecosystems. Ecotourism, defined as "responsible travel that conserves natural environments and sustains the well-being of local people," is a good start, but **community-based ecotourism** goes one step further. Community-based ecotourism initiatives are led by local people, with the income going directly to them, enabling them to preserve their ecosystems and culture. This is in contrast to some ecotourism projects, where local people are employed, often as cooks, cleaners, and drivers, but see only a tiny fraction of the income generated in their ancestral territories and are not involved in decision making. With community-based ecotourism, often a percentage of the proceeds goes toward improving the quality of life for the community, funding health care, education, and conservation projects. Visitors are usually invited to share aspects of daily life, providing an authentic cultural experience. A good community tourism project should be well organized; should reinforce collective identity and revitalize culture; should practice economic solidarity; and should strengthen the defense of territory. This type of tourism is especially important in indigenous communities, whose ancestral cultures, languages, and knowledge of plant medicines are in danger of disappearing. An excellent resource on community tourism is the **Federación Plurinacional de Turismo Comunitario del Ecuador** (www.feptce.com).

Throughout the country, private individuals and organizations, have small reserves, including **Sacha Runa Lodge** in Cotopaxi. Some use income from tourism to purchase and protect hectares of forest.

Environmental solutions are also found in urban spaces. Of note are the restaurants **Tandana** and **Flora** in Quito, both of which are actively implementing creative ecological and social projects. Alliances between urban and rural, mestizo and indigenous causes are also important. A recent program for young leaders in Quito run by human rights organization **INREDH** (www.inredh.org) brought together activists from across the movements, including indigenous, LGBTQ, and anti-extractivist, to work together to find common solutions.

As a visitor to Ecuador, you have the potential to make an enormous impact toward the conservation of its incredible biological and cultural diversity. Think carefully about where you spend your tourist dollars. Consider supporting the projects mentioned here and featured throughout this book. Purchase goods directly from local producers or fair trade stores that stock their products (**Camari** in Quito, for example). Choose hotels and restaurants owned by local families. Look for accommodations with sound environmental policies, which may include renewable energy, recycling, conservation of water and energy, ecological building methods, waste management practices (i.e., gray water systems, composting), use of biodegradable cleaning products, support of local producers, organic gardens, and environmental education. These establishments are included in this guide wherever they were found. If you see examples of incoherence with environmental principles, speak up. For example, boat tours in Machalilla National Park provide information on the threats faced by marinelife, but then serve drinks in single-use plastic cups from disposable plastic bottles. Tour operators are more likely to switch to a more sustainable alternative (such as **EmpaqueVerde Ecuador** products, www.empaqueverde.com) if enough visitors request it. Travel with your own refillable water bottle, lunch container, and cutlery. Say no to disposable plastics and explain why. Reach out to environmental organizations. Consider volunteering at one of the projects listed in this chapter. Learn what you can about environmental problems and solutions in Ecuador and spread the word when you get home.

Plants and Animals

Ecuador is the ninth most biodiverse country in the world. Measured per unit area, it's the most biodiverse. Covering less than 0.005 percent of the planet's surface, it boasts 10 percent of all plant species on earth (almost 20,000, more than in all of North America) and one-sixth of all birds (more than 1,600 species, compared with 844 in North America).

Ecuador is one of the best countries in the world for bird-watching. Of the myriad species, perhaps the **hummingbird** (*colibrí*) deserves special mention, for its presence in all of the mainland regions. They are even spotted buzzing around in Quito. Ecuador is home to over 132 hummingbird species, almost half of the world's total, including the world's second smallest, the *estrellita Esmeraldeña* (or Esmeraldas woodstar). Also of note is the swordbilled hummingbird, which totes a 10-centimeter (4-in) beak.

In the Sierra, the valley interiors were once covered with a thorny woodland, giving way to a low evergreen forest toward the valley edges, then to the grasslands of the *páramo* at higher elevations. The foothills are now mostly covered with a rolling tapestry of agricultural fields, which, sadly, have become more quintessentially Ecuadorian than the forests they replaced.

Situated between the tree line and the snow line at an elevation of 3,000-5,000 meters (9,800-16,500 ft), the windswept grasslands of the *páramo* rise to rocky mountains interspersed with crystalline lakes and streams. Acting as giant sponges, these moorlands give birth to a number of Ecuador's rivers and provide water for many Sierran towns and communities. Much of the *páramo* is sprinkled with wildflowers, but at very high elevations few flowers can survive. A notable exception is the orange thistle-like *chuquiraga*, regarded as the national flower. Another iconic plant is the *frailejón*, a spiky-headed relative of the sunflower that, despite only growing one centimeter every year, can reach several meters in height. Impressive *páramos* can be found near Otavalo in the northern Sierra and in the Cotopaxi National Park in the central Sierra.

The most famous avian resident of the *páramo* is the Andean condor, the world's largest flying bird, with a wingspan of more than 3 meters (10 ft) and weighing up to 15 kilograms (33 lb). The condor is Ecuador's national bird and a symbol of Andean identity. A type of vulture, it is critically endangered, with between 50 and 100 mating pairs in the country. Cotopaxi National Park is the best place to see the carunculated caracara, the largest member of the falcon family, with its bright red face, yellow bill, and black body. Locally known as a *curiquingue*, the caracara was a sacred bird for the Inca.

The mammalian star of the show is the highly endangered Andean spectacled bear, named for white patches around its eyes. The only bear native to South America, the *oso andino* can be found in the cloud forest as well as the *páramo*. The males can reach 2 meters (6.5 ft) in length.

South America's high-elevation relatives of the camel—llamas, vicuñas, and alpacas—were hunted to extinction, but reintroduction programs using animals from Chile and Bolivia have been highly successful in the Chimborazo Fauna Reserve. Wild horses and reintroduced llamas can be seen in Cotopaxi National Park.

The *páramos* are also home to the highly endangered Andean tapir, highland wolves, Andean foxes, and the world's smallest deer, the pudu.

Cloud forests are found on both the eastern and western slopes of the Andes, between the high elevation *páramo* and the lowland rainforest. Cloud forests are cooler than rainforests, characterized by fast-moving, clear rocky rivers and beautiful views due to the mountainous terrain. Rainforests are hotter, with larger, silt-laden, slow-moving rivers and flatter terrain. Rainforests have a greater diversity of trees, but cloud forests have more epiphytes, with mosses on the trunks of trees, orchids between the mosses, ferns and bromeliads growing on branches, and algae covering the leaves.

Andean cloud forests provide some of the best bird-watching in the world. The bright-red feathers of the Andean cock-of-the-rock make it a favorite with birders, who watch their mating displays in courtship clearings called leks. Golden-headed quetzals have bright turquoise plumage and live in tree cavities next to vivid tanagers and toucans, while antpittas skulk in the shadows.

Maquipucuna, a cloud forest reserve north of Quito, is the best place in the country to see Andean bears, as they come to feed in wild avocado trees. Other cloud forest mammals include jaguars, pumas, ocelots, margays, Andean tapirs, mantled howler monkeys, agoutis, Andean coatis, three-toed sloths, and white-fronted capuchin monkeys. Crystalline streams provide habitat for a number of glass frog species and escape routes for the famous basilisk or "Jesus Christ lizard," which can walk on water.

Beautiful cloud forests can be found in the north of the country at Mindo.

History

EARLIEST CULTURES

If you've ever noticed the similarities in features of American indigenous people and Asians, you're not imagining it—most experts agree that the Americas were first colonized by nomadic hunter-gatherers who crossed the Bering Strait from Siberia about 18,000 years ago. They gradually moved south, reaching Latin America a few thousand years later to become the continent's original inhabitants. Archaeologists have found instruments carved from stone and arrowheads made from obsidian and flint dating back 10,000 years, when it is thought that small family groups roamed the area. From then, numerous cultures thrived for thousands of years before the Inca and Spanish invasions.

The pre-Columbian civilization can be divided into four periods: Pre-Ceramic, Formative, Regional Development, and Integration. The best places to see archaeological remains from the pre-Columbian period are museums in Quito and Cuenca.

PRE-CERAMIC PERIOD

The earliest Ecuadorian culture, Las Vegas, can be traced to the Santa Elena Peninsula as long ago as 9000 BC. After starting out as hunter-gatherers, they began farming around 6000 BC. The best-known remains are the skeletons called the Lovers of Sumpa, housed in the Museo Los Amantes de Sumpa in Santa Elena. Around the same time, the area near present-day Quito was inhabited by nomadic hunters known as the Inga.

Pristine areas of Amazon rainforest are usually considered to be ancient, untamed jungles untouched by human hands. But that perception is starting to change, with evidence suggesting that ancient peoples played a key role in the ecological development of the rainforest as long as 8,000 years ago. Like other populations, they changed the land to suit their needs by burning, cutting, tilling, planting, and building. Before European-introduced diseases decimated indigenous populations around 500 years ago, many parts of the Amazon were probably as cultivated as regions in Europe. Research indicates that many rainforest tree species appear to be abundant because they were cultivated for food or building by pre-Columbian cultures, including cacao, rubber, caimito fruit, and tucuma palm.

FORMATIVE PERIOD

Around 4500 BC, people evolved from hunting-gathering and simple farming into more permanent settlements with more developed agriculture and the use of ceramics. Emerging from the Las Vegas culture around 3500 BC, the Valdivia culture inhabited the Santa Elena Peninsula near the modern-day town of Valdivia. They produced some of America's oldest pottery and are best known for producing female ceramic figures known as the Venus of Valdivia. They were followed by the coastal Machalilla culture between the second and first millennia BC, who were experts at crafting objects from shells and practiced skull deformation as a sign of status.

Traces of cocoa dating back to around 3200 BC have been found in ancient pots in the Ecuadorian Amazon; this is the oldest proof of cocoa use ever found, predating the domestication of cocoa by the Maya in Central America by some 1,500 years. This evidence was collected at the Santa Ana La Florida archaeological site near Palanda in the southern Amazon region, where there are traces of a house and a ceremonial site belonging to the Mayo Chinchipe, the oldest known Amerindian civilization in the upper Amazon. The presence of seashells, such as spondylus and strombus, demonstrates that there were communication links between the peoples of the coast and the Oriente.

The Narrio culture appeared in the southern Sierra around 1500 BC and made funeral offerings depicting their ancestors with shells, evidencing commerce between the coast and Sierra. Living on both the coast and in the Andes, the Chorerra (to 300 BC) produced beautiful polished and painted pottery in the form of fruit, animals, and people.

REGIONAL DEVELOPMENT

Between 300 BC and AD 700 several cultures flourished along the coast (Bahía, Guangala, Jambelí, Jama-Coaque, La Tolita) and in the Sierra (Tuncahuán and Panzaleo). The La Tolita people on the northern coast were remarkable craftspeople in metallurgy, using gold, copper, and platinum, this last being worked in Ecuador for the first time in the world. Felines were their principal deity and were represented in their art. Their famous gold sun-mask is the symbol of the Banco Central.

INTEGRATION PERIOD

Coastal cultures reached their peak between AD 700 and 1460. The Manteños were the last of the pre-Columbian cultures in the coastal region and are famous for making U-shaped stone chairs, thought to have been used by shamans during ancient ceremonies. Theirs was a trading culture, and they were specialists in diving for spondylus shells.

In the Sierra, the Cara people arrived in what is now Quito in the 10th century, defeating the local Quitu tribe. The combined Quitu-Cara culture was known as the Shyris or Caranqui civilization and thrived until the Inca invasion, against which they fought valiantly. The Cañaris, descended from the Narrio culture in the southern Sierra, would also put up fierce resistance to the invaders.

THE RISE AND FALL OF THE INCAS

The Incas, or "Children of the Sun," had roots in two previous great empires: Tiwanaku (circa AD 300-1100), based around Lake Titicaca between Peru and Bolivia; and the

Wari (circa AD 600-1100), who occupied the Cuzco area for about 400 years. By about AD 1250, the Incas began to expand from Cuzco. By the 14th and 15th centuries they had built an empire called Tawantinsuyu that stretched from what is now northern Chile to the southern edge of present-day Ecuador.

In 1463 the ruling Inca, Túpac Yupanqui, began the push into Ecuador from Peru. In the Sierra, Inca armies met fierce resistance, notably from the Cañaris and Quitu-Caras. It wasn't until Yupanqui's son, Huayna Capac, continued his father's campaign that the Incan Empire finally conquered these territories. Following their victory, the invaders had enough respect for the Cañari to build a community together at Ingapirca.

Once a complex with ceremonial, astronomical, political, and administrative functions, Ingapirca is Ecuador's most important Inca site. It is thought that the Temple of the Sun, which is still standing, was used as a site for rituals and determining the agricultural and religious calendars. The most important Inca event was Inti Raymi, the Festival of the Sun, which is still celebrated by indigenous communities across Ecuador every June solstice.

Ingapirca also includes a fragment of Inca road, part of a 40,000-kilometer (25,000-mi) network that once connected religious and administrative centers across Ecuador, Peru, Colombia, Bolivia, Argentina, and Chile, described by *Smithsonian Magazine* as "arguably the biggest, most complex construction project ever undertaken." Paved in parts with stone, the roads allowed teams of relay runners to make the 470-kilometer (290-mi) journey from Cuenca to Quito in two or three days, crossing suspension bridges and resting in stone shelters along the way. Messages carried over longer distances would have involved hundreds of oral exchanges, and to preserve the correct meaning of the original message, *quipu*—coded assemblies of strings and knots—were probably used to help the memory of the runners. One of the highest sections of the Inca road passes through what is now Sangay National Park, reaching an elevation of 4,200 meters (13,780 ft), and can be hiked on the three-day Inca Trek from Achupallas to Ingapirca. Another fragment of Inca road can be seen in El Cajas National Park. El Salitre, a small Inca *pucara* (fortress), can be visited on the eastern edge of Cotopaxi National Park.

Huayna Capac chose to build the empire's northern capital where Cuenca is today. Modeled on Cuzco, the city was called Tumebamba, and the ruins can be visited at Pumapungo. Most of the city was destroyed shortly before the Spanish conquest, in a war between Huayna Capac's sons, Atahualpa and Huáscar, in 1532.

That same year, the arrival of the Spanish conquistadores coincided with the Inca's weakest moment, divided as they were by war. The Spanish were able to defeat the Children of the Sun, putting an end to their 50-year reign in Ecuador. During this brief period, the Inca left a strong imprint on the culture and landscape. Agriculture was diversified and centralized, grown on terraced fields watered by complicated systems of irrigation. Though the Quechua language (which evolved into Kichwa) predates the Incas, they enforced it as the official language of the empire. The Incas are thought to have brought the ancestors of the

Andean Saraguro and Salasaca people from southern Peru and Bolivia in the 16th century as part of the *mitma* system of forced resettlement. Saraguros believe that they are descended from members of Huayna Capac's closest circle, who were sent here to start a new colony that would adhere faithfully to their leader's beliefs. To this day, the majority of the 30,000 Saraguros in Ecuador wear black—the color worn by the Incas on special occasions.

THE CONQUISTADORES
THE SPANISH CONQUEST BEGINS

Most conquistadores (literally, "conquerors") were low-ranking Spanish noblemen heading to the New World for wealth, fame, and adventure. Of these, Francisco Pizarro went on to lead an expedition that conquered the Inca empire and claimed the lands for Spain. Pizarro was an illiterate and illegitimate fortune-seeker who accompanied explorer Vasco Núñez de Balboa on a 1513 expedition that was credited with the European "discovery" of the Pacific Ocean. A decade later, Pizarro received permission from the Spanish crown for a voyage along the west coast of South America with fellow adventurer Diego de Almagro.

In 1526, while Pizarro was exploring what is now Panama and Colombia, his main captain, Bartolomé Ruiz, sailed down the Ecuadorian coast on a reconnaissance mission and captured a Manta merchant vessel laden with gold and jewels. This news convinced Pizarro that the region contained untold riches. Following several largely unsuccessful voyages, Pizarro returned to Spain to ask King Charles I for permission to undertake a conquest. He traveled again to the New World having been granted all the authority of a viceroy, arriving in Tumbes in northern Peru in 1532 with 180 men. After meeting with hostility from the Incas, Pizarro's party relocated to the island of Puná in the Gulf of Guayaquil. Here, he met even fiercer resistance from the indigenous inhabitants, resulting in a full battle. Despite being hopelessly outnumbered, the Spanish massacred the locals with superior fighting skills and firepower that included muskets and cavalry. Over 400 natives died, but just three Spaniards did. Pizarro sailed back to Tumbes and decided to move inland in the hope of avoiding further battles and finding the riches he craved.

ATAHUALPA'S FATE

After defeating and capturing his half-brother Huáscar in the civil war of 1532, the Inca leader had decamped to Cajamarca in the mountains of northern Peru. As Pizarro was heading inland, he was alerted to the whereabouts of Atahualpa and a meeting was arranged. The ensuing scene would have been fascinating to witness: Two leaders meeting in the sunbaked central plaza under the eyes of dozens of Spanish soldiers and thousands of Inca warriors, with tension resonating in the air. Atahualpa, considered a living god by his people and with an army of thousands at his disposal, made the fatal mistake of underestimating a band of less than 200 Spaniards. Upon the Inca leader's refusal to accept Christianity and Charles V as his master, Spanish soldiers fired cannons and charged their horses into the heart of the Inca garrison. Within hours, the Incas had been defeated, the Sun King had been taken captive by Pizarro, and the fate of South America's greatest empire had been sealed.

During the nine months of his imprisonment, Atahualpa learned Spanish, chess, and cards while retaining most of his authority. Thinking that Pizarro planned to depose him in favor of Huáscar, Atahualpa ordered his captive half-brother killed. When it became clear that his own life hung in the balance, Atahualpa offered to buy his freedom with the wealth of his entire kingdom. He is said to have reached high on the wall of a room 5 meters wide by 7 meters long (16 by 23 ft), offering to fill it once with gold and twice with silver. The ransom—one of the largest the world has ever known—was assembled and was on its way to the capital when Pizarro went back on his word, fearful of the Inca leader's power. Atahualpa was put on trial for polygamy, idolatry, and crimes against the crown and was sentenced to be burned at the stake. He reacted with horror at this news because he believed that such a fate would prevent his body from passing into the afterlife. He agreed to be baptized and was strangled with a garrote on July 26, 1533, in Cajamarca. The ransom, quickly hidden en route from Cuzco, has never been found.

THE CONQUEST IS COMPLETED

In November 1533, just four months after Atahualpa's death, Cuzco fell to Pizarro and the Inca empire was finished. The Spanish victors were welcomed as liberators by many indigenous groups, who had resented and fought against the yoke of the Incas. A few battles remained to be fought: In May 1534, Sebastián de Benalcázar

(Pizarro's second in command) found himself facing 50,000 Inca warriors under the guidance of Rumiñahui, the greatest Inca general, who had deserted and burned Quito rather than surrender it to the invaders. Benalcázar, aided by Cañari soldiers, defeated "Stone Face," whose capture, torture, and execution signaled the end of organized indigenous military resistance.

By 1549, fewer than 2,000 Spanish soldiers had defeated an estimated 500,000 indigenous people. Although these numbers seem unbelievable, they can be explained by a combination of battle tactics, epidemiology, and luck. In the 16th century, Spanish soldiers were among the best in the world, almost invulnerable to attack from the ground when mounted on their war horses in full battle armor. A dozen mounted soldiers could hold off and even defeat hundreds of Inca foot soldiers. In addition, European diseases, to which the indigenous people had no immunity, killed them by the thousands.

THE END OF THE CONQUISTADOR ERA

Victory did little to dampen the Spanish conquerors' lust for power, and they quickly began fighting among themselves. In 1538, Diego de Almagro contested Pizarro's right to govern the new territory of Peru. He was defeated, tried, and sentenced to death in Lima, garroted in the same way as Atahualpa. Francisco Pizarro was stabbed to death in his palace in 1541 by the remaining members of Almagro's rebel army, led by his son.

The Spanish crown tried to restore order by imposing the New Laws of 1542, aimed at controlling the unruly conquistadores and ending the enslavement of the indigenous peoples, already a widespread practice. A new viceroy, Blasco Núñez Vela, was sent to oversee the budding colonies in 1544, but Gonzalo Pizarro (Francisco's brother) organized resistance and fought and killed Núñez in the battle of Añaquito near Quito in 1544. Pizarro, in turn, was defeated by royal troops near Cuzco in 1548 and beheaded on the field of battle.

THE COLONIAL PERIOD

From 1544 to 1720, Ecuador existed as part of the Viceroyalty of Peru, one of the divisions of Spain's New World colonies. In 1563, Quito became a royal Audience of Spain, thus, permitting it to deal directly with Madrid on certain matters instead of going through the Viceroyalty in Lima. The territory of the Audience of Quito greatly exceeded that of present-day Ecuador, encompassing the north of present-day Peru, the city of Cali in the south of present-day Colombia, and much of the Amazon River Basin east of present-day Ecuador.

FARMS AND SLAVES

As Spanish settlers replaced the conquistadores, and female immigrants evened the balance of the sexes, a new form of land tenure was born in the Sierra. The *encomienda* system gave settlers (*encomenderos)* the title to tracts of the best land, along with the right to demand tribute and labor from the indigenous people who lived there. In exchange, the *encomendero* agreed to defend the land and convert its inhabitants to Christianity. The Spanish crown strove to impose rules governing the treatment of the native Ecuadorians, but, in many cases, they were forced into virtual slavery,

subjected to extreme punishment and death if they resisted. By the early 17th century, about 500 *encomenderos* controlled vast tracts of the Sierra, with around half of the population living on them. The rich volcanic earth of the Andean highlands bore bumper crops of wheat, corn, and potatoes, which thrived in the mild climate, along with cattle, horses, and sheep. Another important source of income for the Spanish in the Sierra was textile *obrajes* (workshops), where indigenous people were forced to weave from dawn to dusk, often chained to their looms in brutal conditions. The hacienda system was also introduced, consisting of large privately owned estates, often owned by minor Spanish nobles. Local indigenous laborers were tied to the haciendas by various forms of debt peonage that continued well into the 20th century.

On the coast, the main crops were bananas, cacao, and sugarcane, though agriculture was hampered by rampant tropical diseases like malaria and yellow fever and a subsequent lack of natives to enslave. Instead, the coastal economy revolved around shipping and trade. Despite being destroyed by fire several times, Guayaquil became a thriving port city and the largest ship-building center on the west coast of South America.

In 1553, a ship en route from Panama to Peru ran aground off the Ecuadorian coast at Portete near Mompiche. The 23 African slaves on board rebelled and escaped into the forests. Despite clashes with local indigenous people, the region became a safe haven for escaped slaves and, by the end of the 16th century, the community had declared themselves to be a republic of *zambos* (curly-haired people). They lived autonomously for most of the colonial era, intermarrying with the local indigenous population and giving rise to today's population of Afro-Ecuadorians, who still mostly live in Esmeraldas province.

The Roman Catholic Church was a cornerstone of life during the colonial period for indigenous people and immigrants alike. By a majority vote, the Vatican had decided that indigenous people actually did have souls, making their conversion a worthwhile endeavor. A sweltering climate, impassable terrain, and fierce indigenous groups kept most settlers out of the Oriente except a few missionaries, many of whom were speared to death or ended up as shrunken heads.

INDEPENDENCE FROM SPAIN
FIRST SPARKS

During the colonial period, the Spanish stood at the top of the social ladder, whether they were born in Spain (known as *peninsulares*) or the New World (*criollos*). Mixed-blood mestizos were in the middle, keeping the urban machinery going as shopkeepers, craftspeople, and skilled laborers. This middle class, aspiring to wealth and status as they looked down on the native masses, was politically unstable and easily provoked by fiery rhetoric—a ready source of fuel for the spark of independence. Following the conquest, countless numbers of indigenous people had died of imported diseases like smallpox, measles, cholera, and syphilis, to which they had no natural immunity. Those that remained, numbering 750,000-1 million by the 16th century, made up most of colonial society and provided the forced labor.

Just as things had settled into a routine of oppression in the colonies,

a series of events unfolded that would eventually shake the continent. From 1736 to 1745, the French mission to measure the shape of the earth at the equator spread ideas of rational science and personal liberty, courtesy of the Enlightenment. Revolutions in the United States (1776) and France (1789) set the stage for the wars of independence in South American countries.

In Ecuador, the physician and writer Eugenio Espejo was a liberal humanist who demanded freedom and a democratic government for the colonies. Hailed as one of the fathers of independence, Espejo was thrown in jail repeatedly and even exiled for his books and articles, before contracting dysentery in a Quito prison and dying in 1795. Across the country, uprisings among both indigenous people and mestizos protested their treatment at the hands of Spain.

The 18th century was a period of economic hardship in Spain, and thus its colonies. The wealthy were harder hit than the poor, resulting in the *criollos* joining the revolutionary movement. The final straw came in July 1808 when Napoléon invaded Spain, deposed King Ferdinand VII, and installed his brother Joseph Bonaparte on the throne. Monetary demands on the colonies—always a source of friction—skyrocketed as Spain sought funds to fight for the deposed Ferdinand, and the colonists decided enough was enough.

EARLY UPRISINGS

Resentful of the privileges afforded to the *peninsulares*, on August 10, 1809, a group of elite *criollos* jailed the president of the Audience of Quito and seized power, but the coup was short-lived and brutally quelled. In the decade that followed, the *criollo*

EL LIBERTADOR

Revered and despised, **Simón Bolívar** embodied all the contradictions of the continent he helped free from Spain. Whether as the heroic liberator of South America or the tyrannical despot chasing an impossible vision of continental unity, Bolívar is considered by many as the most important figure in Latin American history. At his death, his dream remained only half fulfilled: He had freed his beloved land, but he couldn't unify it.

Born in Caracas on July 24, 1783, to a wealthy family of planters, Simón Antonio de la Santísima Trinidad Bolívar y Palacios saw both his parents die before his 10th birthday. Relatives and friends helped raise him in the cultured circles of the New World's upper class. His early teenage years were spent in military school, where his records reveal innate martial talent. His studies continued in Europe, and his attention was soon captured by the rising star Napoléon Bonaparte, who had just crowned himself emperor of France for life. As he soaked up the rhetoric of Rousseau and Voltaire, advocating the sacred duty of a monarch to protect the common man by means of the law, Bolívar was solidifying his own ideas for South America. He came to believe that the best way to organize the struggling republics would be through a strongly centralized, even dictatorial government. At the helm would preside a lifetime ruler with limitless power who would labor for the greatest good—a "moralistic monarch."

When Bolívar returned to Venezuela in 1807, he found a population divided between loyalty to Spain and independence. When Napoléon invaded Spain in 1808, many Venezuelans felt that they no longer owed allegiance to Spain. Bolívar was an important advocate for independence during this time, and indeed, on July 5, 1811, the First Venezuelan Republic voted for full independence. The Spanish quickly regained control, however.

Bolívar, defeated, went into exile, heading to New Granada (now Colombia) to become an officer in the growing independence movement there. With 200 men, he aggressively attacked all Spanish forces in the area, and his prestige and army grew. By the beginning of 1813, he was ready to lead a sizable army into Venezuela and rode victoriously into Caracas, quickly establishing the Second Venezuelan Republic. The

population unsuccessfully tried several times to take control of the Audience of Quito.

THE BATTLE FOR INDEPENDENCE

Simón Bolívar's success in Bogota inspired the faltering independence struggle in Ecuador. In 1820, a junta in Guayaquil under the leadership of poet José Joaquín Olmedo declared Ecuador's independence from its colonial master. Unlike in earlier independence attempts, Olmedo appealed for outside assistance, asking Simón Bolívar and his Argentinian counterpart, José de San Martín, for support. In response, Bolívar sent his best general, Antonio José de Sucre, at the head of an army. The combined Ecuadorian and foreign forces won a number of successive victories against the Spanish before finally being stopped in Ambato. In the nick of time, San Martín's reinforcements arrived and Sucre's army went on the offensive again, heading for Quito via an arduous climb over the Pichinchas. On the muddy slopes of the volcano, within sight of the capital, they fought the largest Spanish force in Ecuador. After three hours and 600 lives lost, Sucre's army prevailed and the Audience of Quito formally surrendered. The Battle of Pichincha was the decisive victory that forever drove the Spanish from Ecuador.

Simón Bolívar arrived in Quito

people named him El Libertador (The Liberator) and made him leader of the new nation.

Spain struck back, occupying Caracas in 1814, and Bolívar went into exile once again. When he returned, he found Venezuela devastated by fighting between pro-independence and royalist forces. He turned his sights to Bogota, where he planned on destroying the Spanish base of power in northern South America. After an arduous two-month crossing of the Andes, Bolívar and his army marched into Bogota in 1819, winning the battle of Boyaca en route. After that, it was only a matter of time before the remaining Spanish forces in New Granada and Venezuela were defeated. On June 24, 1821, Bolívar crushed the last major royalist force in Venezuela and declared the birth of a new republic: Colombia, which would include the lands of Venezuela, New Granada, and present-day Ecuador, with himself as president. After driving the Spanish out of present-day Ecuador and Peru, the nation of Bolivia was created and named after him. Bolívar now ruled over the present-day nations of Bolivia, Peru, Ecuador, Colombia, Venezuela, and Panama. It was his dream to unite them all, creating one unified nation, but it was not to be.

It was in peace that the newly freed nations would disappoint him, and his noble-minded revolution soon dissolved into a bloody struggle between disparate factions. In a last-ditch attempt to reconcile the warring populations, Bolívar organized a peace congress in Panama in 1826. Only four countries showed up.

Bolívar became depressed by his failure to build a united continent, and in April 1830 he resigned as leader of Colombia, declaring: "America is ungovernable; all who served the revolution have plowed the sea." He planned to go into exile but lost his final battle, with tuberculosis, at age 47 on December 17, 1830. He never answered the question of whether a South America unified under a monarch would have prospered, or if he simply would have recreated in the New World the system he fought to dispel. Shortly before he died, the fiery general seethed with bitterness at what he saw as the betrayal of his dream: "There is no good faith in America, nor among the nations of America. Treaties are scraps of paper; constitutions, printed matter; elections, battles; freedom, anarchy." Even on his deathbed, though, his thoughts were full of hope for his beloved federation: "Colombians! My last wishes are for the happiness of our native land."

three weeks later and arranged his famous meeting with José de San Martín in Guayaquil on July 26, 1822, commemorated with a monument on the city's waterfront. It was decided there that Bolívar would lead the charge into Peru, the last Spanish stronghold on the continent. Bolívar and Sucre's subsequent victories at the Battle of Junín and the Battle of Ayacucho sealed South America's independence. Spain was beaten and withdrew its administrative apparatus from the Americas.

For eight years, Bolívar ruled over what was then known as Colombia, encompassing the present-day nations of Bolivia, Peru, Ecuador, Colombia, Venezuela, and Panama. His grand plan for a united South America soon succumbed to regional rivalries, and he resigned as leader April 1830. In August of that year, Ecuador withdrew from Colombia and became fully independent. A constituent assembly drew up a constitution for the State of Ecuador, thus named for its proximity to the equator. A general, Juan José Flores, was put in charge of political and military affairs.

EARLY YEARS OF THE REPUBLIC

Ecuador's childhood as a nation was marked by power struggles among *criollo* elites, in particular aristocratic conservatives from Quito and free-enterprise liberals from Guayaquil. Meanwhile, the new republic had little effect on most of the country—the poor, in other words, stayed poor.

Juan José Flores ruled ruthlessly 1830-1845, either directly as president or through puppet figures, until widespread discontent forced him to flee the country. Between 1845 and 1860, 11 governments and three constitutions came and went, as the economy stagnated and the military's influence in politics grew. By 1860 the country was on the brink of chaos, split by provincial rivalries and tension over border disputes with Peru and Colombia.

THEOCRACY AND CONSERVATISM

In 1860 a new player rose to the top. Gabriel García Moreno so much embodied devout Sierra conservatism that some historians have dubbed his regime a theocracy. He grew up during the chaos of the preceding decades and was determined to impose religious and political order on Ecuador.

Conservatives loved him, seeing him as a great "nation-builder" who saved Ecuador from falling into chaos. Under his iron rule, the economy improved and corruption was dramatically decreased. An improved education system now accepted women and *indigenous people, and* new roads, hospitals, and railroads were built (often using forced indigenous labor). Deeply religious, García Moreno established Roman Catholicism as the official state religion, with membership a prerequisite for citizenship and voting. Free speech was tightly controlled and political opposition squashed.

Not surprisingly, García Moreno's firm stance made him many enemies among liberals, who dubbed him a ruthless tyrant. In 1875, after being elected to a third term, he was hacked to death on the steps of the presidential palace. His last words were reportedly "God doesn't die."

INTO THE 20TH CENTURY
SECULARISM AND LIBERALISM

Two decades of jousting between the Liberal and Conservative Parties ended with the ascension to power of General Eloy Alfaro. Both his terms as president, 1897-1901 and 1906-1911, started with armed coups. Credited with separating church from state, Alfaro embodied the Radical Liberal Party as much as García Moreno typified conservatism. He toppled the Catholic Church from its domination by seizing church lands, instituting freedom of religion, secularizing marriage and education, and legalizing divorce. Civil rights, such freedom of speech and the rights of workers and indigenous Ecuadorians, were expanded, with native slaves being freed from haciendas. He also completed the Quito-Guayaquil railroad and rode triumphantly aboard it in 1908. However, as with García Moreno, Alfaro made many enemies and became a hated figure for conservatives. He lost power in a coup in 1911 and was exiled. Upon re-entering the country and attempting another coup, he was arrested and brought to Quito. An angry mob broke into the prison where he was held and shot him dead, dragging his body through the streets and burning it in Parque El Ejido. It was a barbaric end for the "old warrior," who is considered the hero of Ecuador's liberal revolution. There is a museum dedicated to Eloy Alfaro in Montecristi, his birthplace.

Following Eloy Alfaro's death until 1925, a number of Liberal presidents took power, including his bitter party rival General Leónidas Plaza Gutiérrez. During this second half of the Liberal rule, however, the power was really held by a plutocracy of agricultural and banking interests. According to Ecuadorian historian Oscar Efrén Reyes, the Commercial & Agricultural Bank of Guayaquil was so powerful that presidential and ministerial candidates had to seek its approval before running for office.

CRISIS AND WAR

In 1926, the Ecuadorian Socialist Party (PSE) welcomed indigenous activists to its 1926 congress. At the time, Sierran indigenous communities were engaged in land struggles with haciendas, demanding better conditions and salaries for sharecroppers (*huasipungueros*) who, in exchange for a plot of land, were required to provide labor to hacienda owners; their wives were also obliged to work as domestic servants. A number of indigenous activists considered their efforts to be part of a broader class struggle and joined forces with the nascent PSE.

That same year, Isidro Ayora was elected as president. He restructured fiscal and monetary institutions, bringing a prosperous half decade that saw the establishment of several social agencies and progressive social programs. His skillful financial management couldn't survive the 1929 Great Depression, however, putting an end to his presidency. The 1930s saw another 13 presidents come and go, including José María Velasco Ibarra, who said, "Give me a balcony, and I will become president." The first leader to appeal to both liberals and conservatives, he was elected a total of five times between 1934 and 1961, though was overthrown from four of his five terms.

The border between Ecuador and Peru, outlined only roughly by the colonial Audience of Quito, had been a bone of contention since Ecuador became a country. Boundary talks broke down into skirmishes, and in 1941 Peru took advantage of the rest of the world's focus on World War II by seizing Ecuador's southern and easternmost provinces. Fearing a coup, President Carlos Alberto Arroyo del Río kept the best troops in Quito during the border fighting, and the Ecuadorians were easily defeated. In 1942, Peru and Ecuador signed the Protocol of Peace, Friendship, and Boundaries, also known as the Río Protocol, overseen by the United States, Chile, Argentina, and Brazil. Not only did Ecuador have to sign away more than 200,000 square kilometers (75,000 sq mi) of territory to its neighbor, but it also lost the Amazon River port of Iquitos, its main river access to the Atlantic. Ecuador continued to dispute the Río Protocol, and the border between the two countries was militarized. Running through the ancestral lands of the Siekopai people, it divided communities and families.

Between and 1920s and 1940s, indigenous communities started to collaborate, regionally consolidating their struggles against agrarian capitalism and organizing several protest marches against forced hacienda labor that converged on Quito. The fledgling indigenous movement was supported by the PSE, which included demands for expropriation of hacienda lands in their general platform; raised funds for local indigenous causes; publicized their struggles in the socialist press; provided logistical support for the 1931 First Congress of Peasant Organizations; and assisted indigenous organizations in presenting demands to the government. In return, socialist candidates received electoral support from indigenous organizations. In 1944, the Federación Ecuatoriana de Indios (FEI, Ecuadorian Federation of Indians) was founded, representing the first successful attempt to establish a national organization by and for indigenous peoples.

POSTWAR ECUADOR: INSTABILITY AND MILITARY RULE

Ecuador sided with the Allies in World War II, during which the United States built a naval base in the Galápagos and tried to remove all German settlers from the archipelago. After the war, Ecuador enjoyed a decade of relative political stability and prosperity, despite a massive earthquake that completely destroyed the city of Ambato and the surrounding villages in 1949. Even old Velasco Ibarra was finally able to finish a full term—his third—in 1952. When a wave of disease ravaged Central America's banana crop, Ecuador stepped in to supply the huge U.S. demand with the help of the United Fruit Company. Exports jumped from $2 million in 1948 to $20 million in 1952, and Ecuador's position as world banana king became official.

By the late 1950s, however, the banana boom was over and political chaos returned. Velasco Ibarra, who was re-elected in 1960, began a proud Ecuadorian political tradition by renouncing the Río Protocol in his inaugural address, to the delight of the crowd. His left-leaning policies proved ill-timed, however, coming at the height of the Cold War. A gunfight in the congressional chamber proved how bad things had become at the top. In November 1961, the military removed Velasco Ibarra from power; two years later it replaced his successor with a four-man junta.

Ecuador's first experiment with outright military rule was short-lived, barely managing to pass the well-intentioned but ultimately ineffectual Agrarian Reform Law of 1964. Though land distribution was minimal, the new law did end the brutal *huasipungo* system of forced indigenous labor on haciendas. After flourishing for two decades, the Ecuadorian Federation of Indians started to decline after achieving this key aim. Instead, new indigenous organizations surfaced that focused on defending their culture, religion, medicine, and bilingual education. The first significant of these was the Shuar Federation, formed in the early 1960s, followed by the Federación Nacional de Organizaciones Campesinas (FENOC, National Federation of Peasant Organizations) and Ecuarunari (Confederation of Kichwa Peoples of Ecuador). The latter represents Sierra Kichwas, and the name is a shortened version of a phrase meaning "to awaken the Ecuadorian Indians."

After the military government succumbed to concerns over another economic slump, Velasco Ibarra was re-elected in 1968 for the fifth time with barely a third of the popular vote. For two years he enjoyed military support as he dismissed Congress and the Supreme Court, suspended the constitution, and dictated harsh and unpopular economic measures, before being once again overthrown by the military in 1972.

A few years earlier, it had been discovered that Ecuador had the third-largest petroleum reserves in Latin America. In 1972, the military government paraded the first barrel of oil through the streets of Quito, extracted from the jungle by a consortium between Texaco and the fledgling state oil company, and hailed as the answer to Ecuador's economic woes. The junta instituted a firm strategy of modernization and industrialization. While the middle class grew in numbers and power, further attempts at land reform met the stone wall of the landholding elite. Not surprisingly, the poor and indigenous suffered from the oil-boom inflation and environmental devastation without reaping the attendant benefits.

THE RETURN TO DEMOCRACY

Coups in 1975 and 1976 caused splits within the military, and they sought to return Ecuador to civilian rule. In January 1978 a national referendum voted for a new constitution, universal suffrage, and guaranteed civil rights. The following year, highly popular and charismatic left-winger Jaime Roldós Aguilera took office in a landslide election victory. During an era of military dictatorships throughout Latin America, he embodied the hope for change. He found himself at the wheel of a country unfamiliar with democracy, but with a government budget increased more than 500 percent by the oil windfall. Roldós's center-left government began programs of improving rural literacy and housing. He championed human rights, formed a friendship with the Sandinista government in Nicaragua, challenged the oil contracts negotiated with foreign companies, and turned down an invitation to Ronald Reagan's inauguration. In May 1981, shortly after presenting a draft reform of the hydrocarbons law in favor of national interests, Roldós

and his wife were killed in a mysterious plane crash, which has never been properly investigated by the authorities. Left-wing Panamanian leader Omar Torrijos died in a similar incident a few months later. Both leaders had failed to toe the U.S. line, and a common view is that they were assassinated by the CIA. You can read about these theories in John Perkins's 2004 book *Confessions of an Economic Hitman*. An excellent documentary, *La Muerte de Roldós* by Manolo Sarmiento, also examines Roldós's life and tragic death.

In 1980, the Shuar Federation joined other organizations to form the Confederación de Nacionalidades Indígenas de la Amazonía Ecuatoriana (CONFENIAE, Confederation of Indigenous Nationalities of the Ecuadorian Amazon) to battle for the common interests of all Amazon communities, including the lowland Kichwa, Shuar, Achuar, Siona, Secoya, Kofán, and Waorani.

The early 1980s brought a succession of crises. Border fighting with Peru flared up and the disastrous 1982-1983 El Niño climate pattern caused enormous drought and flood damage, ruining rice and banana crops along the coast. Sudden declines in petroleum reserves left the country with a foreign debt of $7 billion by 1983, when inflation hit an all-time high of 52.5 percent.

Conservative León Febres Cordero defeated eight other candidates to win the presidency in 1984. A neoliberal, Febres Cordero favored a pro-U.S. foreign policy, free market economic policies, and strong-arm tactics that led to accusations of human rights abuses. In January 1987, Cordero was kidnapped by air force troops under orders from an imprisoned mutinous general. Only by granting them general amnesty was the president able to secure his own release after 11 hours in captivity, a move widely perceived as cowardly by Ecuadorians. That same month, an earthquake in Napo Province killed hundreds and ruptured the all-important oil pipeline, causing Ecuador to suspend interest payments on its $8.3 billion foreign debt.

In 1986, CONFENIAE joined Ecuarunari in the highlands to form the Confederación de Nacionalidades Indígenas del Ecuador (CONAIE, Confederation of Indigenous Nationalities of Ecuador) to combine all indigenous peoples into one national pan-indigenous movement. CONAIE's central and most controversial demand was to revise the constitution to recognize the plurinational character of Ecuador. Other fundamental objectives were to consolidate the indigenous peoples and nationalities of Ecuador; to defend indigenous territories; to fight for bilingual education (in their native tongues and Spanish); to combat the oppression of civil and ecclesiastical authorities; to protect the cultural identity of indigenous peoples against colonialism; and to uphold the dignity of indigenous peoples and nationalities.

In 1988, social democrat Rodrigo Borja Cevallos won the presidency and introduced reforms, including a literacy program and legislation to protect civil liberties.

In 1990, indigenous peoples led by CONAIE organized the largest ever uprising in the country's history, frustrated by stalled talks with the government over the recognition of Ecuador as a plurinational state, land reforms, and other issues. The protests blocked roads, cut off the food supply to the cities, and effectively shut down the country for a week. In 500 years of struggle, it was the first time the indigenous movement had articulated itself nationally, and it rocked Ecuador's white and mestizo power base. President Borja Cevallos agreed to meet with CONAIE to negotiate and, while the talks failed to meet the key demands, bilingual education was restored and an Indigenous Affairs Office established. Ecuador's indigenous movement had established itself as a force to be reckoned with. Over the next couple of decades, it would become one of the strongest on the continent, due to its ability to mobilize and inclusion of a diverse range of ethnic groups.

Ecuadorian voters swung back to the right in 1992, electing Christian Socialist Sixto Durán Ballén as president. Harsh austerity measures were masterminded by vice president Alberto Dahik, who fled to Costa Rica in a private plane, accused of embezzling millions of dollars in state funds. A government cover-up, which involved the seizure of Central Bank vaults that held incriminating microfilm, led to the resignation of ministers and the impeachment of one Supreme Court judge.

In 1992, two thousand Kichwa, Shuar, and Achuar peoples embarked upon a 385-kilometer (240-mi) march from the Amazon to Quito to demand legalization of land holdings. Two years later, indigenous organizations again organized a "Mobilization for Life" campaign in protest of an agricultural reform law that would allow communal land to be divided and sold, jeopardizing indigenous territories. Protests were prolonged and violent, with 15 of the 21 major transport arteries closed. In response, the law was reformed in consultation with CONAIE.

The political turmoil was compounded when tensions with Peru erupted into outright war in January 1995. During six weeks of combat near the headwaters of Río Cenepa, elite units of Shuar soldiers distinguished themselves, enabling Ecuador to claim victory.

After a decade of rejecting politics, in 1995 CONAIE made a U-turn and helped form a political movement, Pachakutik, in coalition with non-indigenous social movements. Identifying itself as part of a new Latin American left, the party opposed the government's neoliberal economic policies and favored a more inclusive and participatory political system. In both the 1996 and 1998 elections Pachakutik candidates won seats at all levels of government, from town councils to Congress.

EL LOCO

Desperate times led the voters to desperate choices. In 1996, the same year Jefferson Pérez became Ecuador's first-ever Olympic medalist by winning gold for speed walking, Abdalá Bucaram became president. The grandson of a Lebanese immigrant, he had carved out a successful political career as founder of the Partido Roldista Ecuatoriano (PRE), named after his brother-in-law Jaime Roldós. Bucaram had been mayor of Guayaquil and built a reputation for his eccentric style and rousing speeches. His nickname was "El Loco" (The Crazy One), and he was an energetic campaigner who often used to sing at political gatherings. He was seen as a political outsider, an image that he exploited to perfection,

marketing himself as the people's hero who would lead them out of poverty.

From the start, it was clear that El Loco wasn't firing on all cylinders. His inaugural address was described as a two-hour "hysterical diatribe." One day he was raising money for charity by shaving his mustache on live TV; the next he was having lunch with Ecuadorian American Lorena Bobbitt, who infamously cut off her husband's penis in 1993. The president released an album titled *A Madman in Love* and crooned at beauty contests. More importantly, he outraged his supporters by introducing austerity measures that led to skyrocketing utility bills, and he was accused of large-scale corruption. A general protest strike paralyzed the country, with an estimated 3 million indigenous people participating, and on February 6, Congress determined that he was unfit to govern on grounds of mental incapacity. Bucaram holed up in the presidential palace for days before finally fleeing to exile in Panama, allegedly with suitcases filled with public money, a mere six months after taking power.

Vice President Rosalía Arteaga became Ecuador's first woman president for two days before the male-dominated Congress re-wrote the constitution to allow the president of the Congress, Fabián Alarcón, to be installed. He repealed the austerity measures and muddled through for another year or so until another election was called.

INTO THE 21ST CENTURY
ECONOMIC CRISES AND DOLLARIZATION

After the pantomime of Bucaram's brief presidency, Ecuadorians thought that things couldn't get much worse, but how wrong they were. A second El Niño hit the country in 1998, washing out roads, devastating the country's farming and fishing industries, and killing off wildlife in the Galápagos. In August, an earthquake of magnitude 7.1 hit near Bahía de Caráquez, knocking out water and electricity supplies and even more roads.

It was a good year for the indigenous movement, however, when the new 1998 constitution finally recognized Ecuador as a multicultural and multiethnic nation. After the Texaco lawsuit and several other instances of oil drilling on indigenous territories without their permission, it also decreed that communities must give consent before any project is carried out on their land. The government almost immediately violated this last right, as successive regimes have continued to do, by selling two blocks of Achar, Kichwa, and Shuar lands to an oil company without their consent.

The new constitution came into effect on the same day as the new president, former Quito mayor and Harvard graduate Jamil Mahuad, came to power. Things began well when Mahuad finally laid to rest the longstanding border dispute with Peru. Indigenous Siekoya communities and families who had been divided by the militarized border were reunited after 50 years. However, the rising cost of El Niño, depressed oil prices, and plummeting confidence of foreign investors led to Ecuador's worst economic crisis in modern times. The country's currency, the sucre, fell dramatically, the economy shrank by more than 7 percent, and inflation rocketed to 60 percent. Mahuad pressed ahead with deeply unpopular economic austerity measures, and in a disastrous decision, froze more than $3 billion of bank deposits, preventing millions of Ecuadorians from making withdrawals. Worse news came when Ecuador became the first country to default on its Brady bonds. Filanbanco, the country's largest bank, then folded, taking $1.2 billion in public funds with it. Mahuad's last-ditch policy was to adopt the U.S. dollar as Ecuador's official currency, causing massive unrest.

Mahuad likened the situation to the sinking of the *Titanic* in a state-of-the-nation speech. Widespread protests ensured that the captain went down with the ship, including roadblocks by CONAIE and a coalition of indigenous groups. On January 21, 2000, a thousand protesters, mostly indigenous, burst through a military cordon and rushed the National Congress building. Some of the soldiers who had previously placed barbed wire around the building had stepped aside, indicating that a faction of the military had shifted allegiance. By mid-morning, the rainbow-colored flag of the indigenous movement was hanging from the roof of Congress. The protesters proceeded inaugurate their own National Peoples' Parliament, joined by a high-ranking army colonel and about 200 army officials. A short time later, a three-member junta was declared, composed of Army colonel Lucio Gutiérrez, a former Supreme Court judge, and the president of CONAIE, Antonio Vargas (marking a key moment in the indigenous movement). Later that afternoon, Mahuad was informed that the security of the presidential palace could no longer be guaranteed, forcing him to flee. The rebellion was short-lived, however, as Colonel Gutiérrez lacked the confidence of the military high command. He was replaced in the junta by

General Carlos Mendoza, the armed forces chief of staff, who announced that Vice President Gustavo Noboa would assume the presidency.

Noboa pressed ahead with the dollarization plan and introduced austerity measures to obtain $2 billion in aid from the International Monetary Fund. By 2001, the economy had begun to stabilize, but by then 500,000 Ecuadorians had already emigrated to North America and Europe.

In 2002, Colonel Lucio Gutiérrez was elected president. His campaign painted him as a friend of the downtrodden, and his ascent was seen as part of a general leftward political shift in Latin America, but it didn't last long. As soon as he got into power, Gutiérrez's policies moved markedly to the right. He dropped his early opposition to the adoption of the U.S. dollar, befriended U.S. president George Bush, and introduced austerity measures to finance the country's massive debt. He then filled Supreme Court positions with political allies and announced plans to allow his old ally Abdalá Bucaram to return, prompting massive public demonstrations. After being ousted by the National Congress and losing the support of the army in April 2005, Gutiérrez was forced to flee in fear for his life, leaving by helicopter from the roof of the presidential palace in Quito. On the positive side, the country's economy grew by 7 percent in 2004, in part due to higher oil prices.

RAFAEL CORREA AND 21ST-CENTURY SOCIALISM

Alfredo Palacio took over from Gutiérrez and managed the country until the next election in 2006, when a new figure burst on to the political scene. A young economist, Rafael Correa, appeared during a time of political vacuum, founding a new party, Alianza Pais. He exploited perfectly the anti-elite feeling of the time, raising anti-establishment banners and reviving leftist narratives based on social justice. He reached out directly to indigenous and environmental movements, wearing a poncho, speaking Kichwa, and promising to "create a country where humans could live as part of nature, not as its principal destroyer."

Correa took office in January 2007 and, true to his election campaign promise, quickly pushed through a referendum to replace Congress with a constituent assembly, tasked with drafting a new constitution. The 2008 constitution was the first in the world to grant legal rights to nature and to define water as a human right. Controversially, it also substantially consolidated executive powers to levels never experienced before in Ecuador.

Within his first months in office, Correa transferred control over the public oil corporation, PetroEcuador to the military. Vowing to end "the long dark night of neoliberalism," he closed the U.S. military base in Manta and declared the World Bank representative "persona non grata." The rhetoric against U.S. imperialism, however, gave way to a new wave of Chinese investments, as Correa negotiated a series of billion dollar loans and megaprojects in preserved areas. With record oil profits, his government enjoyed the biggest economic boom in Ecuador's history. In what Correa termed the "Citizen's Revolution," the administration oversaw the construction of highways, hospitals, schools, hydroelectric dams and other mega infrastructure projects. Access to public education and health care improved, while poverty, infant mortality and illiteracy rates fell. Correa was riding high, in 2009 becoming the first Ecuadorian president in 30 years to be re-elected, finally bringing some political stability to the country.

Cracks soon started to show, with allegations of financial irregularities in government construction projects. The much-touted new roads turned out to be among the most expensive in the world, with the price per kilometer over 15 times what it would cost in Germany. The Anti-Corruption Commission denounced the lack of accountability when the Manduriacu dam project came in US$102 million over budget, 82% higher than the contract. This overpricing became a characteristic of Citizen Revolution projects, with little transparency over the missing money. In early 2019, an audit commissioned by the UN announced that roughly half of the $5 billion the state had paid for oil-related infrastructure projects over the previous decade was lost to corruption.

In 2012, international oil companies were invited to bid for 3 million hectares of largely virgin rainforest in the southern Amazon in an auction known as the Ronda Sur. After his 2013 re-election, Correa announced plans to drill for oil in the Yasuní National Park, a UNESCO World Biosphere Reserve. He passed a draconian decree regulating rights of association, allowing the government to control NGOs. He used this legislation to shut down the National Teachers Union and one of the country's most prominent organizations, the Pachamama Foundation, which had been active in efforts to preserve the Amazon.

While the government positioned itself in the international media as a champion of free speech by offering asylum to Julian Assange in 2012, at home it implemented the most repressive media legislation in Latin America. In 2013, Congress passed a law granting broad powers to regulate, censor and prosecute the country's news outlets. Correa branded the private media his "biggest enemy" and used his weekly public address to name and threaten journalists, activists and opponents. Several journalists received death threats, sometimes in deliveries of flowers. What set Correaism apart from prior authoritarian regimes was a world class marketing department that proactively defined Ecuador's brand. Public relations and marketing were the biggest ministerial expenditures, used to generate a smokescreen behind which the government could largely implement its own agenda. Nonetheless, public discontent started to build. Protests against Correa's environmental policies, attacks on freedom of expression and labor laws were met with brutal police force.

By 2015, the oil boom was over and the country was in economic crisis. That August, Correa was faced with the most widespread and vociferous civil unrest of his time in office, sparked by a proposed package of 16 constitutional amendments. Confirming his increasingly dictatorial style, the most controversial of these allowed the indefinite re-election of the President and other government officials. These protests were inconveniently timed, coming just ahead of the Pope's state visit. The Cotopaxi volcano chose that moment to erupt and the government declared a State of Emergency, not just in the affected province but nationwide. Under cover of the decree, the military and police brutally quelled protests across the country, with multiple arrests and injuries. Homes were raided in the indigenous community of Saraguro, over 500 kilometers from the volcano. Despite the protests, and polls indicating that 82% of the people wanted the constitutional changes decided by a referendum, the amendments were pushed through by the National Assembly, where the ruling party had an absolute majority. Though a provision was adopted to prevent Correa from running in the 2017 election, many expected him to install a puppet leader for the following term and then return to power.

In line with the fall of 21st century socialism across Latin America, Correa's reign ended in authoritarianism and widespread allegations of corruption and financial mismanagement. Although his government cannot be compared to the violence of military regimes like Pinochet's, it was nonetheless a totalitarian regime that criminalized almost one thousand journalists, dissident politicians, indigenous authorities, and social activists over its decade in power. Correa's major legacy is the largest licensing of land for extractive industries in the history of Ecuador, not just for oil exploitation but also mega-mining, much of it in indigenous territory. This has increased Ecuador's dependency on the export of raw commodities, especially oil. It also led nature defenders to redefine Correa's regime as neither right or left wing, but extractivist.

MORENO AND THE RETURN OF NEOLIBERALISM

Lenín Moreno, who served as Correa's Vice President from 2007 to 2013, was nominated to run as his successor in the 2017 election, with center-right banker Guillermo Lasso his major contender. With Moreno promising a continuation of Correa-ism, many normally left-leaning Ecuadorian civil society groups, indigenous organizations, academics, activists and NGOs united behind Lasso. After Moreno narrowly won in a contentious second round, Lasso contested the results, providing evidence of election fraud. Nevertheless, Moreno assumed office on 24 May 2017, becoming the world's only currently serving head of state to use a wheelchair, after being shot in a 1998 robbery attempt.

Once in office, Moreno unexpectedly broke with Correa-ism by pardoning several indigenous activists who had been jailed for their involvement in protests in 2015. Through a referendum, he reversed several key pieces of legislation passed by the previous administration, most notably the constitutional amendment allowing indefinite reelection, thereby blocking his predecessor from returning to power. He allowed the prosecution of Vice President Jorge Glas (a loyal Correa-ist), who was sentenced to six years in prison for pocketing $13.5 million in bribes, part of the Odebrecht scandal that engulfed the continent. Moreno, branded a traitor by Correa, was sacked from the Alianza Pais party, but continued as head of state.

In sharp contrast to Correa's fiery, divisive rhetoric, Moreno adopted a conciliatory style, easing pressure on the media and advocating engagement with civil society. However, Ecuador remains a dangerous place for nature defenders, with several being threatened and attacked in 2018. Crucially, Moreno is also accelerating Correa's extractivist policies. The referendum that ended indefinite re-election also included proposals to decrease oil drilling in the Yasuní National Park and to ban metal mining in protected areas. Although both received nearly 70 percent public support, it appears that the Moreno administration is doing exactly the opposite, expanding drilling in Yasuní and licensing more protected areas to mining. In 2018, he appointed a former oil executive to head the Ministry of the Environment, indicating the priority given to extractive investments.

Moreno's government marks a rupture with the "pink tide" of 21st Century Socialism that swept across Latin America. While Ecuador has not joined those countries that have elected far right leaders in the backlash, it appears that Moreno is moving the country back towards neo-liberalism. During a June 2018 visit by U.S. Vice President Mike Pence, the two leaders agreed to improve U.S.-Ecuador relations, which had been strained under Correa. They announced a joint security effort, with Ecuador buying weapons, radar, helicopters and other military equipment. According to Defense Minister Oswaldo Jarrin, co-operation will include training and intelligence sharing. In a further sign of a closer relationship with the U.S., Moreno has taken a much harsher stance towards Julian Assange than his predecessor. He has reached a financing agreement with the World Bank and has met with the IMF, as well as continuing Correa's pattern of borrowing from China.

Shortly after coming to power, Moreno was forced to admit that the public debt was over twice the $28 billion admitted by Correa at the end of his tenure, at nearly $58 billion. In 2018, a criminal investigation was opened against Correa and other officials for concealing the extent of the debt. Correa is also being investigated for ordering the 2012 kidnapping of political opponent Fernando Balda in 2012 and is currently a fugitive from justice after ignoring an injunction to appear in Quito every two weeks as a preventative measure. The judge has requested Interpol to capture the former president, who has applied for asylum in Belgium, where he has lived since the end of his presidency.

Government and Economy

POLITICS

The Republic of Ecuador is a representative democracy with compulsory suffrage for all literate persons aged 18-65, optional for all other citizens. There are three main branches of government: executive, legislative, and judicial. The executive branch is made up of the president and vice president, 28 ministers, provincial governors, and councilors.

The legislative branch, the National Assembly, is responsible for passing laws and consists of 130 assemblypersons representing the country's 24 provinces. The president and assemblypersons may be re-elected once and serve a four-year term. The president must be elected by at least a 50 percent majority, frequently leading to runoff elections. The judicial branch is made up of the National

Court of Justice, provincial courts, and lower courts.

Added to these are the electoral branch, which organizes, conducts, and controls elections and referendums; and the Transparency and Social Control branch, which combats corruption and promotes accountability via overseers such as the comptroller general and the ombudsman.

Twenty-four *provincias* (provinces) are ruled by governors who oversee 219 *cantones* (counties) and around 1,000 *parroquias* (parishes). There are also around 2,000 *comunas*, like mini municipalities that are governed by their own laws and regulations, with communally owned territories.

Ecuador's tumultuous political history is characterized by instability, corruption, and inequality. Since independence from Spain in 1822, there have been nearly 90 changes of power and almost 20 constitutions. Less than a quarter of those governments came to power as a result of a democratic election, and many regimes have been toppled by the military or mass civilian protest. Without the opportunity to mature, any well-intentioned governmental institutions have been unable to address Ecuador's constantly re-emerging problems. The economy is also in constant flux due to its dependence on a few export commodities, such as oil. The vast majority of the nation's wealth sits in the hands of a very few, with a highly inequitable economic and social structure that has existed since the colonial era. Due to large-scale corruption, any periods of economic boom tend to further enrich the wealthy, while more than half of the country's population hovers at or below the poverty level.

While Correa brought a decade of relative political stability to Ecuador,

he did so by concentrating all state powers. Any party or candidate that opposed his government was forced to confront all the state apparatus, making it very difficult for a credible opposition to exist. Of the 137 seats in the National Assembly, 74 are held by Alianza Pais and pro-government independents. Only two other parties hold more than 10 seats, both center-right: CREO, founded in 2012 by former presidential candidate Guillermo Lasso, holds 32 seats, and the long-standing right-wing Social Christian Party, has 15. Pachakutik, a coalition of indigenous and social movements, holds 4 seats.

ECONOMY

Ecuador is substantially dependent on its petroleum resources, which have accounted for more than half the country's export earnings and approximately 25 percent of public sector revenues in recent years. Frozen shrimp have overtaken bananas as the country's second largest export earner after petroleum. Ecuador is still the largest banana exporter in the world, exporting more than twice its closest competitors, the Philippines and Costa Rica. The cut flower industry, especially roses, has grown substantially, with the country now occupying third place in the world after the Netherlands and Colombia. Cacao is another key export.

According to government statistics, the monthly cost of basic food for a family (known as *la canasta básica*) stood at over $700 in 2018, while the average monthly income is $437 and the minimum wage just $386 ($11/day). Unemployment may be relatively low at 4.6 percent, but this doesn't tell the whole story. Informal craftspeople and vendors make up close to 40 percent of the workforce, and the real problems are precarious employment, underemployment, and low pay. The poverty rate fell from 49.9 percent in 2003 to 21.5 percent in 2017, with 9.4 percent of people living on less than $3.20 a day. Indigenous peoples are much more likely to experience poverty, with 63 percent impoverished.

In the two years after Ecuador began to export petroleum in 1971, government income quadrupled. However, the initial bonanza was relatively short-lived, and just five years after production began, a flood of foreign borrowing was needed to sustain economic growth. Ecuador has been able to secure large loans for its size because of its oil reserves and has accumulated a staggering foreign debt. At the same time, the benefits of oil development have not been well distributed. Ecuador's wealth is concentrated with a few people at the top of the social ladder with little trickling down to the rest. Furthermore, oil development has accentuated Ecuador's dependence on export markets and foreign investment, technology, and expertise rather than providing the answer to its economic difficulties.

After the devastating economic crisis of 1999-2000 the economy recovered well in the early 2000s, with GDP growth peaking at 7.9 percent in 2011. Rafael Correa's government, which came to power in 2006, benefited from the biggest economic boom the country has ever known, managing $400 billion in 10 years. Record oil profits and massive borrowing enabled Correa to preside over the construction of highways, hospitals, schools, and hydroelectric dams.

In 2008, Correa expelled the World Bank representative and allowed the country to default on its U.S.-backed debt, deeming it "immoral and illegitimate." A year later, he turned to China to fill the void, with an initial $1 billion loan from PetroChina to Petroecuador. After that, Chinese money began to flow for massive infrastructure projects across the country, but with stringent conditions. Along with steep interest payments (up to 10.5 percent, making the loans among the most expensive on the planet), Ecuador is usually required to use Chinese companies and technologies on the projects. Much of the financing has to be paid back with oil, meaning that Ecuador has pre-sold almost 100 percent of its exportable surplus of Amazon crude to meet repayments. This led to an unprecedented situation in 2015, where Ecuador was forced to import 30 million barrels of oil for use in its own refinery in Esmeraldas.

In December 2009, Ecuadorian debt totaled $10.199 billion, equivalent to 16.3 percent of GDP. By November 2015, that figure had risen to $32.8475 billion, representing 32.9 percent of GDP. When Correa left power in May 2017, he admitted to a $28 billion public debt. Just two months later, in July 28, 2017, his successor, Lenín Moreno, conceded that the figure was actually $57.8 billion, a difference of nearly $30 billion. In 2018, a criminal investigation was opened against Correa and other officials for concealing the extent of the debt. The same year, Correa's successor, Lenín Moreno, reached a $400 million dollar financing agreement with the World Bank and secured a new $900 million loan from China. This brings China's total lending to Ecuador in the last 10 years to over $19 billion, which doesn't include $6 billion in cash-for-oil payments.

For the first eight years of Rafael Correa's government, oil prices were high, averaging $70 a barrel but at times reaching $140. In 2014, the country experienced a severe crisis caused by falling oil prices, which were dependent on the market, and high extraction costs, which were locked into service contracts signed by the government with international corporations such as Halliburton. With the cost of extracting a barrel of oil higher than its market worth value, the industry collapsed. The 3.8 percent GDP growth rate in 2014 fell to 0.1 percent in 2015 and -0.12 percent in 2016. Following the introduction of austerity measures growth was 2.4 percent in 2017.

After the oil crash in 2014, the government's focus turned to mining; thus, the value of Ecuador's mining industry is forecast to jump from $1.1 billion in 2017 to $7.9 billion in 2021.

People and Culture

DEMOGRAPHY

Ecuador's population stands at nearly 17 million, fairly evenly spread between the coast and the Sierra. Two-thirds of the population lives in densely populated urban areas.

Ecuador's population continues to grow at over 1 percent per year, and large families are still considered normal, not least because the predominant Roman Catholic religion frowns on birth control, and abortion is illegal. Sadly, Ecuador has the highest rate of teenage pregnancy in South America; 16.9 percent of girls aged 15-19 are mothers. People still tend to marry young and have children quickly, resulting in a very young population—35 percent are under age 15—in contrast to the aging populations of North America and Europe. However, things are beginning to change, particularly in the wealthier classes, with people marrying later and having fewer children. Life expectancy stands at a respectable 76.6 years.

The largest racial group is mestizo—people of mixed Spanish and indigenous heritage—making up 72 percent of the population. According to 2010 census, 6.8 percent of the population self-identify as indigenous, though other estimates are considerably higher. The Confederation of Indigenous Nationalities of Ecuador (CONAIE) states that indigenous peoples make up 25-30 percent of the population. Similarly, there is a gap between the official figures for Afro-Ecuadorians (5 percent) and NGO estimates (10 percent). These differences have to do with questions of classification of Afro-descendants and indigenous peoples, including the self-identification of those who have intermarried with non-black or non-indigenous people, and those who live in urban areas. Whites are estimated at 6.1 percent, mostly of colonial-era Spanish origin, known as *criollos*.

Between the 1980s and mid-2000s, a series of economic crises led 10-15 percent of the population to emigrate overseas. Today, an estimated 1.5-2 million Ecuadorians live abroad, mostly in Spain, Italy, and the United States. In the early 2000s, thousands of Colombians migrated to Ecuador.

More recently, Ecuador has seen a massive influx of Venezuelan migrants escaping the humanitarian crisis there, with 2,000 entering the country every day in 2017 and 2018. Around 20 percent of these stay in Ecuador, while the others are en route to other countries.

RACISM AND REGIONALISM

Ecuador is far from being a racially equal society, and a look back at history reveals why. Many of the country's richest and most influential families can trace their power directly back to colonial times, when their Spanish ancestors took ownership of the choicest plots of land. The brutal systems of forced indigenous labor implemented by the colonizers would continue for 400 years, only being finally abolished in the 1960s. While indigenous people are often still treated as second-class citizens, and the word *indio* is used in a derogatory way, it's more common to hear overtly racist comments from older people about Afro-Ecuadorians and immigrants from Colombia and Venezuela. Happily though, things are changing and the younger generation is much more open minded. There were both anti-immigration and anti-xenophobia protests in 2018.

Regional prejudice between the mountains and the coast, particularly between Guayaquil and Quito, is just as pervasive. Traditionally, *costeños* view *serranos* as uptight, conservative, two-faced, and hypocritical, whereas *serranos* see *costeños* as brash, lazy, uncultured, and frivolous. A *serrano* who moves to the coast may never really be accepted into their new community and vice versa. Again, though, things are changing with the younger generations. It's certainly true that young people on the coast laugh at the Andean visitors, in their jeans and closed shoes, but it's more good natured than malicious.

INDIGENOUS GROUPS

Indigenous nationalities inhabited mainland Ecuador for thousands of years before the Inca invasion and are still found all over the country, which is officially recognized as a plurinational state. While each has its own culture and customs, most of these groups are struggling to defend their ancestral territory from the ravages of oil exploitation, mining, industrial agriculture, and development. Indigenous leaders who spearhead these resistance efforts are often criminalized. Another common struggle is for bilingual education. Many ancient languages are in danger of dying out, and some have already been forgotten. Some of today's coastal residents are direct descendants of the region's pre-Inca civilizations, but they have lost not just their native tongue but most of their traditions. Indeed, they are rarely recognized as "indigenous." At the other end of the spectrum are the country's last two remaining groups who have never had contact with the outside world and live a seminomadic life as hunter-gatherers in Yasuní National Park. Most of Ecuador's indigenous groups are somewhere between the two extremes, having adapted to various degrees to the western way of life while preserving some of their ancestral customs. Most indigenous communities have a church and at least one shaman, blending Catholic and animist beliefs. Many maintain a strong connection to nature and the Pachamama (Mother Earth), and an encyclopedic knowledge of medicinal plants is often passed down the generations. Ecuador's indigenous peoples are represented by the Confederation of Indigenous Nationalities of Ecuador (CONAIE, https://conaie.org), which fights for social change and land rights. CONAIE is best known for its organization of popular uprisings (*levantamientos populares*) that include marches and road blockades. See the *History* section for more information on the indigenous struggle.

Seven communities of **Tsáchila** people live near Santo Domingo after their ancestors relocated from Quito in the 1600s following a smallpox epidemic, which they cured with paste from the achiote fruit. In tribute, the men still color their hair with achiote and style it in the shape of the red fruit. To represent the knowledge of their shamans, or *ponés,* they wear a *mushily,* a cotton doughnut perched on top of their head. The Tsáchila still maintain many of their ancestral traditions, especially the practice of ancient healing techniques, including steam baths with medicinal plants and ayahuasca ceremonies in a subterranean chamber. Education is bilingual, in Spanish and Tsafiki. The Chigüilpe community has a well-organized tourism project, the Centro Turístico Mushily.

The majority of Ecuador's indigenous people live in the Sierra and are of Kichwa nationality. The Sierran Kichwas are subdivided into numerous groups, including the Natabuelas, Otavalos, Karanquis, Kayampis, Kitu Karas, Pastos, and Paltas in the northern Sierra; the Panzaleos, Salasacas, Chibuleos, Puruhás, Gurangas, Kisapinchas, and Warankas in the central Sierra; and the Cañaris and Saraguros in the southern Sierra. The majority of these groups are represented by Ecuarunari, the Confederation of Kichwa Peoples of Ecuador, and between them, six dialects of Kichwa are spoken. Each group has its own traditions and style of dress, often featuring woollen shawls and ponchos, embroidered shirts and skirts, felt hats, and beaded necklaces. Hair is often long and braided. Many highland Kichwas are small-scale farmers (campesinos), growing crops such as corn, potatoes, and beans or keeping cattle for milk. Others make a living with traditional handicrafts such as weaving, embroidery, and jewelry-making.

At the heart of the Andean indigenous cosmovision is the concept of *sumak kawsay,* or good living in harmony with nature and community—a concept that was adopted in the 2009 Ecuadorian constitution but not upheld. As part of community life, people work together to complete agricultural, construction, and maintenance tasks in joint efforts known as *mingas.* A traditional Andean way of eating is the *pampamesa,* where food is eaten communally on a long strip of fabric on the ground.

It is thought that the **Saraguros** and **Salasacas** are descended from people relocated from southern Peru and Bolivia in the 16th century as part of the Inca *mitma* system of forced resettlement. Other indigenous groups were present in Ecuador long before the Incas and fought valiantly against the invasion, such as the **Cañari**. In fact, the Inca had so much respect for the Cañari that, after finally defeating them, they built a community together at Ingapirca and added a Temple of the Sun to complement the existing Temple of the Moon. Also at Ingapirca is the tomb of a Cañari priestess and 10 of her servants, who were buried alive with her upon her death.

Probably the most famous of the Andean Kichwa groups is the **Otavalos,** who, after being brutally oppressed by the Incas and Spanish, found financial success in the 20th century due to their weaving skills. Otavalo and the nearby villages are great places to participate in traditional indigenous celebrations such as Inti Raymi. Farther north, the **Pastos** are stewards of the eerily beautiful El Ángel Ecological Reserve, which protects some of the most pristine *páramo* in the country, where a ghost of a Pasto chief is said to appear at Laguna Voladero at the solstice. Not far from Ibarra, the **Karanqui** village of Zuleta is known for its embroidery, in which intricate, colorful designs are sewn onto white cloth shirts, napkins, table cloths, and wall hangings. The nearby community of San Clemente is a shining example of community tourism, offering the opportunity to discover the Karanqui way of life, their culture and traditions.

In the central Sierra, the communities around Cotopaxi and Quilotoa are **Panzaleo**. Of these, Sasquili is known for its indigenous market, whereas Tigua is famous for its paintings on sheepskin that depict Andean scenes. Nearby, farmers make a yearly pilgrimage to the top of Amina hill, which is shaped like a gorilla, to ask for blessings for their crops. Pujilí is the best place in the country to join in the Corpus Christi celebrations, which blend Catholic and Panzaleo traditions. The **Puruhás** have been living on the flanks of the Chimborazo volcano since time immemorial. Native guides take visitors to the Templo de Machay, a sacred cave at 4,560 meters (14,960 ft) altitude, where their ancestors conducted rituals asking Chimborazo for blessings, a practice still carried out today. The population of Guaranda, the capital of Bolívar province, is largely **Waranka**. The nearby town of Salinas has become a model for self-sufficiency and community development through a number of successful food cooperatives that were set up by the Warankas with the help of a Salesian monk. Near Baños, the **Salasacas** still weave in the ancestral way, using sheep wool and plant dyes, with the women spinning and the men sitting at the looms. Indeed, the women can be seen spinning as they sit outside their stalls in the craft market, or even as they walk along the street.

GENDER AND SEXUALITY

Ecuadorian culture is very sexually polarized, with machismo and male dominance running through society from top to bottom. Girls are brought up to be "princesses" and to spend a lot of time on their appearance. Many women work (often casual, part-time jobs or in the family business), but they are also expected to manage the home and raise the children. Men who get involved in domestic chores are mocked with the derogatory term *mandarina*, which roughly translates as "under the thumb." Traditional indigenous cultures often have especially fixed ideas about gender, with roles very clearly defined.

While it is common to see men out playing football after work, enjoying a few drinks, or gathered around a television watching the game, it is rare to see a group of women out enjoying themselves or having time for hobbies. Most young women are expected to live with their parents until they are married. The few who attempt to live alone, with friends, housemates, or a boyfriend, may face being ostracized by their family. Even those who share an apartment with other students for the duration of their university studies are expected to move back to the family home as soon as they graduate.

It is pretty much expected for men to cheat on their wives and to visit brothels, which are legal and present in every town. Domestic violence and femicide rates are high, with a woman killed every 84 hours, usually by an intimate partner.

Abortion in Ecuador is illegal except in the case of a threat to the life or health of a pregnant woman (when this threat cannot be averted by other means) or when the pregnancy is the result of the rape of a mentally disabled woman. Not surprisingly, unsafe abortion is a leading cause of injury and death. Women can be sentenced to up to two years in prison for having an abortion, and even harsher penalties apply to medical professionals who perform them. Ecuador's former president, Rafael Correa, threatened to resign if Congress passed a law decriminalizing abortion in cases of rape, and the congressmember who proposed the motion was accused of treason and sanctioned to 30 days of silence.

See the *Women Travelers* section of the *Essentials* chapter for advice on dealing with machismo and staying safe as a foreign female visitor.

Until just over 20 years ago, homosexuality was considered a crime punishable by prison in Ecuador, but fortunately things have changed dramatically since then. In fact, the 1997 constitution included some of the world's most progressive LGBTQ-friendly legislation, including full anti-discrimination laws on grounds of sexual orientation, and the equalization of the age of consent (which now stands at 14 for everyone). Since 2008, same-sex couples can legally register their civil union and receive the same rights/benefits as straight couples (except for adoption), but the arrangement is not yet officially referred to as a marriage.

Nevertheless, Ecuador's largely conservative and macho culture tends to view gender queerness negatively, especially the older generations. Many traditional indigenous cultures have especially fixed ideas about gender identity. Anti-gay humor is common, with the word *maricón* used to derogatively describe gay or effeminate men. Many LGBTQ people are either in the closet or share their orientation very selectively.

There are some suggestions and advice for LGBTQ travelers in the *Essentials* chapter.

RELIGION

Since the first conquistador planted a cross in honor of God and the king of Spain, Roman Catholicism has been a linchpin of Latin American culture, and Ecuador is no exception. After the constitution of 1869, the official religion became Catholicism and only Catholics could obtain citizenship. In 1899, the liberal government of Eloy Alfaro made a new constitution that respected all faiths and guaranteed freedom of religious choice. The public education is supposedly secular (though sex education regarding contraception is very limited in schools even today).

According to the Ecuadorian National Institute of Statistics and Census (2010), 91.95 percent of the country's people have a religion, 7.94 percent are atheists, and 0.11 percent are agnostics. Of those with a religion, 80.44 percent are Catholics, 11.30 percent Protestants, 1.29 percent Jehovah's Witnesses, and 6.97 percent have other faiths (notably Mormonism).

After the Spanish conquest many indigenous people were pressured into converting to Catholicism for fear of what their new masters would do if they refused. The pressure to convert continued into the 20th century, with missionaries working directly with oil companies in the 1960s and 1970s to "civilize the Aucas" (a derogatory term meaning savages) and clear oil concessions of indigenous peoples. Missionaries are still present in Ecuador today, though their tactics are somewhat gentler. Though churches are found in even the most remote of Amazon communities, many of the ancient traditions have prevailed, resulting in a fusion of animist beliefs and Catholicism. Many indigenous people see no conflict between participating in a shamanic ritual that evokes the spirits of the anaconda and jaguar and then going to church the next day.

A fusion of indigenous and Catholic traditions can also be seen in many of Ecuador's celebrations. For example, in the Corpus Christi celebration in Pujilí, the priest of the rain dances through the streets accompanied by people in animal and devil masks. La Mama Negra celebration in Latacunga exhibits an even more complex racial mix, blending together Afro-Ecuadorian, indigenous, and Catholic beliefs.

While an increasing number of young people are not religious, the older generations tend to frown upon atheism, so it may be best to keep your beliefs, or lack of them, to yourself.

LANGUAGE

Spanish is Ecuador's official tongue and is spoken by the vast majority of the population. As a plurinational country, there are also 21 indigenous languages, comprising nine varieties of Quechua plus Waorani, Shuar, Kofán, Achuar-Shiwiar, Awa-Cuaiquer, Chachi, Tsafiki, Epena, Secoya, Tetete, Sápara, and Media Lengua. Many indigenous people are bilingual, though some elders speak only their native tongue. Conversely, a growing number of young people speak only Spanish, and the ancient languages are in danger of dying out. Only a handful of elderly people in the jungles of Pastaza province still speak Sápara, for example. Some indigenous nationalities, often led by young people, are starting to take measures to rescue their native tongues. For more information on languages in Ecuador, see www.ethnologue.com.

Few people speak English in Ecuador, mainly wealthy Guayaquileños and Quiteños, and some people working in tourism. You will struggle to communicate without some knowledge of Spanish, so it's a good idea to learn some basics before your trip, or take classes once you get here.

ARTS AND ENTERTAINMENT
VISUAL ARTS

Early colonial sculptors and painters remained anonymous, remembered only for their gloomy but heartfelt images of the Virgin and Gothic-style saints. Indigenous influences began to emerge with the onset of the Renaissance and baroque styles, allowing artists like Gaspar Sangurima, Manuel Chili (aka Caspicara), and Miguel de Santiago more freedom for personal expression in their works. Works by these artists can be seen in the Museo Fray Pedro Gocial, the Museo Nacional de Arte Colonial, and the Museo de San Agustín in Quito and the Convento de las Conceptas in Cuenca.

The Quito School, encompassing the artistic output of the Audience of Quito during the colonial period (1542-1822), is famous for its mastery of polychrome carvings of the Virgin Mary, Jesus, and numerous saints. It was particularly well known for its use of realism, emphasizing the suffering of Christ and even using real human hair. Notable artists include Isabel de Santiago and María Estefanía Dávalos y Maldonado.

The 19th century and independence brought "popular" art to the fore, and the Quito School's influence faded, as it was synonymous with Spanish rule. Concerned with the secular as much as the holy, it consisted of intense colors and naturalistic images of landscapes and people. This was followed in the 20th century by the reverberations of impressionism and cubism. Powerful representations of the dignity and suffering of Ecuador's indigenous peoples dominated the work of Camilo Egas (1889-1962), Manuel Rendón (1894-1982), and Eduardo Kingman (1913-1999). Kingman painted exaggerated renditions of hands that inspired Oswaldo Guayasamín (1919-1999), probably Ecuador's most famous modern artist. Guayasamín's final magnum opus, the *Capilla del Hombre* (Chapel of Man), is dedicated to the struggles of indigenous peoples. Other works include *La Ternura*, depicting the tenderness of a mother and child's embrace, and *El Toro y el Cóndor*, symbolizing the struggle between Spanish and Andean identities.

The Museo Fundación Guayasamín in Quito is located in the artist's former home and is the best place to see his work. Araceli Gilbert (1913-1993) is famous for her brightly colored geometric abstracts.

Originally painted on ceremonial drums, Tigua paintings are now painted on sheep hide stretched over a wooden frame. Common themes include religious festivals and daily Andean life. The Cotopaxi volcano is present in the majority of the work, often painted with a human face, expressing the Kichwa world view of mountains as living beings. The paintings are sold nationwide, but the best place to see them is in Tigua at the gallery of Alfredo Toaquiza, a prominent artist whose father pioneered the use of sheepskin at the suggestion of Hungarian artist and collector Olga Fisch.

Ecuador's most famous graffiti artist is Quiteño Juan Sebastian Aguirre, better known as Apitatán (Facebook @elapitatan), who has painted murals all over the country, Latin America, the United States, and Europe. Many of his distinctive pieces depict indigenous themes.

MUSIC AND DANCE

Made famous throughout South America by Guayaquileño Julio Jaramillo in the 1950s and 1960s, *pasillo* is considered the national music style. To learn more about these melancholic acoustic guitar-based love songs, head to the Museo de la Música Popular Guayaquileña Julio Jaramillo in Guayaquil, where there is also a *pasillo* school that works with young people to keep this music tradition alive.

The haunting melodies and wistful lyrics of the Ecuadorian Andes

CONTEMPORARY ECUADORIAN MUSIC

Listening to contemporary artists is a great way to immerse yourself in the culture and also learn Spanish. All the artists and songs mentioned here can be found on YouTube. With the prevalence of *cumbia, reggaetón*, pop, and salsa, however, you are unlikely to hear any of this music when you're out and about; a lot of Ecuador's music scene remains fairly grassroots and underground.

Ecuador has a thriving hip-hop scene. Quiteño rapper **Chango** (Facebook @medicenchango) rightly won an award for the wonderful video to "Vengo de un País" (I Come from a Country), a love song to Ecuador from his debut album *Me Dicen Chango* (They Call Me Chango). His second album, *Animal*, includes songs written from the perspective of the Andean condor and Lonesome George, the famous Galápagos tortoise. With over 6 million hits on YouTube is **Barrio 593**'s "Hip Hop Ecuador." Their name is a reference to Ecuador's international dialing code. On his album *Polemica*, **Una Voz** (Facebook @unavozqm) addressed a direct message to Rafael Correa in "Sr Presidente, Permítame Faltarle El Respeto" (Mr President, Permit Me to Disrespect You) regarding the exploitation of the Amazon. The video has English subtitles on YouTube. Also speaking out for the Amazon is **Mateo Kingman** (Facebook @mateokingmanoficial) from Macas, who fuses folklore influences with hip-hop. His debut single, "Lluvia," was released in 2016, and "Religar," the first single from his second album, was released two years later. Also from the Amazon region are rapper **Jota Al Cuadrado** (Facebook @jos3phjara) and Kichwa group **Kambak,** whose best known song, "Sikwanka," is about the toucan bearing witness to the oppression of indigenous peoples.

Andean hip-hop group **Los Nin** (Facebook @losninoficial) has been around for over a decade and is still going strong, using pan flutes and rapping alternately in Spanish and Kichwa. Check out their 2009 single "Identidad" and, from 2018, "Unan Las Manos." **La Mafia Andina** is also an Andean hip-hop group mixing Spanish and Kichwa, this time with an indigenous female singer/rapper **Taki Amaru. Curare** is another band using Andean instruments such as pan flutes, but this time to create metal music. Check out their songs "Morenita" and "Tinku." Even heavier is the band **Colapso.** A graduate of Quito's National Music Conservatory, **Lascivio Bohemia** (Facebook @lasciviobohemiaec) samples and remixes Afro-Ecuadorian sounds, coastal beats, and the native music of the Sierra, as can be heard on his 2016 album, *Afro Andes EP*. Starting to make it on the international stage is **Nicolá Cruz**, who fuses music from the Andes to the Amazon with traditional instruments and *cumbia* beats, to create an electronic sound. Check out his tune "Colibria." Another band using traditional Ecuadorian sounds is guitar-based **Guardarraya** (Facebook @guardarraya), whose song "Chuchaqui" is the repentant tale of a hangover.

Da Pawn (Facebook @dapawn) creates folksy low-fi tunes such as "Ballenas de Ruido," which has chalked up well over a million YouTube hits. Influenced by reggae and ska, **Sudayaka** (Facebook @sudakayaec) is amazing live, as are the **Swing Original Monks** (Facebook @swingoriginalmonksofficial), one of Ecuador's better known bands. Check out their song "Caminito." Like the Arctic Monkeys that inspired them, **Lolabúm** (Facebook @lolabum) were teenagers when they got together in 2014 and are still going strong, taking a noisier, darker turn. Iguana Brava is a *cumbia* band from Guayaquil.

are played by groups throughout the highlands. The music can be extremely beautiful, although there is a tendency to churn out the same old songs for visitors, such as "El Condor Pasa," a Peruvian tune made famous by Simon and Garfunkel in the 1960s, and, even worse, panpipe versions of ballads by Celine Dion and Lionel Richie. Flutes were considered holy by the Inca, who provided the original set of instruments and tunes for modern-day Andean music. The *quena*, a vertical flute once made from condor leg bones, is used to play the melody, along with panpipes such as the *rondador* and *zampoña*. Bass drums made from hollow logs or clay are used to keep the beat, with the help of various rattles and bells. Peguche, near Otavalo, is known for its workshops making traditional Andean instruments. The group Los Huayanay is an example of Ecuadorian Andean music.

The colonial Spanish tried their best to suppress indigenous music but only inspired the creation of a whole host of new sounds by introducing the *vihuela*, an ancestor of the guitar, the first stringed instrument seen on the continent. Offshoots include the 10-stringed *charango*, originally from Bolivia and made from armadillo shells, and the 15-stringed *bandolina*.

There are two key types of Afro-Ecuadorian music. Marimba, popular on the northern coast, is played on an instrument of the same name, a West-African wooden xylophone struck to a hypnotic beat. Banned for much of the early 20th century, marimba is seen as an expression of freedom by many Afro-Ecuadorians. *Marimba Esmeraldeña* was declared Intangible Cultural Heritage by UNESCO in 2015. An example is the album *Yo Soy El Hombre* by Don Naza y El Grupo Bambuco. The Chota Valley in the northern Sierra is the birthplace of another Afro-Ecuadorian type of music, *bomba*, which uses a wooden drum of the same name, usually accompanied by other drums and instruments of Spanish origin such as the guitar. Female *bomba* dancers sometimes balance a bottle on their head. *Bomba* bands to check out include Marabu and Mario Diego Congo y Las Chicas del Valle.

Caribbean-flavored *cumbia* from Colombia has indigenous, Afro, and Spanish influences. Ecuadorian *cumbia* began in the early 1990s with Grupo Coctel. In the last decade, one of the key Ecuadorian *cumbia* singers has been Manolo. *Technocumbia* fuses *cumbia* and electronic sounds, with recent Ecuadorian examples including María de los Angeles, Gerardo Morán, Veronica Bolaños, and Delfín Quishpe.

In the latter 20th century, salsa and merengue began to dominate, and they remain extremely popular across the generations. If you are in Ecuador for an extended period, consider taking classes, as dancing is very important at social occasions and a good way to meet people. Locals will be delighted to see you try. Etnia is a band from Esmeraldas who fuse salsa with Afro-Ecuadorian music.

International rock and pop are also very popular in Ecuador, and many top music acts come to Quito to perform. Heavy rock is particularly popular. Quito has a thriving *rockero* scene.

In the past 10 years, the booming beats of *reggaetón* have spilled out from the club scene and are heard blasting out just about everywhere in Ecuador. Originating in Puerto Rico in the 1990s and influenced by Caribbean music and hip hop, *reggaetón* burst onto the international scene in 2017 with *Despacito*. It's famous (or infamous) for its explicit lyrics, gyrating dance moves, and repetitive beat; you'll either love it or hate it. It is inexplicably popular at children's birthday parties, blasting out at earsplitting volume from speakers that are often bigger than the birthday boy or girl.

LITERATURE

Most of the books listed have been translated into English.

Cumandá, a romantic drama set in the rainforest and written by Juan León Mera, is one of Ecuador's most famous

PUBLIC HOLIDAYS AND MAJOR FESTIVALS

Ecuador is a country with a thriving tradition of holidays, festivals, and celebrations: some Catholic, some indigenous (or a blend of the two), others marking important historical occasions. Many Ecuadorians don't have paid vacation and the long weekends created by public holidays or *feriados* are the only chance they have to go on holiday. During these periods, accommodations should be booked in advance and may be more expensive (especially around New Year's Day and Carnival). Traveling is best avoided, as buses will be full and there are more accidents on the roads. Some cities become ghost towns (e.g., Quito), with all the residents gone to the beach; others become overrun (e.g., any beach destination). If the date of a public holiday falls on a weekend or midweek, it will often be moved to the Friday or Monday. In addition to the national festivities, each city commemorates its founding date with street parties. Smaller towns and villages hold annual *fiestas patronales* in honor of their patron saint.

- **January 1: New Year's Day**—a national holiday.

- **February or March** (weekend closest to new moon): **Carnival**—the country's biggest party, with four days of festivities and water fights. The Monday and Tuesday are national holidays. Guaranda is the most traditional place to join in the fun. **Pawkar Raymi** (Blossoming Festival) is the Quechua equivalent of Carnival, celebrating the fertility of the earth. Festivities last for 11 days and include fireworks, parades, musical events, and rituals. Otavalo and the surrounding villages are the place to be.

- **March or April** (40 days after Ash Wednesday): Easter Week or **Semana Santa**—a long weekend with parades on Good Friday (a national holiday) remembering the passion of the Christ, notably in Quito.

- **May 1: Labor Day**—a national holiday with workers parades around the country.

- **May 24: Battle of Pichincha**—a national holiday to commemorate the decisive 1822 battle that resulted in independence from Spain.

- **May or June** (9th Thursday after Easter): **Corpus Christi**—honors the Eucharist, particularly celebrated by indigenous people in the central Sierra. During the festival in Pujilí, the "priest of the rain" dances through the streets in an elaborate costume to the beat of a drum, accompanied by a colorful cast of characters. Cuenca is another fun place to be, with sweet stalls lining the streets, fireworks, and parades.

- **June: Fiesta del Coraza**—celebrated at Laguna San Pablo near Otavalo between June 9 and 15, including a race on the lake between floating horses made of reeds. Key personages are the *coraza,* painted white to represent the Spanish, with his face covered in silver chains to symbolize greed; and the *pendonero,* who represents resistance to the Spanish invasion, dressed as a warrior waving a blood-red flag.

books from the 19th century. Writers in the early 20th century mainly focused on realistic social themes of injustice and race. Jorge Icaza's *Huasipungo* (*The Villagers*, 1934) is considered one of Ecuador's best novels, vividly portraying the hardships of everyday life in an indigenous village. The avant-garde movement in the 1930s was led by Pablo Palacios, who dealt with challenging subjects such as mental illness (of which he had personal experience). One of his most widely read works is *Un Hombre Muerto a Puntapiés* (*The Man Who Was Kicked to Death*). Adalberto Ortiz's *Juyungo* (1942) is a seminal novel on black life in Esmeraldas. Jorge

- **June 21-29: Inti Raymi** (Quechua for Sun Festival) is the Inca festival of the northern solstice and the most important Andean celebration. Every indigenous group has its own specific dates and traditions, but the main event starts on June 21 and continues for several days. There is a celebration at the Inca sites of Ingapirca on June 21.and Las Tolas de Cochasquí on June 22. In the Otavalo area, people gather to bathe in sacred rivers and waterfalls on June 22 to eliminate negative energies accumulated during the previous year, to purify themselves and kick off the festivities. The Peguche waterfall is a popular spot to participate in this cleansing ritual, which also takes place at Laguna Quilotoa.

- **August 10: Independence Day**—a national holiday commemorating the country's first (failed) uprising against the Spanish in 1809.

- **End of August: Fiesta del Yamor**—held in Otavalo from the end of August until the first week of September. This festival dates back to pre-Incan times and centers around a drink, a type of *chicha*, which is made from seven varieties of corn and represents the unity of the people.

- **November 2: Día de los Difuntos**—a national holiday, better known as Day of the Dead. Families bring food, flowers, and offerings to the graves of loved ones, or prepare tables of food for them at home and call for their spirits to come and eat. Don't miss the delicious *colada morada*, a sweet purple fruit drink.

- **November 3: Foundation of Cuenca**—a national holiday and the city's biggest celebration, which merges with the previous holiday.

- **Saturday prior to November 11: Fiesta de La Mama Negra**—a state-sponsored version of a flamboyant festival in Latacunga, combining not only Spanish and indigenous traditions, but also African elements, culminating in the arrival of a blackened man in women's clothing throwing milk and water.

- **December 21: December solstice**—a festival held at the Inca site Las Tolas de Cochasquí.

- **December 24: Christmas Eve**—Most locals celebrate Christmas with a family dinner and gifts at midnight.

- **December 25: Christmas Day,** a national holiday.

- **December 28: Día de los Inocentes**—commemorating the children who were massacred by Herod. To demonstrate the innocence of the people, practical jokes are played.

- **December 31: New Year's Eve**—life-size effigies of prominent figures of the outgoing year are burned at midnight.

Carrera Andrade, from Quito, was one of the most important Latin American poets of the century and can be read in Winds of Exile: The Poetry of Jorge Carrera Andrade.

The English-language compilation Contemporary Ecuadorian Short Stories, edited by Vladimiro Rivas Iturralde, is an easy toe in the water of Ecuadorian literature (and includes the English translation of *Un Hombre Muerto a Puntapiés*). *Fire from the Andes: Short Fiction by Women from Bolivia, Ecuador, and Peru* is another recommended anthology. In 2012, Abdón Ubidia, author of *Sueño de Lobos* (*Wolves' Dream*, 1986) and several other works was awarded the

ECUADOR'S TRADITIONAL CELEBRATIONS

Ecuador is a country that takes great pride in its traditions, and visitors are welcomed into the fun with open arms. **New Year's Eve** is celebrated by burning effigies (*monigotes*), often of cartoon characters or public figures who symbolize the outgoing year (unpopular politicians being a favorite). In a wonderful blend of pyromania and personal reflection, the effigies are stuffed with lists of things that people would like to leave behind. Some people complete a symbolic act at midnight that represents their hopes for the forthcoming year; e.g., walking around the block with a suitcase to manifest travel. In Montañita, the surfers catch a midnight wave. In some Sierran towns, people read out the old year's Last Will and Testament, which is filled with jokes and criticisms of friends, neighbors, and the government.

On the nights preceding New Year's Eve, men dress as widows (*viudas*) of the outgoing year and go around asking for "funeral contributions" (aka a beer fund). This tradition has evolved in recent years, with men now dressing in full drag—a joy to witness in such a macho country.

Día de los Difuntos (Day of the Deceased) on November 2 honors those who have passed away. All over the country, families visit cemeteries with flowers and food, traditionally *colada morada,* a purple corn drink, and *guaguas de pan,* sweet breads shaped as babies. On the coast, people prepare the favorite dishes of their departed loved ones and then call on their spirits to come and eat. They swear that the atmosphere changes when the ghosts arrive and that some of the food disappears. On this day, people go calling from house to house with the words *"Angeles somos, pan pedimos"* ("We are angels, we ask for bread") and are given a plate of food. Visitors are welcome to join this tradition.

Every town and village holds annual *fiestas patronales* in honor of their patron saint, which is usually a real religious effigy miraculously discovered somewhere local that gets paraded through the streets. As with every kind of Ecuadorian celebration, music, beauty pageants, and pyrotechnics play a key role. Fireworks are often attached to a tower (*el castillo*) or sometimes to a person in a cow costume (*la vaca loca*), who charges around shooting rockets into the crowd to frenetic music—a custom stemming from rituals asking for agricultural blessings. Amazingly, under the protective gaze of the patron saint no one gets hurt!

A more private tradition takes place in the early hours of **Mother's Day** (Día de las Madres), when traveling bands individually serenade mothers and grandmothers, often with Julio Jaramillo's beautiful "Para Ti Madrecita."

Eugenio Espejo Award, Ecuador's highest honor for its citizens who have made notable contributions to Ecuadorian culture. Santiago Páez has written several sci-fi novels, including *Profundo en la Galaxia (Deep in the Galaxy)* and *Shamanes y Reyes (Shamans and Kings).* His most recent book, *Ecuatox*, is an ecology-themed satire.

A voice for the Afro-Ecuadorian experience, Luz Argentina Chiriboga's novels explore race, gender, sexuality, class inequality, and the clash of cultures. *The Devil's Nose* (2015) is based on the true story of the Jamaicans who worked on Ecuador's railroads in the early 20th century. Gabriela Aleman, voted one of "Latin America's 40 most promising writers under 40," released the English version of her sci-fi political satire *Poso Wells* in 2018.

María Fernanda Ampuero's *Pelea de Gallos* was listed in the *New York Times'* top 10 publications of 2018, and Mónica Ojeda's *Mandibula* was ranked number 12 in the list of the year's best literary works in Spanish newspaper *El Pais.* At the time of writing, both books were only available in Spanish.

ESSENTIALS

Getting There

AIR

A number of airlines offer flights into the **Mariscal Sucre International Airport,** located near the town of Tababela, about 12 kilometers (7.5 mi) east of Quito. For a list of airlines that fly into Quito, see the *Getting There and Around* sections of the *Quito* chapter.

To find the best deals on flights, use a flight

aggregator (www.booking.com, www.skyscanner.com) and be flexible with your dates if possible. Once in Ecuador, you can travel easily by air or bus. It's a good idea to book well in advance if you want to travel during peak periods (Christmas and the summer holidays in the United States and Europe). If you're a student or under 26, check to see if **STA Travel** (www.statravel.com) has discounted air tickets.

BUS

International buses entering Ecuador will wait outside the immigration offices while passengers complete the formalities. Always check that your passport has been stamped upon arrival. It is fairly common for border officials to forget, and without a stamp you will be in the country illegally. This can cause enormous hassle when it comes to leaving Ecuador or extending a visa.

PANCONTINENTAL BUSES

These buses traverse the continent and can transport you between Ecuador and Venezuela, Colombia, Peru, Argentina, and Chile. Be prepared for long journeys, though; from Buenos Aires in Argentina to Huaquillas in Ecuador, for example, is 84 hours (with stops en route for food). Departures are not daily, so check itineraries well in advance. Tickets can be bought online or at the bus company offices in Quito and other departure cities.

Cruz del Sur (Quito: Av. Santa María 870 y 9 de Octubre, tel. 2/290-5823, and Quitumbe bus terminal, tel. 2/382-4791) is recommended and has a good website with itineraries and prices. Inquiries via Facebook and email are generally responded to within a day. Their routes start in

Argentina and Chile and currently go no farther north than Ecuador (at the time of writing, their services between Colombia and Ecuador had been discontinued but may restart in the future; check the website for information). Popular journeys include Lima to Quito (Tues., $110, 36 hours); Quito to Lima (Thurs., $110, 36 hours).

Another good option is **Rutas de America** (Quito: Selva Alegre O1-72 y Av. 10 de Agosto, tel. 2/250-3611 or 2/254-8142; https://rutasdeamerica. net), with routes between Venezuela and Peru. If you contact them on Facebook or online chat, you will be sent a link to a WhatsApp group and a staff member will respond to your query. Buses also run between Quito and Lima twice weekly (36 hours, $110).

Wanderbus (www.wanderbusecuador.com) offers a hop-on-hop off bus service that tours the country, taking in some of the major tourist destinations, including Quito and Cotopaxi. It's much more expensive than the regular bus, but prices include bilingual guides and stops at attractions en route. Tickets can be bought online.

FROM COLOMBIA

The only recommended Colombia/Ecuador border crossing is 7 kilometers (4.3 mi) north of **Tulcán** in Ecuador and 13 kilometers (8 mi) south of **Ipiales** in Colombia. Situated on a bridge over the Río Carchi at **Rumichaca,** the crossing is open 24 hours. It's necessary to clear both countries' immigration stations, no matter which direction you're crossing, and there is just one line at each immigration station. At the time of writing, the influx of Venezuelans fleeing the humanitarian crisis has increased queues at the border from

15 minutes to several hours, so be prepared to wait. Direct any questions to the Ecuadorian immigration office (open 24 hours) located in the CENAF buildings at the bridge.

In Ipiales take a private taxi (13,000 pesos/$4) or a *colectivo* (1,700 pesos/$0.55) to the border and complete the formalities. Once you're in Ecuador, head to Tulcán ($4 by private taxi, $1 shared taxi, $0.75 microbus). Drivers accept pesos. Money changers in Tulcán's Parque Ayora are more trustworthy than at the border, with better rates. Official Ecuadorian changers should have photo IDs.

Tulcán has buses leaving for just about every major city in Ecuador, including Quito (5 hours, $5). There is even a bus to Huaquillas (18 hours, $22), if you want to bypass Ecuador altogether and go straight to Peru.

FROM PERU

The most common way to enter from Peru is via the Ecuadorian town of **Huaquillas,** where the construction of new immigration offices a few kilometers outside the town center has made the crossing safe and convenient, with Ecuadorian and Peruvian border officials sitting side by side in the same building. Simply join the queue at the "Salida del Peru" desk, then queue up again to enter Ecuador at the "Ingreso al Ecuador" desk.

In addition to the pancontinental bus companies previously mentioned, **CIFA** (www.cifainternational.com) operates services from Peru that cross the border and wait for passengers while they complete the formalities.

Alternatively, to make the crossing independently, the immigration office is easily accessible via Tumbes in Peru ($10 or 33 soles by taxi). Once your passport has been stamped,

Huaquillas is a $5 taxi ride away (the driver will accept soles).

Coming from Peru, it's best to get rid of Peruvian money before crossing into Ecuador, to avoid the dodgy money changers. Once in Ecuador, you can take out dollars at one of the ATMs in Huaquillas (there is a Banco Pichincha near the main plaza). Huaquillas is not a town you want to hang around for long, and luckily there are plenty of buses to shuttle you to more pleasant destinations.

Huaquillas is not the only border crossing with Peru. For a much more scenic experience, consider entering the country in the highlands south of Vilcabamba, either at **Zumba/La Balsa** (convenient if you're coming from the ruins at Chachapoyas or the Peruvian Amazon) or **Macará** (convenient if you're coming from the Peruvian coast or Lima). Both crossings are safe. **Nambija Internacional** (tel. 7/231-5177 or 7/303-9179, Facebook @coop-nambija1987) has a couple of daily departures from **Jaén** in Peru to **Loja** in Ecuador (stopping in **Vilcabamba** en route), which wait while passengers complete the necessary formalities in Zumba/La Balsa. Between **Co-op Loja** (tel. 7/257-1861 or 7/272-9014) and **Union Cariamanga** (tel. 7/260-5613, Facebook @UnionCariamanga), there are three daily departures from **Piura** in Peru to **Loja** in Ecuador (8 hours, $14), which wait at the border while passengers complete formalities in Macará.

CAR OR MOTORCYCLE

To drive a vehicle into Ecuador from Colombia or Peru, you will need to obtain a **Carnet de Passages en Douane** (CPD, www.carnetdepassage. org) in your home country. A CPD is an internationally recognized customs document that allows you to temporarily "import" a car or motorbike into the country. It is valid for three months, with a further three-month extension possible. After that, there are hefty daily fines if you continue to use the vehicle. It is not legal to sell a car that has entered the country with a CPD. To permanently import a vehicle, you may end up paying more than its worth in tax and duty.

In addition to the CPD, you'll need your passport, your driver's license from your home state, and full registration papers. If the car isn't yours, bring a notarized letter signed by the owner authorizing you to use the vehicle. An international driver's license is also helpful.

Until the Pan-American Highway (Panamericana) penetrates the rainforests of the Darién Gap between Panama and Colombia, driving from Central to South America (and thus from North America to Ecuador) will remain impossible. Shipping companies in Panama City will transport your vehicle around the gap by ferry, and some go all the way to Ecuador.

Getting Around

CAR OR MOTORCYCLE

The bus service is so easy, extensive, and economical that few visitors choose to drive. The main roads are in good condition and, outside the heavily congested cities, there is generally little traffic. Out in the country, with the freedom to stop where you choose, driving can be a joy. However, the otherwise laid-back Ecuadorians tend to be rally drivers behind the wheel, and overtaking on blind bends seems to be a national pastime. Standards of driving can be extremely alarming, especially in cities, where driving is only recommended for the most confident of road users.

Cars drive on the right-hand side of the road. The legal driving age is 18 (although the required age for car rental is usually 25). In urban areas, the speed limit is 50 kph (about 32 mph). On highways, the speed limit is 90 kph (55 mph). Speeding may result in a hefty fine and three days in jail. It is technically a legal requirement for everyone in the car to wear a seatbelt, though this is only strictly enforced in the front seats (there are often no seatbelts in the back). Regular gasoline is known as *extra* ($1.90/gallon), and premium is *super* ($2.90/gallon).

Police and military checkpoints are common. Be prepared to stop and show your passport and documents, including the vehicle's registration, proof of insurance, and driver's license. An international driver's license is not required, but having one is a good idea.

It is illegal to bribe a public official, but if you are faced with unscrupulous traffic police (*transito*) looking to make an easy buck, handing over $20 may be considerably quicker and cheaper than the alternative paperwork and hassle. Asking whether a solution might be found ("*¿Es posible encontrar una solución?*") might smooth things along.

In case of an accident, get a copy

of the *denuncia* (report) for insurance and possible legal tangles. Remember that drivers are often assumed guilty until proven innocent, and there is a chance of being put in jail until things are sorted out.

VEHICLE RENTAL

To rent a car, you need to present a passport, a valid driver's license, and an internationally recognized credit card. Minimum age is usually 25. A hefty deposit is charged on the card to ensure that the car is returned in one piece (21-25 years old might be able to negotiate rental upon payment of an even bigger deposit). Prices vary from $15/day or $105/week for a small car, rising to $100/day, $550/week for a larger 4WD vehicle. Check if the quoted rates include tax (IVA), unlimited mileage (*kilometraje libre*) and insurance (*seguro*). The deductible on the insurance is very high, usually between $1,000 and $3,500. Check the car carefully for any dings and scrapes before setting out.

In Quito, **Ecuador Freedom Bike Rentals** (www.freedombikerental.com) offers motorbike hire, which is also available at various agencies in Baños.

TAXIS

Yellow taxis are readily available across most of the country. Some rural Amazonian and Sierran towns have a mix of conventional taxis and white pickup trucks (*camionetas*). Short taxi journeys are usually economical, often $1.50-2. In larger cities, drivers are supposed to use a meter, so insist that yours does ("*el taxi metro por favor*"). If the driver claims it is not working, consider using a different taxi, or negotiate the fare in advance. Where there are no meters, it's a good

idea to ask a local person or your hotel what the approximate fare should be and suggest it to the driver, rather than asking him (or, very occasionally, her) how much it will be. Taxis at airports and bus terminals often have flat rates, which are nonnegotiable. Bear in mind that fares often increase at night in cities.

It is not uncommon for taxistas to play blaring music or to drive alarmingly. Feel free to ask them to turn the music down ("*¿Podria bajar la voluma por favor?*") or drive more slowly ("*¿Podria conducir mas despacio por favor?*") and to find a different taxi if the request is refused. Don't be put off: Many taxi drivers are extremely polite, helpful, a pleasure to talk to, and a great source of local information. Those learning Spanish can make the most of having a captive audience!

Throughout most of the country, taxis are a safe way to travel and it's generally fine to flag them down in the street. In cities at night, however, extra care should be taken. "Express kidnappings," where rogue taxi drivers briefly abduct passengers, relieve them of their valuables, and force them to take cash out of an ATM or hand over their PIN number, are not uncommon. Victims are usually released unharmed, but these incidents are terrifying and can turn violent.

Hiring a taxi by the day could cost anywhere between $50 and $100. Get a few quotes, as prices vary greatly. Using taxis for longer trips allows for tailor-made itineraries without the responsibility or stress of car rental. You'll find that some drivers are knowledgeable, friendly local guides.

HITCHHIKING

While it shouldn't technically be recommended as a safe method of transport, it's fairly common for Ecuadorians to catch rides with passing motorists, especially in remote rural areas. Even though *ir al dedo* ("thumbing it") means the same in Latin America as it does elsewhere, here it's more common to wave down passing cars with a flap of the hand. It can be difficult to tell the difference between an unofficial taxi cruising for passengers and a friendly motorist offering a ride for free, so it's a good idea to clarify when you get in, by asking "*¿Cuanto seria?*" ("How much would that be?"), or to offer to pay when you get out "*¿Le debo algo?*" ("Do I owe you anything?"). Use your own judgment when deciding to get in. A good rule of thumb is to look for a car with a local woman driver or passenger(s).

BUS

Love it or hate it (and you'll probably experience both emotions), bus is the most common, recommended, and economical mode of transport, with journeys costing roughly $1-1.50 per hour of travel. The majority of Ecuadorians don't own cars and depend on the bus service, which is generally reliable. It's also incredibly comprehensive, covering even remote rural areas. Traveling by bus is a wonderful way to admire Ecuador's stunning scenery and travel with the locals.

There are downsides, however. Comfort levels vary widely, from bone-shaking rust buckets to ultramodern vehicles with air-conditioning, Wi-Fi, plug sockets, toilets, reclining seats, and attendants. Drivers often play music or movies at high volume, so take ear plugs if you're sensitive to noise. Inexplicably, the movies are usually ultra-violent and can be fairly sexually explicit, so bring a distraction if you're traveling with kids. Probably

the most common way for visitors to fall victim to theft is to store their belongings in the overhead compartment on a bus; these are easy pickings for thieves. Don't leave any valuables in your main luggage, which will be stored under the bus. Keep anything of value in your day pack or handbag and hold it on your lap. If you put it on the floor in front of your seat, make sure that the person behind you can't access it. Putting it between your feet with a strap wound around your leg should do the trick.

Most journeys over 6 hours have departures during the day or overnight. Traveling by day means you can look out of the window and marvel at the rapid changes in landscape and vegetation, and you always get some unforgettable glimpses of everyday life as you pass by. Traveling at night is a good option for those who can sleep anywhere and are looking to save on a night in a hotel (though it may involve arriving to an unknown destination in the early hours, which can be unsettling).

Larger towns usually have a main bus terminal (*terminal terrestre*), where there is a row of ticket offices. It's often necessary to purchase a separate ticket ($0.25) to get out onto the platform, which goes toward the upkeep of the station. If there is no *terminal terrestre*, there is usually a park or intersection from which buses come and go. Some bus companies have their own office or terminal for arrivals and departures.

Adding to the wonderful flexibility of travel within Ecuador, many buses can be hailed from the roadside with a flap of the hand and will let you off upon request. On these buses, sometimes you pay the driver when you get on, other times when you get off. Most often, a conductor will come around and collect fares. Just watch what the locals do and follow their lead. To ask the driver to stop, say "*¡pare!*" (stop), "*a la esquina*" (at the corner), or simply "*¡gracias!*" (thanks). If you're not sure where to get off, ask the conductor to notify you when you get to your desired destination; they usually remember to do so.

If you prefer a faster, direct service with no unscheduled stops, buy a ticket for a *directo* at the terminal or bus company office. Tickets can be bought on the day of travel, though on public holidays and high season weekends (especially on beach routes), it's advisable to buy it the day before. Most tickets have allocated seat numbers, which may or may not be respected.

Long-distance buses stop for meals, and there is usually a toilet at the back, but you may have to ask the conductor for the key.

Even on short journeys, vendors climb aboard in most towns selling drinks, snacks, and fast food. In fact, Ecuador's buses are the livelihood of many thousands of vendors, selling everything from food to medical products. Although this can be an annoyance, remember that these people make a living from it, so perhaps giving a quarter for a few candies is not unreasonable. Many vendors have a set routine, and you'll be amazed at how much time and effort they put into their sales pitch. First they greet all the passengers, thank God for the beautiful day, and give a long apology for disturbing their journey. This may be followed by a tale of woe about their current economic situation. Then they give a detailed description of the product, its contents, benefits, and instructions for use. The vendor then walks through the bus handing a product to every passenger, emphasizing that this is by no means an indication of intent to purchase (you can refuse to take it or give it back later). The vendor will then try to surprise you with a very reasonable offer (most products are sold for $0.25-2) and then go back through the bus collecting sales. You'll notice that locals are very tolerant of the vendors and frequently make purchases.

Information about bus schedules can be unreliable on companies' websites, but many schedules can be checked online at Andes Transit (https://andestransit.com).

Police occasionally stop buses searching for contraband or criminals. All passengers will be asked to disembark. The men are patted down, everyone has their bag searched, and all are asked to present ID before getting back on the bus.

COLECTIVOS AND RANCHEROS

A *colectivo* is a shared form of transport on a set route, often a converted pickup truck with benches in the back, covered with a canvas awning. This can be an economical way to travel, though they usually only leave when they are full, so there may be a wait. *Chivas* or *rancheros* are open-sided buses with wooden bench seats, also common in rural areas.

METRO AND TROLLEY SYSTEMS

Quito's network of three electric trolley bus lines is cheap, well organized, and usually much faster than traveling by car, especially in heavy traffic. Overcrowding and pickpockets can be a problem, however. Flat fare for all services is $0.25. An underground metro system is currently being built in Quito and is projected to be operational in 2019 (delays not withstanding).

TRAIN

When it opened in the 1900s, Ecuador's railway was used to transport goods and passengers between Quito and Guayaquil. Crossing raging rivers, deep ravines, frosty Andean peaks, dense cloud forests, and rocky slopes, linking the Sierra and the coast was an impressive feat of engineering. The most famous section was christened Nariz del Diablo (Devil's Nose), where a series of switchbacks are so tight the entire train has to back up to fit through, descending over 500 meters (over 1,600 ft) in just 12 kilometers (7.5 mi). With the new transport system, suddenly trade between the two regions was possible in hours rather than days, and, with three classes of ticket, rail travel was affordable for local people, boosting the economy along the whole route. Additional lines were added to Otavalo and other cities and the railway flourished for decades, until the road system rendered it obsolete. The network fell into disrepair and was finally closed in the 1990s.

In 2008, Rafael Correa's government oversaw a multimillion-dollar renovation of the railways, and many sections have since been reopened. Rather than an everyday method of transport, however, a number of scenic journeys are available as tourist attractions, at prices that are out of reach for most Ecuadorians. As well as the Devil's Nose, several other routes are available, most of them round-trip one-day experiences with prices ranging $28-63. These leave from Otavalo and Quito among other cities. For more information, see the **Tren Ecuador** website (http://trenecuador.com/en). Tickets can be bought online, by phone (800/873-637), or in person at the stations.

AIR

Flying within Ecuador is quick, convenient, and relatively inexpensive. With some exceptions, mainland flights are generally economical (from $40 one way). To get the best deal, book in advance and be prepared to be flexible with dates. Some promotional deals only include hand luggage, so check carefully. Compare prices for all three domestic carriers: TAME, Avianca, and LAN.

TAME (www.tame.com.ec) is Ecuador's national carrier and covers the whole domestic network. **LAN** (www.latam.com) and **Avianca** (www.avianca.com) serve Quito.

Visas and Officialdom

TOURIST VISAS

Travelers from the vast majority of countries do not require a visa to enter Ecuador and will be given a 90-day permit stamp upon arrival (exceptions are citizens of Afghanistan, Bangladesh, Cuba, Eritrea, Ethiopia, Kenya, Nepal, Nigeria, North Korea, Pakistan, Somalia, and Senegal, who require a visa). This 90-day permit is only issued once per year (i.e., if you are issued one on April 1, 2019, you cannot request another until April 1, 2020). Citizens of most Latin American countries are issued a 180-day visa upon arrival.

A passport with validity of at least six months is required. Border officials have the right to ask for proof of onward travel arrangements (a reservation for a bus ticket to Peru or Colombia is sufficient), though they often do not. If you are traveling from a country with a risk of yellow fever transmission, including Peru, Colombia, Brazil, Argentina, and Bolivia, you may be asked to show a vaccination certificate. Check with the World Health Organization for the current list of affected countries.

If you enter or exit Ecuador via the border with Peru or Colombia, make sure you are given exit and entry stamps at the border showing the date. Officials are known to forget, and without a stamp, you're officially in the country illegally.

Since February 2018, overstaying a visa involves a fine. At its most severe, the penalty is $772 and expulsion from the country.

If you know beforehand that you would like to stay in Ecuador beyond 90 days, consider applying for a longer visa with your local Ecuadorian embassy before your trip, to avoid formalities in Ecuador.

Alternatively, at the time of writing, the 90-day visa can be extended once, by a further 90 days, when you're in the country. Take your passport to any Migration office on the day your visa expires and you'll be asked to complete a form and pay $129 at a branch of Banco Pacifico. The extension will be granted on the same day. Migration offices can be found in Quito at Ministerio de Relaciones Exteriores, Carrión E1-76 at 10 de Agosto, 2/299-3200. There are also smaller, regional offices in other towns across the country, as listed here: www.cancilleria.gob.ec/coordinaciones-zonales. Go early (8:30am) and be prepared to wait. After this extension it is possible to extend the visa for another 6 months by applying for a Visa Especial de Turismo at the Ministerio de Relaciones Exteriores, which costs $450. Visa rules and requirements change frequently. For up-to-date information, and to download the application form, see www.cancilleria.gob.ec (go to *Movilidad Humanos, Servicios,* and then *Visas*). For requirements in English, visit www.consuladovirtual.gob.ec/en.

If you have the resources, especially if you have limited Spanish or time, it is highly recommended to get some help navigating any kind of visa process. It's usually well worth paying a little extra to save an enormous amount of hassle. Lots of bilingual local people make a living assisting foreigners with these kinds of procedures, but make sure to get a recommendation, as there are some unscrupulous folks working in this area. A recommended and economical lawyer is Joseph Guznay (josephguznay@gmail.com), who is based in Quito but works nationwide. Companies such as EcuaAssist (www.ecuaassist.com) can help with visas and a wide range of bureaucratic and legal procedures.

VISAS FOR LONGER STAYS

A wide range of visas exist for those wishing to stay longer in Ecuador, whether temporarily or as a resident. A list of visas and their requirements, in English, can be found here: www.

consuladovirtual.gob.ec (select Visas from the Consular Services menu). You will certainly need to procure the services of a lawyer, such as Joseph Guznay (josephguznay@gmail.com) or a company such as EcuaAssist (www.ecuaassist.com), to negotiate this kind of red tape.

BRINGING PETS

If you're planning on bringing a four-legged friend, check the country-specific entry requirements here: www.pettravel.com. Have all paperwork on hand going through immigration and customs. The Agriculture Ministry is at customs and thoroughly checks all paperwork.

Sports and Recreation

MOUNTAINEERING

A variety of high-altitude climbing options in Ecuador will delight mountaineers, whether complete beginners or seasoned veterans. Options range from day climbs suitable for anyone with a reasonable degree of fitness, to highly technical snowy ascents, to seven-day expeditions through the wilderness.

It is not recommended to undertake any mountaineering expedition without a guide.

Since 2015, climbers of any glaciated mountain must be accompanied by an accredited, specialized guide and be registered by a licensed tour agency in the Biodiversity Information System (Sistema de Información de Biodiversidad, SIB). This system is strictly enforced. Any reputable agency will take care of this formality, so make sure that yours does.

Recognized mountaineering clubs can apply for climbing permits with SIB (http://sib.ambiente.gob.ec). For more information, contact ASEGUIM, the **Ecuadorian Mountain Guide Association** (www.aseguim.org), or the **Ministry of the Environment** (tel. 2/398-7600, ext. 3001, mesadeayuda@ambiente.gob.ec).

Non-glaciated peaks should not be attempted without a guide either. Even trails that don't require technical knowledge are often poorly marked or nonexistent, and the weather can change rapidly, reducing visibility to near zero. It is very easy to get lost, and helicopter rescue teams are often sent out to search for overconfident tourists, especially Europeans who are accustomed to the Alps but unprepared for the Andes. With nighttime temperatures below freezing, fatalities from exposure have occurred. Don't underestimate the danger of attempting to strike out on your own. Aside from the safety benefit, hiring a local guide, directly or through an agency, is also a great way to learn about Ecuador while providing sustainable income for a fellow lover of the great outdoors.

Guided climbs typically include equipment, permits, transportation, meals, and overnight(s) in a refuge or camping. Check with your guide or tour agency about what you will need to bring: usually hiking shoes, warm clothes, and a waterproof jacket. Mountaineering gear is available at stores in Quito.

The central Sierra is the best region for mountaineering, home to the famous Avenue of the Volcanoes. Machachi and Latacunga both make good bases for the more northerly central peaks, including Corazón, the Ilinizas, Rumiñahui, and Cotopaxi. Two out of Ecuador's big three—Cotopaxi, Chimborazo, and Cayambe—are in the central Sierra. Cotopaxi (5,897 m/19,347 ft) is the country's most popular high-altitude climb because of its relative simplicity; it's mostly an uphill slog. However, less than half of those who attempt the summit actually succeed; climbers need to be in good physical condition, be fully acclimatized, and have a certain amount of luck with the conditions. Chimborazo (6,310 m/20,702 ft), the planet's closest point to the sun, is more challenging. Both require an overnight stay in a refuge. As part of guided tours of the national park, anyone with a decent level of fitness can climb to the snowy refuges on Cotopaxi and Chimborazo at 4,800 meters (15,750 ft) and 5,000 meters (16,400 ft), respectively. Both walks take a breathless 40 minutes from the parking lot.

Near Quito, the two Pichincha volcanoes, Guagua and Rucu, can be climbed as day trips; the latter is easier and more accessible. To the south of the city, within the Pasochoa Protected Forest, it's possible to climb to the lip of Cerro Pasochoa's blasted volcanic crater in six hours. The Pichinchas and Cerro Pasochoa are good starters for acclimating and getting into shape. To the east of Quito, Antisana (5,704 m/18,714 ft) is Ecuador's fourth-highest peak and one of the least climbed. Its reputation for being difficult and dangerous is due in part to the presence of active glaciers and lack of a refuge. Reaching the summit requires a three-day expedition.

In the northern Sierra, Otavalo provides access to Fuya Fuya (4,262 m/13,983 ft), the only peak in the country that can safely be climbed without a guide, on a four-hour round-trip (do go with a companion, though). Tour operators in Otavalo offer day-trip climbs to Fuya Fuya.

Guides can also be hired via the Ecuadorian Association of Mountain Guides (tel. 2/254-0599, www.aseguim.org). Its Members page lists the contact details of guides who speak English, German, French, and Italian.

A very helpful source of information for all things climbing is Wlady Ortiz, the bilingual local owner of Ecuador Eco Adventure (tel. 99/831-1282, www.ecuadorecoadventure.com) in Riobamba. As well as offering climbs of peaks nationwide, Wlady has opened Riobamba Base Camp, a hostel designed exclusively for hikers and climbers.

Wherever you climb, be prepared to deal with the effects of altitude. Even if you're fit, you might experience fatigue, headaches, and breathlessness.

It is not uncommon to suffer some degree of **acute mountain sickness** (AMS), known locally as *soroche,* which feels like the world's worst hangover: headache, nausea, fatigue, insomnia, and loss of appetite. Your guide will know how to deal with this, and anyone suffering acutely will be accompanied back to a lower altitude. A couple of days walking around Quito (at 2,850 m/9,350 ft) is a good way to prepare for a climb. Drink plenty of fluids and avoid alcohol. Before tackling any of the highest peaks, ideally you should trek and sleep at around 4,000 meters (13,000 ft) for a couple of days. All mountaineering tour agencies offer acclimatization climbs.

HIKING AND CAMPING

There are wonderful hikes in all regions of Ecuador, many of which can only be undertaken with a guide. There are also some areas with excellent trails for self-guided hikes. Many national parks and private reserves also have well-marked trails for independent hiking. Entrance to all national parks is free.

Self-guided hikes are usually well marked, and maps are readily available from local hostels or online. Most are out of cell phone range, but if you have a smartphone you can download the application Maps.me (https://maps.me), which can be used offline to help guide your way. Serious hikers can request topographical maps from the Instituto Geográfico Militar (IGM, www.igm.gob.ec) in Quito, either in person or online (see *Servicios* on the IGM website).

Even when setting out for a popular, well-marked, self-guided hike, it's sensible to take some precautions. It's not a good idea to go alone, in case of accident. Many hostels in popular hiking areas are good places to meet up with hiking buddies. Notify your hotel where you're going, your approximate route, and when you expect to be back; don't forget to confirm your safe return. Be prepared for rapid changes in weather, especially in the Sierra. Wear layers and take sunblock and sunglasses. Carry plenty of water; energy rich snacks such as dried fruit and nuts (chocolate is a godsend at altitude); a compass (or compass app on your phone); waterproof clothing (a thin plastic poncho is a good idea, as it folds up small and can also cover your day pack); and bandages in case of blisters.

Unless you're an outdoor survival expert, do not consider striking out on your own into the wilderness. Many trails are poorly marked or nonexistent, and the weather can change rapidly, reducing visibility to near zero if clouds descend. This book indicates wherever possible which hikes can be completed independently and which need a guide.

Several national parks have designated camping areas. Many hostels and lodges also have camping facilities for as little as $3 or $6 per night. Some even provide tents. It's best to bring your camping gear from home, including a water bottle that filters and purifies water. There are outdoors stores in Quito, but good-quality items are expensive. Tents are available for as little as $30 in most large supermarkets (such as Mi Comisariato), though they are only suitable for the kindest of weather (i.e., dry nights on the coast) or covered camping areas. In the Sierra, especially on the *páramo*, be prepared for sub-zero nighttime temperatures.

RAFTING AND KAYAKING

White-water sports are very popular in Ecuador, and the terrain is perfect, with rivers rushing down either side of the Andes to the coastal plains to the west and Amazon basin to the east. From half-day rafting and kayaking trips for complete beginners to week-long advanced-level expeditions, the whole spectrum of activities is available, and the spectacular scenery through gorges, canyons, valleys, and jungles makes these trips as beautiful as they are exciting.

The Ministry of Tourism requires all rafting companies to be certified, so make sure that yours is. Most of the better companies have Class III certification or higher from the **International Rafting Federation** (IRF, www.internationalrafting.com). Trip leaders should have Wilderness Advanced First Aid qualifications.

BIRDING

Ecuador is indisputably one of the best birding destinations in the world with Mindo being the premier location in the country. Incredibly, one-sixth of the planet's types of bird (almost 1,600 recorded species) are found in Ecuador. Perhaps the most iconic is the hummingbird, present in every region from sea level to snowcapped mountains, including the world's second smallest, the Esmeraldas woodstar, or *estrellita Esmeraldeña*. At the other end of the scale is the Andean condor, the world's largest flying bird, with a wingspan of more than 3 meters (10 ft). Other avian stars include the blue-footed booby, the magnificent frigate bird, the long-wattled umbrella bird, the agami heron, the harpy eagle, the Andean cock-of-the-rock, and a variety of toucans, macaws, antpittas,

and tanagers. For more details on Ecuador's birds, see the *Plants and Animals* section of the *Background* chapter.

The nonprofit **Jocotoco Foundation** (http://www.jocotoco. org) has a number of reserves that protect endemic and threatened bird species all over the country. They also have lodges and offer tours. **San Jorge** (www.ecolodgesanjorge.com) owns eight private reserves and four ecolodges in birding hot spots. Specialized agencies such as **Neotropical** (www.neotropicalecuador.com) offer birding tours. Local bird guides are found all over the country and are more economical than an organized tour. Recommended local guides have been included throughout this book.

Robert Ridgely and Paul Greenfield's two-volume illustrated *The Birds of Ecuador: Field Guide* is considered the birding bible here.

SPECTATOR SPORTS

Soccer (*fútbol*) is Ecuador's national game, far more popular than all other sports combined. Informal matches pop up on makeshift fields everywhere—on a narrow strip of beach as the tide comes in, or on a patch of cleared rainforest with bamboo goalposts. Every village has its football pitch (*cancha de fútbol*) for more organized games. Antonio Valencia, an Ecuadorian from Lago Agrio who captains Manchester United, is a national hero.

In Quito, the city's most successful club is the **Liga de Quito,** which plays at the Estadio Casa Blanca. Ticket prices range from around $5 for a seat behind the goal to $25 for a box seat at the main stand. Expect to pay at least $20 for El Clásico. The Ecuadorian national team plays at the Estadio Atahualpa in Quito at an elevation of 2,850 meters (9,350 ft), a huge advantage over teams from lower elevations. Check www.elnacional.ec for details of the next match. Tickets can be bought at the stadiums (*estadios*) and should be purchased ahead of time for popular matches (such as El Clásico).

Whenever there is a big match in Ecuador, men gather around televisions in stores and restaurants to watch. While football violence is known between rival fans in the cities, it is rare elsewhere in Ecuador.

Ecuavolley, the local version of volleyball, is another popular sport, both on the beach and on concrete courts. Big city parks, such as Quito's Parque La Carolina, are a good place to watch games, especially on Sundays.

Learning Spanish in Ecuador

Ecuador has many excellent Spanish schools, and it's worth shopping around to find one that fits your needs. Most provide 2-6 hours of instruction per day, either in groups ($5.50-6.50 per hour) or one on one ($7-13 per hour). An initial registration fee may be required ($20-35).

Most schools offer extra activities such as cooking, salsa classes, surf lessons, volunteering, cultural experiences, and group trips. Some will house you in private or shared accommodations (prices vary) or arrange for a homestay with a local family (typically $20-25 per day for full board, $17-20 for a room and two meals per day). You can make your own accommodation arrangements if you prefer.

The advantage of learning in the Sierra is that the people tend to speak more slowly and clearly than their coastal counterparts, making it easier to practice in public.

To give something back, consider the excellent nonprofit **Yanapuma Spanish School** (www. yanapumaspanish.org), which has locations in Quito. Proceeds go toward sustainable development projects in indigenous and marginalized communities and a scholarship fund for disadvantaged children. It's the only school using the Communicative Language Teaching methodology, which moves away from traditional grammar-based classes. Instead, students learn through interaction with the teacher and (if in a group class) other students. Prices start at $6/hour for group classes and $9/hour for private, individually tailored classes. Study & Travel programs combine classes with exploration of Ecuador with a teacher. Widely ranging volunteer opportunities are available.

In Quito, the following schools are also recommended: **Simon Bolivar Spanish School** (Mariscal Foch E9-20 *y* Av. 6 de Diciembre, tel. 2/254-4558, www.simon-bolivar.com); **Ailola Quito Spanish School** (Guayaquil N9-77 *y* Oriente, tel. 2/228-5657, www.ailolaquito.com); **Guayasamín Spanish School** (Calama E8-54 *cerca* 6 de Diciembre, tel. 2/254-4210, www. guayasaminschool.com); **Instituto Superior de Español** (Guayaquil N9-77 *y* Oriente, tel. 2/228-5657, www.superiorspanishschool.com);

La Lengua (Av. Cristóbal Colón E6-12 y Rábida, Building Ave María, tel. 2/250-1271, www.la-lengua.com); and **South American Language Center** (Amazonas N26-59 y Santa María, tel. 99/520-2158, http://spanishschoolsouthamerican.com). Of note is the **Cristóbal Colón Spanish School** (Colón 2088 y Versalles, tel./fax 2/250-6508, www.colonspanishschool.com), the most economical option for one-on-one classes at $7 per hour.

In Otavalo, **Mundo Andino Spanish School** (Bolívar y Abdón Calderón, 3rd floor, tel. 6/292-1864, www.mundoandinospanish-school.com) and **Otavalo Learning & Adventure** (García Moreno y Atahualpa, tel. 99/700-8542) are recommended. Just north of Otavalo, the excellent **Pucará B&B & Spanish School** (tel. 99/521-6665, www.pucaraspanishschool.com) is in a beautiful rural setting.

Food and Drink

As with everything else, gastronomically Ecuador is a land of diversity, with many small towns and villages having their own specialty dishes. The most traditional food is sometimes made according to recipes passed down the generations. In some towns, you'll find unassuming little cafés where local women have been serving the same dish for 50 years, faithfully following their grandmother's secret formula. Most Ecuadorians are enthusiastic and knowledgeable about their cuisine and will happily point you in the direction of the best spots to try it. If you ask for restaurant recommendations, it may be assumed you're looking for international food and an expat hangout; for a more authentic experience, try asking where the locals eat ("*¿Donde comen los locales?*") or where you can try good local food ("*¿Donde puedo probar buena comida local?*").

Despite the abundance of delicious, economical fruit and vegetables, many Ecuadorians live primarily on a diet of carbohydrates, notably white rice (*arroz*), and meat, especially pork (*carne de chancho/cerdo*), chicken (*pollo*), and fish (*pescado*). Vegetable intake is often limited to a scrap of side salad and some truly delicious soups (*sopas*). Of particular note is *fanesca*, a traditional Easter soup containing salt cod to represent Jesus and 12 different kinds of beans and grains to represent the apostles. Traditional Ecuadorian food is known as *comida típica* (typical food), which is usually a blend of national staples and local dishes. Perhaps the most *típica* is *seco de pollo*, a slow-cooked chicken stew in a sauce of beer, naranjilla juice, onions, garlic, peppers, and tomatoes.

Often the best place to eat *comida típica* alongside the locals is the food court (*patio de comida*) at the central or municipal market (*mercado central/municipal*). If you're cooking for yourself, the markets are also the best source of fresh produce, usually much more flavorsome than at the supermarket. There are bound to be some weird and wonderful fruits you've never seen before. Local markets are also a great way to support small-scale local farmers and vendors.

As with anywhere, a restaurant filled with locals usually means the food is good. Ecuadorians commonly eat out for lunch (*almuerzo*), with many opting for a set meal (*menú del día*) at unfussy restaurants that are sometimes colloquially referred to as *huecos* (holes). These set meals, often available for around $3.50, offer the most economical and filling option for travelers, consisting of a juice or tea, a soup (*sopa*), and a main course (*segundo*). The main course is usually some sort of meat, chicken, or fish with rice and a side dish such as salad (*ensalada*), plantain (*platano*), manioc (*yucca*), or lentil stew (*menestra*). In the Sierra, hominy (*mote*) and avocado (*aguacate*) are popular sides. Occasionally there is a small dessert (*postre*). One o'clock is generally lunchtime. Dinner (*cena*) tends to be smaller and eaten from 7pm on, although many Ecuadorians will eat out as late as 10pm. A set evening meal is called a *merienda* and follows a similar format to lunch.

A number of Ecuadorian dishes tend to be eaten for breakfast (*desayuno*) but are available throughout the day, including *bolón* (a ball of plantain with cheese or ham, best served with fried eggs); *tigrillo* (mashed plantains with cheese and egg); *humitas* (ground corn mashed with cheese, onion, garlic, eggs, and cream and steamed in corn leaves); tamales (corn flour dough filled with pork, egg, and raisins, wrapped in leaves and steamed); *quimbolitos* (a sweet version of a tamale); and *mote pillo* (hominy scrambled with egg, onion, and herbs, available in the southern Sierra). Continental breakfasts (bread, jam, coffee and juice) and American breakfasts (the same, plus eggs) are available everywhere. A bowl of fruit, yogurt, and granola is another popular option.

Perhaps king of Ecuadorian street food is the empanada (pastry turnover filled with cheese or meat). Cheese empanadas, usually fried but sometimes baked, are often sprinkled with sugar.

Ecuador's tourist towns and larger cities have a wide range of international cuisine.

REGIONAL SPECIALTIES

The most famous specialty in the Sierra is *cuy* (guinea pig) roasted whole on a spit, though pork is much more commonly eaten. There is fierce competition among Sierran towns over which makes the best *hornado* (slow-roasted pork) and *fritada* (pork cooked in water and orange juice until the water is reduced and the meat is browned in its own fat). In Latacunga, the specialty is *chugchucara*, with chunks of pork, crispy skins, potatoes, plantains, and corn. A wide variety of potatoes and corn are grown in the Andes, with the former being used to make the region's famous *locro de papa*, a thick soup served with avocado. Another Sierran soup is Loja's *repe*, made from green bananas.

Ecuadorians don't generally eat dessert, though in the southern Sierra meals are traditionally followed with *miel con quesillo* (honey with soft unsalted cheese). Cakes are popular for special occasions, including *tres leches* (three milks), made with evaporated milk, condensed milk, and cream. Wonderful fruit salads can be found all over the country, especially the coast. Regional sweet specialties include *helado de paila* (fruit sorbet originating in Ibarra); *helados de Salcedo*

TIPS FOR VEGETARIANS

ESSENTIALS
FOOD AND DRINK

An increasing number of vegetarian and vegan restaurants are popping up in Ecuador and have been featured in this book wherever they were found. A good online resource is www.happycow.com, which has a database of meat-free establishments searchable by town. Quito has an especially good range. Vegetarian options in restaurants are also improving, with some having a special section on the menu, most often with pasta or rice dishes. Most tourist towns have decent Italian restaurants, which always have veggie pizza and pasta. Even the least touristy midsized towns have Chinese restaurants, known as *chifas*, which reliably serve noodles with vegetables (*tallarines con verduras*) and rice with vegetables (*chaulafan con verduras*), which you can be sure will be meat-free. The servings at *chifas* are usually big, service is fast, and they are often the only option on Sunday, when many places are closed.

Off the beaten track, asking for vegetarian food (*comida vegetariana*) might result in a blank stare, but the situation is rarely hopeless; there are usually veggie options, it's just that they are not known as such. In the set lunch (*almuerzo*) places, the soup of the day (*sopa del día*, known as *crema* if it's smooth) might be of the vegetable variety, in which case you're in for a treat because Ecuadorian soups are generally very good. It's worth checking that it doesn't contain any animal products ("*¿Esto contiene productos de origen animal?*"). The same should be asked of *menestra* (lentil stew), which is widely available. Most places can rustle up a plate of rice, lentil stew, fried eggs (*huevos fritos*), and plantain fries (*patacones*). An omelet is another life saver for veggies, known as *tortilla de huevos*, especially good with vegetables (*con verduras*). Some street food options are meat-free, including *empanadas de queso* (pastry turnover with cheese) and *choclo* (corn on the cob).

In the Sierra, the *llapingachos* (fried potato patties) are delicious, but they are nearly always cooked in pork fat. Beans (*habas*), potatoes (*papas*), hominy (*mote*), and avocado (*aguacate*) are popular Sierran sides that can be put together to make a meal. *Locro de papa* (potato soup with avocado) is so filling it can make a meal in itself. In the Oriente—the most challenging region for vegetarians—you'll probably end up eating a lot of rice, yucca, and plantain. Wherever you go, the fruit salads (*ensalada de fruta*) are generally good, but the regular salads (*ensaladas*) are usually pitiful, consisting of iceberg lettuce, raw onion, and tomato. Vegetarians with access to a kitchen, the local market, and some cooking skills will be delighted by the cheap and plentiful abundance of vegetables, legumes, and grains.

(ice cream on a stick made of layers of coconut, blackberry, mango, taxo, naranjilla, and milk flavors, originating in Salcedo); *cocadas* (balls of coconut with *panela*, or raw sugar, originating in Esmeraldas); and *bocadillos*, squares of raw sugar syrup and peanut that look like fudge, originating in Loja).

DRINKS

One of the highlights of a trip to Ecuador is the vast range of fresh fruit available, which is made into *jugos* (pure juice or blended with water) or *batidos* (fruit blended with milk). They're often made very sweet,

and you can ask for less sugar (*menos azúcar*). Especially popular are *mora* (blackberry), *maracuyá* (passion fruit), *naranjilla* (a tart Andean fruit), and *tomate de arbol* (tree tomato).

Ecuadorian coffee is among the best in the world, but sadly instant Nescafé is prevalent. You're more likely to get a cup of real coffee in the Sierra. Large supermarkets and small organic stores all over the country sell organic ground Ecuadorian coffee.

Tea, often referred to as *agua aromatica*, is widely available. The most common flavors are *manzanilla* (chamomile), *menta* (mint), *anis* (aniseed), *cedrón* (lemongrass), and *horchata,* a pink infusion of various medicinal herbs that originated in Loja. English breakfast tea is known as *té negro* (black tea), and you need to order milk separately, which often causes confusion. Brits might need to use two tea bags per cup to get it up to strength!

Sold by street vendors everywhere is *morocho,* a thick, sweet drink rather like rice pudding, made from *morocho* corn, milk, cinnamon, sugar, and raisins. Served hot, it's filling and comforting. *Avena polaca* is another thick milk-based drink, this time made with oats and served cold. Originating in Santo Domingo, it's wickedly creamy and sold by mobile vendors everywhere.

A popular juice in the central Sierra is *borojó,* a fruit with energizing properties, laughingly referred to by the locals as the natural Viagra.

A quick look in any store refrigerator will confirm the fact that 71 percent of Ecuador's drinks market is controlled by Cervecería Nacional (the national brewery) and Coca Cola. National beers include Pilsner and Club Verde, both of which will disappoint beer connoisseurs. Happily, craft beer is popping up everywhere and tends to be local. Ecuadorians often buy a big bottle of beer and share it among friends. Any alcohol imported from the United States or Europe is prohibitively expensive. Ecuadorian wine isn't very good (except for the sweet *vino de uva* in Patate), so Chilean is your best bet, but it's not cheap. Head to the big supermarkets for the best deals. The most popular brand is the boxed wine Clos, with the accompanying joke, "It's not wine but it's clos(e)," though the merlot is actually pretty good.

Rum is very popular in Ecuador, but the more traditional sugarcane liquor, known as *caña* or simply *trago,* is the alcohol of choice in most of rural Ecuador. Heated and mixed with cinnamon and sugar, the potent concoction is called *canelazo,* to which fruit is sometimes added. Also comforting on a chilly Sierran night is *vino hervido,* hot mulled wine, most commonly found in Quito. If you get too *borracho* (drunk) the night before, you may wake up *chuchaqui,* a Quechua word meaning "hungover" that proves even the Incas knew the perils of "the morning after."

Accommodations

The entire spectrum of overnight lodging is represented in Ecuador. Accommodations fall into the following categories, which the Ministry of Tourism is working to standardize according to the services offered: *hotel, hostal, casa de huespedes, hostería, hacienda, lodge, resort, refugio,* and *campamento.* In a hotel, all bathrooms are private and there should be a restaurant or café. A *hostal* (hostel) may have some dormitories and/or shared bathrooms and might not have a restaurant or café (though might have a shared kitchen). A *casa de huespedes* (guesthouse) sleeps a maximum of six people, usually in the converted home of the owner or manager. A *hostería* (inn) should have private rooms and/or cabins, gardens, green areas, and parking. These tend to be outside town and fairly swanky. *Haciendas* are even swankier, usually historical and out in the countryside. Many were converted into tourist lodging after the end of forced indigenous labor. They usually have expensive restaurants and activities such as horseback riding. Lodges will be out in nature, offering activities such as hiking and visiting local communities. A resort is a tourist complex with diverse facilities that offers recreational activities. A *refugio* (refuge) is usually found on mountains and in protected natural areas, offering basic accommodations for tourists engaged in activities such as trekking and climbing. *Campamentos* (campgrounds) provide a camping area, shared bathrooms, and outdoor areas for preparing food. Some provide tents, but most do not.

Not included in these categories are *centros de turismo comunitario* (community tourism centers, or CTCs), which are owned and run by communities, with the income distributed among members and going toward improvements in education and health care. These are usually fairly basic. An excellent resource on community tourism is the Federación Plurinacional de Turismo Comunitario del Ecuador (www.feptce.com, Facebook @ TurismoComunitarioEc). Homestays, where visitors lodge with local families, are another great way to experience community life. These can be arranged by most Spanish schools and many community tourism projects throughout the country, By stepping outside the normal world of hotels and restaurants, and branching out beyond the same conversations with fellow travelers, you can gain firsthand knowledge of the country as well as improve your Spanish.

Look for accommodations with sound environmental policies, which may include renewable energy, recycling, conservation of water and energy, ecological building methods, waste management practices (graywater systems, composting), use of biodegradable cleaning products, support of local producers, organic gardens, and environmental education. These establishments are included in this guide wherever they were found.

Be aware that all over the country are "love motels" aimed at lovers rather than travelers, where rooms are rented by the hour. This is a necessary service in a country where most people live with their parents until they are married. These establishments, which are also popular for conducting extramarital affairs, can usually be identified by tacky names and hearts somewhere on the sign.

Some general tips on accommodations are as follows:

- Prices in this book have been given for dorm beds (where they exist), single rooms (s), and double rooms (d). Many of the places listed also offer private rooms for groups. Contact individual establishments for details and prices.

- Prices vary depending on the time of year, so be aware of national holidays and high season, when prices rise sharply, before planning your trip. New Year's, Carnival, and Easter are especially expensive.

- Prices are not usually fixed in cheaper hotels, so bargaining is possible, especially if you're staying a few nights.

- A 22 percent tax is levied in more expensive accommodations (included in the prices quoted in this book), along with a 10-20 percent surcharge for paying by credit card.

- Electric showers in less expensive places can be dangerous if improperly wired; *don't* touch the shower head with wet hands. Remember that C stands for *caliente* (hot) and F means *frio* (cold). If there are no letters, the left tap is usually hot.

Many establishments have cranky hot water that may have a knack to it; the receptionist can usually help.
- The plumbing in Ecuador can't handle toilet paper, so be sure to throw it in the garbage instead of flushing it down the toilet.

Conduct and Customs

Ecuadorians are generally warmly welcoming of visitors and often lack the social reserve that prevents many Europeans from striking up a conversation with a stranger. While much leeway is given to the peculiar ways of foreigners, an effort to learn some of the local etiquette will be very much appreciated. It's also a basic way to show respect for your host country.

Keep your eyes open and you'll see that there is a lot to learn from Ecuadorian culture. Note that even though many people live in poverty, there are very few homeless people, a mark of the strong sense of community that has been lost from so many "developed" nations. Outside the cities, you will be met with incredulity if you mention that many people in your home country do not know their neighbors. Note how peaceful people are in public; this author has seen more fights in one night in the United Kingdom than in a decade of living in Ecuador. Note the respect that young people have for the elderly, or how all the generations socialize together.

GREETINGS AND GENERAL POLITENESS

Ecuadorians are renowned for their laid-back attitude and often smile through frustrations that can leave many gringos fuming. In other ways, the culture can be quite formal, such as the importance of greetings. Outside cities it is common to wish complete strangers "*buenos días/tardes/noches*" as you pass them in the street, and people entering a store or bus often announce "*¡Buenos días!*" to everyone inside. When meeting someone for the first time, shake their hand, say "*mucho gusto*" ("pleased to meet you"), and tell them your name. In informal situations among younger generations, people may introduce themselves with a kiss on the cheek. Two female friends will greet each other with a kiss on the cheek, as will a man and a woman. Two men usually shake hands or might embrace if they are close friends or family. If you're dining informally in a group, a new arrival will probably come around the table to kiss everyone's cheek in turn. If you approach a group and only know one person there, it is polite to introduce yourself to everyone. Ecuadorians often have social graces that can be hard to emulate for more awkward Brits such as this author!

Say "*buen provecho*" ("enjoy your meal") to your companions before a meal or to fellow diners when entering

SAY WHAT?

A lot of Ecuadorians have **nicknames,** and these often refer to their most obvious physical feature. It can be shocking for visitors from more politically correct countries to hear people referred to as *"El Gordo"* (fatty) or *"La Negra"* (dark skinned). Locals with Asian-looking eyes are almost invariably nicknamed *"Chino"* (Chinese); unusually light skinned people are *"Colorado"* (colored); and those with light eyes are usually *"El Gato"* (the cat). These terms are often suffixed with the colloquial *"ito"* or *"ita"*; e.g., *"La Flaca"* (skinny) becomes *"La Flaquita"* for a woman. While people rarely have any choice over their nickname (it seems unlikely that the guy with protuberant ears would relish being called "Dumbo" every day), these names are not meant offensively. As one local commented "I wouldn't call him Fatty if I didn't like him." Some of these words are also used as casual terms of address: *"¡Hola, Negra!"* or *"¡Hola, Flaquita!"* is a common way for a young person to casually address a close female friend of any skin color or size. The only word that is used in a derogatory way is *"indio"* to refer to an indigenous person. While some indigenous people believe in reclaiming the word (there is a hotel in Otavalo called El Indio, for example), visitors should avoid using it.

or leaving a restaurant. When arriving at someone's home, especially for the first time, it is polite to say *"permiso"* and wait for permission before stepping over the threshold. *"Permiso"* is also used as "excuse me" if you need to squeeze past someone or ask them to move out of the way. Yawning in public is considered rude, as is pointing or beckoning with a finger. Ecuadorians may point by puckering or pursing their lips or pointing with their chin, while beckoning is a downward flap of the hand.

There are various terms of address in Ecuador. Greatly respected older people are known as *"Don"* or *"Doña"* and then their name (e.g., "Doña Elena"). Women who are well into middle age can safely be addressed as *"Señora,"* whereas young women are *"Señorita"*; if you're not sure, it's best to avoid any term of address. Men are referred to as *"Señor."* In more informal situations, you can't go far wrong addressing someone as "friend" (*"amigo"* or *"amiga"*). Even more informal are *"chico"* and *"chica,"* which roughly translate as "guy" and "girl." Young women will often greet each other with *"¡Hola, chica!"*

SOCIAL OCCASIONS

Note that if an Ecuadorian uses the word invite (*"te invito"*), this usually means that he or she will pay. Equally, if you invite someone, you will be expected to foot the bill. If your hosts want to pay, it's best to let them and then return the favor on another occasion.

Guests are not expected to be punctual for social gatherings and should arrive 30 minutes to an hour late. Parties probably won't get going until after midnight and the dancing will likely continue into the early hours. Many a gringo has missed out on a great party by going home too soon.

Often, Ecuadorians will order a big bottle of beer and pour a glass for everyone. It will be appreciated if you get the next bottle.

DRESS

Andean people are much more formal in dress than their coastal counterparts. Modest shorts with a T-shirt is fine, but skimpy clothes should be avoided. Even in sweltering heat, it's best for women to avoid plunging necklines and short shorts. On the beach, skimpy clothes are perfectly acceptable, even the tiniest of bikinis, but topless sunbathing is definitely not.

Ecuadorians generally dress smartly for any kind of official occasion. This might be tricky for backpackers, but it's a good idea to brush up as much as possible for visits to the immigration office, or anything but the most informal invitation to someone's home.

CHALLENGES

The famous lack of punctuality in Ecuador can be difficult for gringos. This fluidity with time keeping can even extend to simply not turning up. Ecuadorian bureaucracy can also be extremely frustrating, to the point of incredulity, but it's vital to maintain good humor; losing your temper will not get you anywhere. You will be required to present a dismayingly long list of documents, letters, references, and copies of ID (possibly notarized) to complete any kind of official business, such as visa extension. This author had to take six trips into the city to open a bank account. If you have good Spanish and plenty of time and patience, you may be able to handle "*tramites*" (the collective term for bureaucratic procedures)

independently. Otherwise, it is highly recommended to take a local person with you who is used to navigating red tape.

There is a tolerance for noise in Ecuador that can be charming or challenging. For example, when this author's neighbors threw a party to baptize their twin girls, they closed the whole road, erected a marquee, and hired a band; the whole community salsa-danced until the early hours. Rather wonderfully, no one complained about the road closure or the music. On the other hand, it can be unbearable when someone decides to play thumping *reggaetón* all day from the back of their car, often so loud that it prevents any kind of thought, let alone conversation, nearby. This author has even visited some remote jungle communities where earsplitting *technocumbia* is played from dawn until dusk. The concept of "noise pollution" does not really exist in Ecuador, so, if you're sensitive to noise, bring good earplugs because they are hard to find locally. If you can afford it, noise-canceling headphones would be a good investment.

Queuing is not a popular pastime in Ecuador. Don't be pushy but be prepared to be firm.

Health and Safety

The information in this section is current at the time of writing. Before your trip, it's recommended to check for up-to-date information on the websites of the **U.S. Centers for Disease Control and Prevention** (www.cdc.gov/travel) and the U.K. government's **Travel Health Pro** (https://

travelhealthpro.org.uk), both of which offer country-specific advice.

Most visitors to Ecuador suffer nothing more serious than some sunburn, a couple of altitude headaches, some itchy mosquito bites, and perhaps an upset stomach. Having said that, there are risks of much more significant health problems, many of which can be mitigated with basic precautions.

Before your trip, make sure you have adequate **travel insurance** that covers medical expenses and any activities that you are planning on undertaking (surfing, scuba diving, mountaineering, etc.). Stock up on any prescription medication you require (including oral contraceptives). Bring copies of prescriptions for eyewear, just in case.

VACCINATIONS

If possible, see a health professional at least 4-6 weeks before you leave for Ecuador. All visitors should make sure their routine immunizations are up to date, along with **hepatitis A** (a viral infection transmitted through contaminated food and water or by direct contact with an infectious person) and **tetanus** (often called lockjaw, a bacterial infection introduced through open wounds).

Those whose activities may put them at extra risk should also consider vaccinations against **hepatitis B** (a viral infection transmitted via infected blood or body fluids); **rabies** (a viral infection usually transmitted via the saliva of an infected animal); **typhoid** (a bacterial infection transmitted through contaminated food and water); and **tuberculosis** (a bacterial infection transmitted by inhaling respiratory droplets from an infectious person).

DISEASES FROM BITING INSECTS OR TICKS

Ecuador is considered high risk for the **Zika virus,** which is usually mosquito-borne, though a few cases of sexual transmission have been reported. Zika only causes mild symptoms in most people, but there is scientific consensus that it can cause babies to be born with microcephaly (a small head and undeveloped brain) and other congenital anomalies. At the time of writing, the official advice is that pregnant women should postpone nonessential travel to Ecuador until after pregnancy. Women should avoid becoming pregnant while in Ecuador and for eight weeks after leaving. The risk can be reduced by visiting areas over 2,000 meters (6,500 ft) altitude, where the infected mosquitoes are unlikely to be present.

Dengue fever, another mosquito-borne disease that causes flu-like symptoms, is common. It can occasionally develop into a more serious life-threatening illness, but usually just means an unpleasant few days of fever, headaches, joint pain, and skin rash. The only treatments are rest and fluids. If you want to take pain relief, choose medication with acetaminophen and avoid aspirin. Medical attention is recommended, if only for diagnosis. The symptoms of **chikungunya,** which is also mosquito-borne and fairly common, are similar to dengue. Again, it is rarely serious and there is no treatment apart from rest and fluids.

Less common insect-borne diseases include **leishmaniasis** (an infection caused by the leishmania parasites, transmitted by the bite of infected phlebotomine sandfly) and American trypanosomiasis (also known as **Chagas disease,** an infection caused by the *Trypanosoma cruzi* parasites, transmitted by the bite of a triatomine insect. The most common form of leishmaniasis is cutaneous and starts with a red sore at the site of the sandfly bite, which may then develop into a lesion or ulcer. Common symptoms of Chagas disease are headaches, muscle aches, fever, and a rash. Both are potentially life threatening if not treated and are only prevented by bite avoidance.

It sounds obvious, but the best strategy for avoiding all these diseases is to reduce your likelihood of being bitten. If it's not too hot, wear long sleeves and pants, especially in the evenings. Light colors are less attractive to insects. Socks are a good idea, as ankles and feet are particularly prone to bites. This may not be practical on the beach, where repellent is a better strategy. DEET-based products are widely available. The higher the percentage of DEET, the more effective the repellent, but also the more toxic for your skin. Bring lemon eucalyptus or citronella oil from home if you're looking to avoid these harsh chemicals. Air-conditioning or a bedside fan can prevent nighttime bites. Mosquito nets are available in some general stores.

Most bites are nothing more than an itchy annoyance, but if a bite becomes infected or you start to feel unwell, seek medical assistance.

CONTAMINATED FOOD AND WATER

If you're going to get sick, it will probably be from contaminated water or food. As a tropical country, Ecuador is full of bacteria and parasites. The most common problem is **traveler's diarrhea,** which is unpleasant but not usually the sign of anything serious. Stay near a bathroom, drink plenty of water, and maybe get some oral rehydration solution such as Pedialyte, which is available in most pharmacies. Many travelers swear that a glass of flat cola and a banana is the best remedy. If symptoms persist or you have stomach pains, seek medical assistance. It may be a good idea to get tested for parasites, which are common and easily treated.

The precautions you take will depend on how sensitive your stomach is. In most of the country, water from the faucet is not drinkable, even by local people. If you have an easily upset stomach, use filtered water to brush your teeth and to wash fruits and vegetables. Many hostels provide free filtered drinking water in blue 20-liter bottles, which can be used to fill up your personal bottle. Most restaurants will also fill up small bottles upon request after a meal, to save on buying bottled water. Generally, ice cubes in Ecuador can be trusted. Other culprits are shellfish, pork, and undercooked or poorly prepared meats. Popular ceviche carts and seafood restaurants are usually fine, as they have a high turnover of produce, but less frequented places might reheat yesterday's shrimp. A place full of locals is a good sign. You might want to avoid food from street vendors, especially meat and fruit salads. Get in the habit of washing your hands several times a day. Many public restrooms do not have soap, so consider carrying hand sanitizer. Many travelers get away without taking any of these precautions and are just fine; you'll soon find out how careful you have to be!

HIV AND STDS
Human immunodeficiency virus (HIV) is transmitted by direct contact with the bodily fluids of an infected person, most often through sexual contact, intravenous injections, or blood transfusions. There is a high incidence of HIV in Ecuador, especially in coastal regions. This is due to

a combination of poor sex education; the unpopularity of, or lack of access to, condoms; and the prevalence of men having extramarital sex, often at brothels. Sadly, there is such a stigma attached to HIV in Ecuador that many people are too ashamed or afraid to seek treatment or even diagnosis, leading to unnecessary deaths from AIDS. Preventing HIV is straightforward: Do not have unprotected sex or share needles.

For the same reasons, other types of **sexually transmitted diseases (STDs),** such as chlamydia, gonorrhea, syphilis, and herpes are also common. Prevention is the same: Use a condom.

OTHER CONCERNS
CONTRACEPTION AND UNWANTED PREGNANCY

Condoms (*condónes*) and **contraceptive pills** (*píldoras anticonceptivas*) are available at pharmacies (though not in some rural areas, so stock up when you're in a town or city). Condoms are of variable quality in Ecuador, so it's best to buy a recognized brand or bring them from home. The **morning after pill** (*el píldora del día después*) is also available and can be taken effectively up to 72 hours after unprotected sex (though the sooner it is taken, the more effective it is). Remember that the morning after pill does not protect from STDs.

Abortion is illegal in Ecuador, and as a result, unsafe abortion is a leading cause of injury for women and girls. Black market abortion drugs from Argentina are available, but many of them are fake and/or life threatening. Some private clinics do offer clandestine abortions in good faith for $800-1,000, but if something goes wrong, no one will take responsibility. If you find yourself in the difficult situation of an

unwanted pregnancy in Ecuador and come from a country where abortion is legal, it is probably best to cut your trip short and head back home for the procedure. If you need to have an abortion in Ecuador, make discreet inquiries with as many local women as possible before making a decision about where to go. A new helpline set up by Salud Mujeres Ecuador 2.0 (Facebook @SaludMujeresEcuador 2.0) can also provide information (9/9830-1317, 5pm-10m daily).

SUNBURN AND HEATSTROKE

Never underestimate the power of the equatorial sun, even on a cloudy day, wherever you are in Ecuador. The coastal sun is more obviously brutal, whereas seemingly weaker Andean rays can be deceptively burning. A nasty **sunburn** can be very painful and seriously limit further outdoor activities. At the extreme end of the scale, **heatstroke** can be fatal. Limit your time in direct sunshine between 11am and 3pm, especially on the coast. Use high sun protection factor (SPF) sunscreen, sunglasses, and a hat. Drink plenty of water.

ALTITUDE

Most people who visit Quito (at 2,850 m/9,350 ft above sea level) will notice the effects of being at **altitude,** especially breathlessness upon physical exertion. Also common are headaches, fatigue, appetite loss, nausea, a bloated stomach, and sleep disturbance. Take it easy for a couple of days, avoid alcohol, drink plenty of water, and you should acclimatize. Then, if you're planning on going higher, take it gradually if you can, increasing sleeping elevation by no more than 500 meters (1,600 ft) per day. Acetazolamide can be used to assist with acclimatization but should not replace gradual ascent.

The symptoms mentioned are signs of **acute mountain sickness** (AMS), the least serious of three altitude illnesses. The other two, **high-altitude cerebral edema** (HACE) and **high-altitude pulmonary edema** (HAPE), require immediate descent and emergency medical treatment. Signs of HACE include confusion, altered consciousness, and incoordination. Signs of HAPE include increasing breathlessness, breathlessness lying flat, cough (initially dry then wet), chest tightness, and blood-tinged sputum. These illnesses are just two of many reasons why you should only attempt very high altitude expeditions with a licensed guide, who will be trained in dealing with them.

PHARMACIES, DOCTORS, AND HOSPITALS

Provided you speak some Spanish, **pharmacies** in Ecuador can often be trusted to recommend treatments and medicines for minor ailments that require a prescription back home. However, if your problem is more serious, you need the expertise of a **doctor.** Ask around locally for a recommendation, as there are some charlatans out there. An appointment with a local private doctor might be $20; check beforehand to avoid any surprises. Take a Spanish speaker with you if you don't speak the language. The doctor will probably write you out a prescription for some kind of medication, which is usually economical, from the local pharmacy. Make sure to look everything up on the Internet before purchasing anything. This author was once prescribed a drug which, upon further investigation, turned out to be "licensed for veterinary use only in the majority of countries." If you're not sure, get a second opinion from another doctor.

If you think you are being prescribed too many drugs, you might be right. Some dodgy doctors are in cahoots with shady pharmacists to prescribe and sell unnecessary drugs and split the profits between them. If a doctor gives you a long prescription and then a "special offer" flyer for a specific pharmacy nearby, there is a good chance that something fishy is going on. This is why it's a good idea to ask around locally and get a few recommendations for the same doctor before making an appointment.

Health care at public hospitals is free for everyone, including visitors. Bear in mind that you may have a long wait to see a doctor, facilities are usually basic, and bedside manner is generally nonexistent. You (or a friend) will have to go to the closest pharmacy to purchase any medication that is not held in the hospital, but these items are usually inexpensive. In an emergency, consider taking a taxi to the closest private hospital or clinic, or at least the public hospital in the nearest big town. For any complex medical issue, it's best to go private. Good health care isn't cheap, which is why it's a good idea to have adequate insurance. Private hospitals will demand a credit card guarantee for admission. Be ready to pay up front, even if you have insurance coverage. Make sure to get a detailed, comprehensive receipt—in English, if possible—for making a claim.

Dental care is economical and generally good quality. If you're coming from a country where it's prohibitively expensive, consider making an appointment with a recommended dentist in Ecuador; you might save yourself hundreds or even thousands of dollars.

POST-TRAVEL REMINDERS

Pay close attention to your health for at least six months after your trip, since many exotic diseases have long incubation periods. Symptoms may resemble other illnesses, such as the flu, causing doctors unfamiliar with tropical medicine to misdiagnose. If you have any mysterious symptoms, tell your doctor where you've been— a fever in particular should call for a blood test.

CRIME

On the whole, Ecuador is a safe place to visit, and the majority of travelers experience no difficulties with security. Outside of the cities, violent crime is infrequent. It is, however, worth being aware of the risks and taking precautions to mitigate them. There are more thefts and assaults during public holidays (*feriados*), due to a lot of people moving around and high alcohol consumption, so be extra vigilant during these times.

The information in this section is current at the time of writing. Before your trip, especially if traveling to known areas of unrest (see *Danger Spots*), it's recommended to check for up-to-date security advice on the websites of the U.S. Department of State's **Bureau of Consular Affairs** (www.travel.state.gov) and the **British Foreign Office** (www.fco.gov.uk/travel). U.S. citizens can register with the Department of State for free before taking a trip (http://travelregistration.state.gov), so that their information is on file in case of an emergency.

THEFT AND ROBBERY

Pickpocketing and **opportunistic theft** are by far the most common crimes against visitors, and the most preventable. Muggings also happen but are less frequent. Watch out for distraction techniques that allow pickpockets to go to work (e.g., spillages, staged fights, and pushing or shoving). Be especially alert in cities, on public transport, in crowded areas and at popular tourist attractions. In these places, especially on public transport, strap your backpack to your front. If you have valuables in there, don't keep them in easily accessible pockets, but at the bottom of the main section. Don't keep anything of value in your pockets. Don't wear expensive jewelry or a valuable watch (consider not bringing these to Ecuador). For any valuables that you do bring with you (cell phone, tablet, camera, MP3 player, etc.), write a list of the models and serial numbers and keep one copy with you and another back at home. Keep your cell phone out of sight. If you need to look at your phone (as this author constantly had to, for online maps), don't do it while walking along the street. Find somewhere to stop, have a careful look around, and then briefly consult your phone. In cities, you might be better off asking directions or having a printed map.

Don't carry large amounts of money. Have some emergency cash hidden away somewhere. It's a good idea to have a small purse with small denominations so that you don't reveal the whereabouts of your main wallet when paying small amounts like bus fares and snacks. If you have a debit card and a credit card, consider taking one out with you and leaving the other back at your hotel. Carry a color copy of your passport, including the visa entry stamp page, and keep the original safe. If your hostel or hotel has a security box (*caja fuerte* or *caja de seguridad*), you can leave valuables locked away while you explore. If there is no safe but your accommodations are secure and trustworthy, you may choose to leave valuables padlocked in your backpack and locked in your room.

Probably the most common way for visitors to fall victim to theft is to store their belongings in the overhead compartment on a bus; these are easy pickings for thieves. Don't leave any valuables in your main luggage, which will be stored under the bus. Keep anything of value in your day pack or handbag and hold it on your lap. If you put it on the floor in front of your seat, make sure that the person behind you can't access it. Putting it between your feet with a strap wound around your leg should do the trick.

Much more sinister are **"express kidnappings"** (*secuestro express*), where rogue taxi drivers briefly abduct passengers, relieve them of their valuables, and force them to take cash out of an ATM (or threaten them into revealing the PIN number and hold them while accomplices empty their account). Victims are usually released unharmed, but these incidents are terrifying and can turn violent. These robberies are fairly common in Quito, especially at night. To avoid this kind of incident, ask your hotel, restaurant, or bar to call you a radio (prebooked) taxi. If you have a cell phone, save the number of a reliable taxi company and call one yourself. If a radio taxi isn't available, airports, bus terminals, large supermarkets, and expensive hotels generally have taxi ranks with registered drivers. Look for the Transporte Seguro logo, meaning that

video cameras, panic buttons, and GPS should be installed. Check for the cameras when you get in; there should be one on the right of the dashboard and one in the back. They are spherical with a ring of red lights that should be visible at night if the camera is working. The panic buttons are on either side of the car between the front and back seats. If they are activated, the video and audio footage from inside the taxi will be streamed to the police and the GPS tracker activated. If you decide to flag down a city taxi at night and discover there is no camera, feel free to say "*no gracias, no tiene camera.*" Other signs of a legitimate taxi include the municipality registration number sticker displayed on the windscreen and doors; the orange license plates; or the new white plates with an orange strip on the top. The driver should also have an ID, usually on the back of the driver's seat.

Also fairly common is the **use of drugs to subdue robbery victims.** This technique is usually employed in areas with bars and nightclubs. Don't accept anything from a stranger, including food, drinks, leaflets, perfume samples, telephone cards, or cigarettes, no matter how friendly or well-dressed they appear. These items may be covered with a substance known as *scopolamine,* which is absorbed through the skin and leaves victims in a subdued, compliant state. The most frequent targets of this kind of crime are young men on nights out. A number of local men died in 2018 as a result of these robberies.

Armed robbery is not unheard of, particularly in Quito. Robberies have also been reported at some remote hiking areas known to be frequented by tourists. If you are confronted by an armed robber, hand over your valuables without discussion or resistance. Aside from keeping valuables out of sight, the best defense is to walk confidently and stay alert. In cities at night, stay on the main, well-lit, populated streets in the center. Pay attention to your gut instincts: If something tells you to avoid a certain street or leave a certain area, do it.

The Ecuador District Attorney's Office (Fiscalia General) now has an English online tool for tourists to report robbery, theft, and loss of belongings and documents: www.fiscalia.gob.ec/denuncias-on-line-para-turistas.

SEXUAL ASSAULT

Unwelcome attention in the street is common in Ecuador but rarely turns into anything more sinister. Sexual assaults and rape are not unheard of, however. Women should avoid walking on beaches late at night, even in pairs. Follow the rest of the advice in this section about staying safe in cities and taxis. Be especially alert around public holidays. Don't leave any drinks unattended or accept drinks from strangers.

If the worst happens and you are attacked or raped, you may not receive much help from police. It is worth filing a report, however, especially if you can describe your attacker(s). Women's health clinics (*clínicas de la mujer*) in larger cities can provide specialized treatment and gather evidence for the police report. The morning after pill (*el píldora del día después*) is available from most pharmacies and should be taken as soon as possible in the case of rape.

DRUGS

Most of the foreigners in jail in Ecuador are there for drug offenses, usually cocaine related. If you're caught with drugs, don't expect much support from your embassy or the Ecuadorian legal system. Jails are often hellholes, the judicial process can take years, and penalties are steep. Steer clear.

DANGER SPOTS

Most of Ecuador can be roamed freely and relatively safely, taking the precautions already mentioned in this section. However, there are some areas which should be avoided, or should only be visited with the utmost precaution.

The northern part of Esmeraldas province is probably Ecuador's most dangerous region, and travelers are advised to completely avoid the area north of the city of Esmeraldas. The Colombian border zone has long been a hotbed for drug traffickers and FARC splinter groups (often one and the same) and was the setting for two car bomb attacks against military targets in early 2018, leaving four soldiers dead and 39 people wounded. In March 2018, two journalists from a leading newspaper who were investigating the attacks were kidnapped, along with their driver, by a dissident drug-trafficking faction. The three men were subsequently killed when the Ecuadorian government refused the kidnappers' demands to release imprisoned gang members and end anti-narcotics cooperation with Colombia. A month later, the same gang kidnapped and killed an Ecuadorian couple. While these events happened in or near the border town of San Lorenzo, the violence has also spread farther south. In April 2018 a homemade explosive was detonated in the town of Viche, 150 kilometers (90 mi) south of the border and only 50 kilometers (31 mi) from Esmeraldas city, on one of the main roads connecting the highlands to various popular beach destinations. In response to these incidents, President Moreno has boosted security for the region, sending 12,000 soldiers and police to combat drug gangs. Travelers are advised to completely avoid the area north of the city of Esmeraldas.

Other provinces that neighbor Colombia are Carchi and Sucumbíos, and the U.K. Foreign Office recommends avoiding the 20-kilometer (12-mi) strip of land that runs alongside the border, with the exception of the official crossing town of Tulcán, which is considered safe. However, there are destinations that fall within the exclusion zone that you may decide are worth the risk to visit. The general consensus in Ecuador is that the recommendation to avoid Lago Agrio, for example, is out of date. This author, a lone female traveler, felt safe enough to use it as a base from which to visit the surrounding Amazon communities, but was careful to not stray from the city center or to go out after 8pm. Similarly, the beautiful El Ángel Ecological Reserve in Carchi province falls within the exclusion zone but was a highlight of the northern Sierra region.

The situation in these provinces can change quickly, and travelers are advised to monitor the U.K. Foreign Office website (www.fco.gov.uk/travel) for the latest developments.

Drunken street violence, noticeably absent from the vast majority of the country, is present in Quito's La Mariscal and the northern coastal towns of Canoa and Atacames. All three are also high-risk areas for robbery and sexual assault.

Many midsized towns have very specific areas that are best avoided after dark, often around markets. These have been indicated in this book wherever local people indicated they exist. It's a good idea to ask your hotel about any places to avoid, especially if you're planning on exploring on foot.

IF SOMETHING HAPPENS

In an emergency, call 911 for police, ambulance, or the fire service. It's worth bearing in mind that Ecuadorian police do not provide the same safety net that those of us from many European countries are accustomed to. Some police are helpful and honest. The tourist police in Quito are a good example. They respond quickly and in good faith to calls for assistance. However, generally speaking, corruption and inefficiency are rife. If you are in Ecuador for a while, it may be a good idea to have someone local to call in an event of an emergency, as the police may not show up. Choose someone who will answer their phone at any time of day or night.

If you are a victim of crime, head to the nearest police station to report it, even if just for insurance purposes. You may be redirected to the public prosecutor (*fiscalia*) to file a report (*denuncia*). If your bank cards have been stolen, call your bank immediately to block them. If your passport is lost or stolen, contact your embassy by phone or in person in Quito. Your embassy may also be able to help if you need emergency funds to get home or a lawyer. If the unthinkable happens and you are dealing with a fatality, embassies can also be extremely helpful in notifying the deceased's family back home and making other arrangements.

NATURAL DISASTERS

Ecuador is situated in an area of intense seismic activity. Aftershocks are still being felt following the April 2016 earthquake, which measured 7.8 on the Richter scale. In the event of a natural disaster, you should monitor the social media channels of the Ecuadorean National Geophysical Institute (www.igepn.edu.ec) and the National Service for Risk and Emergency Management (www.gestionderiesgos.gob.ec) (both Spanish only) and follow the advice of local authorities.

ROAD SAFETY

Ecuador has one of the highest rates of road accidents in Latin America, mainly due to careless driving, speeding, badly maintained vehicles, mobile phone use, and drunk driving. As with crime, road accidents are more frequent on public holidays. Apart from asking drivers to slow down ("*¿Es posible conducer mas despacio por favor?*"), there isn't a lot that visitors can do to mitigate this risk.

OCEAN SAFETY

People drown every year off Ecuador's beaches, many of which have strong currents and riptides. There is a lack of funding for lifeguards, so it's often local surfers who end up pulling people out of the water when they get into trouble. The main thing to remember is that a riptide is a narrow channel of water that is heading out to sea, so if you get stuck in one, swim parallel to the shore and you will quickly escape it. If there are red flags on the beach, don't go in the ocean.

TOILETS

There are public toilets in bus stations and in many tourist areas, often signposted SSHH (*servicios higiénicos*). You usually have to pay $0.15-0.25 to enter, which includes a handful of toilet paper from the attendant. In free public bathrooms and gas stations, there will probably be no toilet paper, so it's a good idea to carry your own at all times. This goes in the wastepaper bin, not flushed down the toilet. There may or may not be soap.

Travel Tips

WHAT TO PACK

It can be a challenge packing for Ecuador. For the Sierra, bring layers, including warm sweaters. For high altitude towns and cities such as Quito, you will be glad of a warm jacket or coat in the evenings. You'll also need something waterproof. A lightweight plastic poncho is a good idea, as it can also cover your day pack (some are as thin as a garbage bag and roll up very small; they're very cheap and fine for moderate day hikes). Bring a comfortable pair of shoes or sneakers and broken-in hiking boots if you plan to trek.

Anywhere you go, you will need sunglasses and sunblock (cheaper and better quality if brought from home). A hat or baseball cap is also a good idea; the midday sun can be brutal. Insect repellent is widely available in Ecuador, though bring lemon eucalyptus or citronella oil from home if you're looking to avoid DEET.

Bring a flashlight in case of power

outages. A water bottle that filters and purifies water is an excellent investment and will enable you to safely drink water from the faucet, even rivers and streams. This will save you from buying water (and thus creating plastic waste) or constantly looking for places to fill your bottle. Ecuador can be noisy, so a few pairs of earplugs will probably save your sanity. If you have the budget, consider noise-canceling headphones. Remember power adaptors to charge your devices. These are available in airports, but expensive. A padlock for your main luggage (one for each zip) is also sensible.

Finally, bring small-denomination U.S. dollar bills. Leave room in your luggage for souvenirs if you like to visit markets.

MONEY
CASH AND CARDS
The currency in Ecuador is the U.S. dollar. Outside the international airports, it's not easy to change money in Ecuador, so it's best to bring dollars with you or get money out of ATMs once in the country. If you are bringing cash from home, make sure to get small-denomination bills. It can be almost impossible to find a store that will accept a $50 or $100 bill. A lot of vendors will have trouble changing even a $20 when it comes to small purchases. There are ATMs in all cities and most towns that accept Visa and Mastercard. Most reliable for international cards are Banco Pichincha and Banco Internacional. Banco Guayaquil works for most cards but not all. The locations of these ATMs can be found on Google Maps, so check ahead of time if a destination has a cash machine, especially if you're headed to a small town or village. There are few ATMs on the Galápagos Islands.

Many ATMs in smaller towns have a $100 withdrawal limit per transaction, so for $300 you may have to withdraw three lots of $100. If you need a large amount of cash, you may need to get it out over several days, due to withdrawal limits with your bank and/or the dispensing (this author pays $2.50 per transaction). It is not uncommon for ATMs to be out of service, so it's a good idea to have enough cash on you for a couple of days, or you may end up having to make a quick dash to the nearest big town. Remember to tell your bank in advance that you are traveling, otherwise they may block your card if you try to use it abroad.

Outside major supermarkets and high-end stores, hotels, restaurants, and travel agencies, credit cards are not widely accepted in Ecuador, except to get cash out of ATMs. Just because an establishment sports a credit-card sticker doesn't mean it necessarily takes them; always ask. It's best to use cash wherever possible and have a credit card as a backup.

Money Transfers
Western Union is widely used all over Ecuador and there are branches everywhere. If you need to send money to someone, you will need their name exactly as it appears on their ID and the name of the town where they are located. Go into any Western Union branch, present your ID, and hand over the cash, plus the transfer fee (it costs around $6 to send $50). You will be given a code, which you send to the person receiving the money. They then take the code and their ID to a Western Union branch and withdraw the cash. Some jungle lodges and hotels (especially those requiring deposits to secure high-season bookings) may request advance payment via

Western Union. Make sure to keep hold of the receipt in case of any issues.

Tipping

A *propina* (tip) isn't required or expected, but it doesn't take much out of your pocket and can make someone's day. Remember that most restaurant and bar staff earn minimum wage ($11/day) or even less if their employer has hired them informally (sadly, a situation faced by many Venezuelan immigrants). Any tip, even a dollar or two, will be appreciated. Some establishments have a tip jar at the cash register, which will get shared among the staff. Fancier restaurants add 10 percent for *servicio* (service) and the 12 percent IVA (value-added tax). It's not unheard of for the restaurant owner to pocket the service charge, so if your server has been particularly helpful, it will certainly be appreciated to leave an extra tip in cash. Airport and hotel porters should be tipped $0.50 or $1, as should the people who watch your car if you've parked in the street. Taxi drivers are often very patient about waiting outside a store, providing a wealth of local information, or helping load and unload bags, and will certainly appreciate a tip for these efforts. Guides are tipped depending on the cost and length of your stay or trip, from a couple of dollars to over ten in luxury jungle lodges and on Galápagos cruises.

Taxes

Shops, hotels, and restaurants must charge a 12 percent IVA (value-added tax), which should be noted separately on the *cuenta* (bill). When making reservations in advance for hostels and hotels, ask if the price quoted includes this charge, as many people receive a surprise when paying the bill.

Wherever it was known, IVA has been included in the accommodation prices quoted in this book.

Receipts

When paying for things, especially in supermarkets, the cashier may ask you *"¿Con datos o consumidor final?"* If you would like your printed receipt to have your name and ID number on it say *"con datos"* ("with data"). Ecuadorians who are planning on submitting the receipt to the tax office will request this. For most visitor purposes, *"consumidor final"* is fine and quicker to process.

Budgeting

Ecuador is a comparatively inexpensive place to visit (with the exception of the Galápagos Islands). Serious budget travelers can get by for under $25 per day, staying in dorms, traveling by bus, and eating set meals. If you have $50 per day, you will be able to stay in a private room, eat at tourist restaurants, have a few drinks, and factor in some taxi travel.

Generally speaking, dormitory beds cost $8-10, though they are found only in the major tourist hubs. Decent single and double rooms are usually $15-25, occasionally as low as $10-12, some with shared bathrooms. Many hostels include breakfast and/or have kitchens so you can prepare your own food. Fresh produce from local markets is good quality and cheap. Most markets also have an economical food court (*patio de comida*) serving basic local fare. A basic breakfast (coffee, bread, jam, eggs) in a café might cost $3. Set lunches (*almuerzos*) in local restaurants are filling and economical ($2.50-3.50), usually consisting of a juice, a soup, and a main course (rice with chicken, fish, or meat, plus a side such as plantain or lentil stew). Less common are set dinners (*meriendas*), following a similar format. A main course in a tourist restaurant might cost $6-9. Cheap, filling street food is everywhere. Vegetarians traveling on a low budget should check *Tips for Vegetarians* in this chapter for meat-free local dishes to avoid more expensive tourist restaurants. Larger cities and tourist towns often have veggie restaurants with set lunches for $3.50-4. A large bottle of local beer is around $3.

The bus is an economical way to travel, with short local journeys usually costing $0.30 and longer distance trips around $1-1.50 per hour. Passing motorists will often offer a ride but may expect a small donation in return, so check in advance if you're very short on funds. A short taxi ride within a town might be $1.50-2.

Volunteering is often an economical way to experience Ecuador and give something back. Most programs cover expenses by charging to participate, but the cost is sometimes minimal. Check out *Volunteering in Ecuador* for some ideas.

TRAVELERS WITH DISABILITIES

After being shot in a 1998 robbery attempt, Ecuador's president, Lenín Moreno, is the world's only currently serving head of state to use a wheelchair. During his time as vice president (2007-2013), he increased the budget for people with disabilities more than fifty-fold and oversaw the initiation of some accessibility infrastructure. Despite these advances, however, Ecuador is still behind the times in making structural changes to address the needs of its own citizens with disabilities, not to mention

visitors. Budget travelers especially may find themselves severely restricted. Many hotels and some tourist attractions with accessible facilities do exist in Ecuador, but getting around is a challenge.

In most cities, sidewalks are narrow, crowded, and uneven (sometimes cobbled). Public buses are not equipped to handle those in wheelchairs, with steep stairs that can be difficult to navigate for those with limited mobility. The Quito trolley system can handle wheelchair passengers, although its near-constant overcrowding makes this better in theory than in practice. Taxi drivers are often helpful, but there are no adapted taxis or rental cars. There are some wheelchair ramps and toilets in international airports, major bus stations, and some gas stations but their presence certainly cannot be relied upon.

A couple of options exist for those with the available budget, such as going with an organized tour. **South America for All** (www.southamericaforall.com) specializes in adapted tours and is recommended. If you prefer to travel independently, you could hire a driver or travel by taxi and take a companion without disabilities with you. **DisabledTravelers.com** (www.disabledtravelers.com) has a directory of companies offering trained, professional travel companions.

There are good online resources for disabled travelers. **Wheelchair Traveling** (http://wheelchairtraveling.com) has some excellent country-specific information about travel in Ecuador, so check there first. The government has created an online tourist guide for visitors with disabilities (http://turismoaccesible.ec) that is available in English. The translation leaves quite a bit to be desired, but

VOLUNTEERING IN ECUADOR

Some organizations offer a range of nationwide volunteer placements, acting as middleman between visitors and the NGO or nonprofit that is seeking volunteers. One good example is the **Yanapuma Foundation** (www.yanapumaspanish.org), which charges a one-off fee of $85 to match volunteers with a variety of pre-screened placements, which includes an orientation in Quito, accompaniment to the placement, and ongoing support throughout. The fee goes toward Yanapuma's work in sustainable development among indigenous and marginalized communities. Another example is **Ecuador Volunteer** (www.ecuadorecovolunteer.org), a volunteer work agency set up by the owner of climbing tour company Ecuador Eco Adventure in Riobamba, who charges no fee for the service. Details of placements are on both organizations' websites.

The following organizations accept volunteers directly. See the websites or contact them for more information about duties, length of placement, accommodations, food, and costs. Many other opportunities exist all over the country; this is just a small selection.

Both **Jatun Sacha** (www.jatunsacha.org) and **Jocotoco** (www.jocotoco.org) have a number of private nature reserves across the country that accept volunteers.

The **Maquipucuna Reserve & Bear Lodge** (www.maquipucuna.org) is the best place in the world to see Andean bears and protects over 6,000 hectares (15,000 acres) of pristine rainforest in one of the earth's top five biodiversity hot spots. In the crater of the Pululahua volcano, the **Pululahua Hostal** (www.pululahuahostal.com) is an eco-hostel, organic farm, and restaurant that uses solar, wind, and biogas energy systems. Just west of the city center, the **Centro Tinku Escuela de Permacultura** (Facebook @centrotinku.escueladepermacultura) is a school that provides workshops on permaculture, bio-construction, agro-ecology, and related topics.

there is information about the accessibility of various tourist attractions, plus a directory of accessible recreational activities, hotels, restaurants, and bars.

In addition to the hotels in the directory, the following have accessible facilities: **Hostería Mandála** (www.hosteriamandala.info) in Puerto López, **La Bicok** (Facebook @ BicokLodge) in Mindo; and **Huasquila Amazon Lodge** (www.huasquila.com) outside Tena. The last even has a lift at the swimming pool and Jacuzzi, and off-road wheelchairs for jungle tours.

WOMEN TRAVELERS

Ecuador is generally a safe country for female travelers, but it is common practice for men to whistle and make comments at women in the street. Foreigners, especially blondes, are often singled out for extra attention. This can be annoying but rarely turns into anything more sinister. How you deal with this is up to you. Ignoring it is the safest strategy. This author sometimes stops and says loudly enough for all passersby to hear *"Señor, las mujeres solo quieren caminar en paz, sabe."* ("Sir, women just want to walk in peace, you know.")

If someone goes as far as to touch you, if there are other people around, the best strategy is probably to say loudly *"No me toques!"* ("Don't touch me!"). Ecuadorians generally want visitors to have a good time in their country and will be horrified at this kind of behavior.

Female travelers may find the central and northern coast more challenging than the south. From Manta and up, there is noticeably more unwelcome attention from men in the street. Women, especially those traveling alone if not accustomed to it, might consider heading to the beach destinations farther south. Montañita is considerably safer than Canoa, where sexual assaults are fairly common but unreported. Women should not walk on any beach late at night. While many genuine relationships occur between visitors and locals, it's wise to remember that the coastal area is home to some men who may not exactly be gigolos but do expect foreign women to pay for everything, from new surfboards to expensive holidays.

Wherever you go, take the usual precautions. Don't leave your drink unattended or accept drinks or anything else from strangers. Particular care needs to be taken around public holidays, due to the influx of people in tourist destinations and high alcohol consumption. See the *Crime* section for general information on staying safe in Ecuador.

Women should not be put off traveling alone in Ecuador. As a blonde lone female traveler, I have been happily exploring Ecuador for nearly a decade, and I feel safe setting out alone for most destinations across the country (see the *Crime* section for any notable exceptions). It's one of reasons I love living here. Off the established tourist trail, I have often been the only visibly foreign person in a town and felt welcomed and comfortable. Walk confidently (even if you don't feel it) and you are much less likely to be a victim of any crime. Meet people with a friendly open manner and a smile, and you will usually get the same in return, which helps you to feel safer anywhere you go.

Lone female travelers should be prepared to respond to questions such as "Where is your husband?" and to be met with incredulity about traveling solo or not having children. How you respond is up to you. I usually take the

opportunity to explain that, for me, motherhood and marriage are not the only valid choices for women and that I have opted to do other things with my life. If the questions make you feel uncomfortable, you could always say *"esa es una pregunta muy personal"* ("that is a very personal question"). If a combination of questions makes you feel unsafe (e.g., "Do you have a boyfriend?" "Where are you going?" and "Where exactly are you staying?"), it's probably best to invent a boyfriend, cut the conversation short, and go somewhere you feel secure (a busy restaurant, for example).

TRAVELING WITH CHILDREN

Ecuador is a great choice for traveling with children. It's safer and more compact than many other Latin American countries. If you're looking for resorts and theme parks, it's probably not the destination for you, but there's plenty of real-world excitement here, in terms of nature, wildlife, and adventure activities. There are lots of easily accessible opportunities to experience different indigenous nationalities as well, with world views very different to the western way of thinking. Many of these peoples live with few economic resources, but not in traumatizing poverty. A visit to Ecuador will provide your kids with plenty of food for thought and likely keep them thinking and questioning long after they return home.

People in Ecuador love children, so families traveling with youngsters will enjoy a warm welcome. If you're hoping to find other gringo families for your kids to play with, you may be out of luck. But, there is noticeably little bullying and social exclusion among Ecuadorian children, who will often play happily with visiting kids who speak no Spanish whatsoever. Outside cities and big towns, many Ecuadorians have the kind of childhood that many of us are nostalgic for: playing in the street with homemade toys, no parents in sight, no fear about "stranger danger" in small tightly knit communities. Older kids will enjoy picking up and learning a few words in Spanish and will be met with a kind audience upon which to practice.

A lack of safety regulations means you'll have to be extra vigilant about things like unexpected holes in the street and hazardous play equipment in parks. Safety seats are generally hard to come by in rental cars (be sure to arrange one ahead of time), and in taxis they're unheard of. Seatbelts in the back are also a rarity. This is, after all, a country where a family of four can blaze across town on a motorcycle with no helmets. Movies on buses are often very violent and/or sexually explicit. Drivers may or may not respond to pleas to put on something more child friendly.

Children pay full fare on buses if they occupy a seat, but they often ride for free if they sit on a parent's lap. The fare for children under 12 years is greatly reduced for domestic flights (perhaps half fare, and they get a seat), while infants under 2 cost around 10 percent of the fare (but they don't get a seat). Many tourist attractions have discounted tickets for children. Changing facilities are rare but sometimes exist in airports and newer bus terminals. Breastfeeding is accepted in public.

LGBTQ TRAVELERS

Although enormous progress has been made with LGBTQ rights in the last 20 years, Ecuador still has a largely conservative and macho culture, and gender queerness continues to be viewed negatively, especially by older generations. LGBTQ travelers are advised to keep a low profile and avoid public displays of affection.

There isn't much of an organized LGBTQ community in Ecuador. Quito has the most developed scene, with several gay clubs. Younger people tend to frequent these, with the older generation preferring more discreet places like gay saunas. Quito has held a pride event every June since 1998, and there is a gay film festival every November. Some hotels specifically state that they are LGBTQ friendly, including Anahi Boutique Hotel (www.anahihotelquito.com/en) in Quito; and the luxury ecological wellness retreat My Sachaji (www.mysachaji.com), just outside Otavalo.

The Nomadic Boys' website (https://nomadicboys.com) has an excellent section on the gay scene in Ecuador (especially Quito), and the Facebook pages @EcuadorGayPride and @OrgulloEcuador are good places to look for upcoming events.

SENIOR TRAVELERS

Age is respected in Ecuador, so senior travelers will generally be treated considerately. Those over 65 are entitled to discounts on bus travel and entrance to most museums and tourist attractions. Inquire in advance about the physical demands of tours, especially at altitude.

TRAVELING WITH PETS

If you're traveling with a really small "handbag-sized" dog, you probably won't encounter too many difficulties getting around, but anything bigger can be a challenge. Many bus

- 911   General emergency number for ambulance, fire, or police
- 131   Ambulance
- 102   Fire
- 101   Police

companies have a No Pets policy or will insist that pets go in the luggage compartment, which is not an option for anyone with the slightest bit of compassion for their animal. Some bus companies can be persuaded if you have a dog crate, offer to buy a ticket for it, and put it on the seat next to you. Buses in rural areas are more open to carrying pets. Taxi drivers might flat-out refuse to carry an animal or will try to insist that it goes in the trunk. Others will accept with no qualms or ask you to carry your pet on your lap. Check in advance whether hotels accepts pets, as policies vary widely.

To bring a pet into Ecuador, check the country-specific entry requirements here: www.pettravel.com. Have all paperwork on hand going through immigration and customs.

COMMUNICATIONS AND MEDIA
TELECOMMUNICATIONS

If you plan to bring your cell phone from home to use during your trip, you will need to first "unlock" it for international use. Once you are in Ecuador you can buy a local SIM card (known locally as a *chip*) for around $5 with one of the local service providers. Of the two main companies, Claro and MoviStar, the former has better coverage and more branches nationwide. At the Quito airport, there is a Claro *chip* vending machine in the airport center across the road. With your SIM card you will be issued an Ecuadorian number and you can add credit (known as *saldo*) to your "account" in newsagents, pharmacies, and supermarkets everywhere. If you use a lot of data, consider creating an online account with Claro (https://miclaro.com.ec) and purchasing a data packet (e.g., 1GB for 30 days for $10). If the site doesn't accept your credit card, you can purchase credit with cash in a store and use your balance for online purchases. Another option is to buy a cheap local cell phone for about $40, but these only have capability for calls and text messages. WhatsApp is widely used in Ecuador. Some rural areas have no cell phone coverage.

If you don't have a cell phone, you can make national and international calls from pay phone booths known as *cabinas,* which are often part of Internet cafés. Per-minute local calls cost about $0.11, domestic calls $0.22. Calling an Ecuadorian cell phone costs $0.25 per minute, while calling North America costs from $0.20, Europe from $0.40, and Australia from $0.80. To make a call within Ecuador, dial 0 followed by the regional prefix code and the seven-digit phone number. In this book, the regional prefix codes come before the slash (/); e.g., if the number is written 6/239-1234, the regional code is 6. Cell phone numbers have a two-digit prefix starting with 9. To call Ecuador from abroad, the international dialing code is 593.

TELEPHONE PREFIXES

Prefixes listed by province, with major cities in parentheses:

Prefix	Region
2	Pichincha (Quito), Santo Domingo de los Tsáchilas (Santo Domingo)
3	Bolívar (Guaranda), Cotopaxi (Latacunga), Chimborazo (Riobamba), Pastaza (Puyo), Tungurahua (Ambato, Baños)
4	Guayas (Guayaquil), Santa Elena (Salinas)
5	Los Ríos, Manabí (Manta, Portoviejo, Bahía de Caráquez), Galápagos (Puerto Ayora, Baquerizo Moreno)
6	Carchi (Tulcán), Esmeraldas (Atacames), Imbabura (Otavalo, Ibarra), Napo (Tena), Orellana (Coca), Sucumbíos (Lago Agrio)
7	Azuay (Cuenca), Cañar (Azogues), El Oro (Machala), Loja (Loja), Morona-Santiago (Macas), Zamora-Chinchipe (Zamora)
93, 95, 97, 98, 99	cell phones

Internet

There are Internet cafés or *cybers* in every town and most villages. Many are open 8am-10pm daily and charge $1-1.50 per hour. Quality of equipment and Internet speed vary widely. Most offer printing, copying, and scanning services. *Cybers* can get busy with local kids at school closing time (around 2:30pm). For the at sign (@), press Alt 64.

Wi-Fi is available in hotels, hostels, and restaurants all over the country but is often unreliable. Outside the main cities and tourist destinations, digital nomads may struggle to find decent connection (especially for video calls). If you need the Internet for work, it's a good idea to have a mobile device and purchase a data package to fall back on. In very rural areas, there may be no cell phone signal or Internet. Many buses claim to have Wi-Fi, but most do not. There is free Wi-Fi in some public places such as main squares; keep an eye out for signs. Monthly Internet is expensive in Ecuador ($40-50 for a basic service).

Mail

Most people in Ecuador do not have a mailbox, house number, or street address. To send something within the country, head to a branch of the national postal service, **Correos Ecuador** (www.correosdelecuador.gob.ec) or the private courier company **Servientrega** (www.servientrega.com.ec). Items can be sent to another branch for collection by the recipient or to a nonresidential building that has an address (a large hotel or a lawyer's office, for example). Long-term visitors could rent a mailbox at the local branch of Correos Ecuador for an annual fee (around $25). To send something overseas, it's best to use an international courier such as FedEx, DHL, or UPS. Any packages that come in from abroad are routinely opened by customs and may be liable to customs fees. There is almost no online shopping in Ecuador (no Amazon deliveries, for example).

WEIGHTS AND MEASURES
ELECTRICITY

As in North America, electricity in Ecuador is 120 volts, 60 hertz alternating current, and plugs are type A (two flat prongs) and type B (two flat prongs with a third grounding prong). Power outages are fairly common, even in major cities, and it's a good idea to bring a surge protector for expensive equipment.

TIME
The Ecuadorian mainland is five hours earlier than UTC or Greenwich mean time, the same as North American eastern standard time. Because days and nights on the equator are almost the same duration year-round (with sunrise around 6am and sunset around 6:30pm), daylight saving time is not used in Ecuador.

BUSINESS HOURS
Typical business hours are 8am or 9am to 5pm or 6pm Monday-Friday, with a lunch break 1pm-2pm. Banks usually open on Saturday mornings, but government offices and most tour agencies do not. Many small businesses keep fairly irregular opening hours.

TOURIST INFORMATION
MAPS
Both **International Travel Maps** (www.itmb.com) and **Longitude Maps** (www.longitudemaps.com) offer a variety of Ecuador maps that can be ordered online. In Ecuador, the best resource is the **Instituto Geográfico Militar** (IGM, www.igm.gob.ec), where maps can be purchased at the office in Quito or online (see *Servicios* on the IGM website). Maps of city centers and popular attractions are available at tourist offices nationwide. If you have a smartphone you can download the application Maps.me (https://maps.me), which can be used offline and is a great tool for hikers.

TOURIST OFFICES
Most towns and cities have official tourist offices, often called iTur. These are usually located in the municipal building on the main square or at major bus terminals. Most are only open Monday to Friday. Some are extremely helpful, with English-speaking staff and excellent websites with information about attractions, activities, accommodations, restaurants, tour agencies, etc. Others only really want to hand out maps. The Ministry of Tourism can be found online (www.ecuador.travel, www.turismo.gob.ec) and on Facebook (@MinisterioTurismoEcuador).

RESOURCES

Glossary

aguardiente: sugarcane alcohol

aguas termales: hot springs

almuerzo: lunch

artesanías: handicrafts

cabaña: cabin

cabina: pay phone, often inside an Internet café

camioneta: pickup truck taxi, usually white

campesino: rural resident

canelazo: hot, sweet alcoholic drink made with sugarcane

cc or centro comercial: shopping center or mall

chicha: drink, often made from manioc, sometimes fermented with human saliva

chiva: open-sided bus with wooden seats, also known as a *ranchero*

colectivo: shared form of transport, often a converted pickup truck with seats in the bed

con datos: printed receipt with the name and ID number of the purchaser, for tax purposes

consumidor final: printed receipt without the name and ID number of the purchaser

cordillera: mountain range

criollo: originally a person of pure Spanish descent born in the colonies but now applied to anything traditional, especially food

curandero/a: medicinal healer

cyber: Internet café

denuncia: legal complaint or police report

ecuavolley: the local version of volleyball

feria: fair, usually selling artisanal goods or food

feriado: public holiday

gringo: term for North Americans, but applied to most white foreigners; not particularly derogatory

hacienda: farm or country estate

helado: literally means "iced"; can refer to ice cream, sorbet, or a cold coconut to drink (*coco helado*)

indígena: indigenous person (note that *indio* is considered insulting)

malecón: riverside or seaside promenade

merienda: supper, also used for cheap set-menu dinners

mestizo: person of mixed indigenous and European blood

minga: community voluntary work

mirador: viewpoint

municipio: town hall or city hall

obraje: textile workshop

Panamericana: Pan-American Highway

páramo: high-elevation grasslands

pasillo: Ecuador's national music

peña: bar with traditional live music

Oriente: the Amazon region

ranchero: open-sided bus with wooden seats, also known as a *chiva*

saldo: mobile phone credit

Sierra: Andean region

SS HH: sign for public restroom (*servicios higiénicos*)

terminal terrestre: bus terminal

tienda: shop

tramites: any kind of bureaucratic procedures; e.g., opening a bank account, obtaining visa extension

tsantsa: shrunken head

yucca: cassava or manioc

Spanish Phrasebook

PRONUNCIATION

Once you learn them, Spanish pronunciation rules—in contrast with English—don't change. There are 27 letters in the Spanish alphabet: the familiar English 26, plus ñ. Every letter is pronounced. The capitalized syllables below are stressed.

VOWELS

a as 'ah' in "hah": *agua* AH-gwah (water), *pan* PAHN (bread), *casa* KAH-sah (house)

e as 'e' in "bet:" *mesa* MEH-sah (table), *tela* TEH-lah (cloth), *de* DEH (of, from)

i as 'ee' in "need": *diez* DEE-ehss (ten), *comida* ko-MEE-dah (meal), *fin* FEEN (end)

o two sounds: either the short "o" sound in British English "hot": *comer* KO-mare (eat); or like a longer "oh," as in *poco* POH-koh (a bit). *Ocho* has both sounds: O-choh (eight).

u as 'oo' in "cool": *uno* OO-noh (one) and *usted* oos-TEHD (you); when it follows a *q*, the u is silent; when it follows an *h* or has an umlaut (ü), it's pronounced like "w."

CONSONANTS

b, f, k, l, m, n, p, q, s, r, t, w, x, y, z pronounced almost as in English; **h** is silent; **v** is pronounced the same as **b**

c as 'k' in "keep": *casa* KAH-sah (house); when it precedes *e* or *i*, c is pronounced as 's' in "sit": *cerveza* sayr-VAY-sah (beer), *encima* ehn-SEE-mah (on top of).

g as 'g' in "gift" when it precedes *a, o, u*, or a consonant: *gato* GAH-toh (cat), *hago* AH-goh (I do, make); otherwise, g is pronounced as 'h' in "hat": *giro* HEE-roh (money order), *gente* HEHN-tay (people)

j as 'h' in "has": *jueves* HOOAY-vays (Thursday), *mejor* meh-HOR (better)

ll as 'y' in "yes": *toalla* toh-AH-yah (towel), *ellos* AY-yohs (they, them), *llamas* YAH-mahs (llamas)

ñ as 'ny' in "canyon": *año* AH-nyo (year), *señor* SEH-nyor (Mr., sir)

rr like a Scottish rolled 'r.' This distinguishes *perro* (dog) from *pero* (but) and *carro* (car) from *caro* (expensive). Many foreigners have particular trouble with this sound. If you do, try to use a different word; e.g., *auto* for car.

STRESSED SYLLABLES

The rule for where to put the stress when pronouncing a word is simple: If a word ends in a vowel, an *n*, or an *s*, stress the next-to-last syllable; if not, stress the last syllable.

Pronounce *gracias* GRAH-seeahs (thank you), *orden* OHR-dayn (order), and *carretera* kah-ray-TAY-rah (highway) with stress on the next-to-last syllable.

Otherwise, accent the last syllable: *venir* veh-NEER (to come), *ferrocarril* feh-roh-cah-REEL (railroad), *edad* eh-DAHD (age).

Exceptions to the accent rule are always marked with an accent sign: (á, é, í, ó, or ú), such as *teléfono* teh-LAY-foh-noh (telephone), *jabón* hah-BON (soap), and *rápido* RAH-pee-doh (rapid).

BASIC AND COURTEOUS EXPRESSIONS

Most Spanish-speaking people consider formalities important. When approaching anyone for information or any other reason, do not forget the appropriate salutation—good morning, good evening, and so on.

Hello. *Hola.*

Good morning. *Buenos días.*

Good afternoon. *Buenas tardes.*

Good evening. *Buenas noches.*

How are you? *¿Cómo está?* (formal)
¿Cómo estás? ¿Qué tal? (informal)

Very well, thank you. *Muy bien, gracias.*

OK; good. *Bien.*

So-so. *Más o menos.*

Not OK; bad. *Mal.*

And you? *¿Y usted?* (formal) *¿Y tu?* (informal)

Thank you. *Gracias.*

Thank you very much. *Muchas gracias.*

You're very kind. *Muy amable.*

You're welcome. *De nada.*

Good-bye. *Ciao* ("CHOW") or *Adios.*

See you later. *Hasta luego.*

please *por favor*

yes *sí*

no *no*

I don't know. *No sé.*

My name is . . . *Me llamo . . .*

What is your name? *¿Cómo se llama usted?*

Pleased to meet you. *Mucho gusto* or *Encantado* (more formal and stronger).

Just a moment, please. *Momentito, por favor.*

Excuse me, please (when you're trying to get attention). *Disculpe* or *Con permiso* (for moving past someone).

Sorry (when you've made an error). *Disculpe* or *Lo siento* (stronger and more formal).

Enjoy your meal. *Buen provecho.*

How do you say . . . in Spanish? *¿Cómo se dice . . . en español?*

Do you speak English? *¿Habla usted inglés?*

I don't speak Spanish well. *No hablo bien el español.*

I don't understand. *No entiendo.*

Could you speak more slowly please? *¿Podría hablar más despacio por favor?*

ECUADORIAN SLANG

Ecuadorians love slang (*jerga*, pronounced "yerga") and creative word play. Phrases come and go, some of them only used in a particular town or village. A few of the most popular, longstanding, non-offensive slang terms are listed below. Dropping these into casual conversation is a simple way to delight local people and make them laugh.

pana a close friend, a buddy

¡Tranquilo! Don't worry about it! (Use *¡Tranquila!* when talking to a woman.) Can be shortened to *¡Tranqui!*

bacán/chévere cool

buenazo awesome

The suffix *-azo* means "big" or "very"; e.g., *olazo* to refer to a big wave, *solazo* to mean "strong sun." The suffix *isimo* also means "very"; e.g., *riquisimo* (very delicious), *bacánsisimo/chéverisimo* (very cool). The suffix *-ita/-ito* is used to mean "little" or just to soften what you're saying; e.g., *animalito* (little animal), *panita* (affectionate way to say "buddy").

¡Que bestia! "How crazy!" or "That's wild!" (literally, "What a beast!")

¡Habla serio! Be serious! Used like "You must be kidding me!"

¡Chuta! Damn! Shoot! (Not be confused with "*¡Chucha!*" which is offensive and refers to female genitals)

¡Que huevada! ¡La misma huevada! What cr*p! The same old cr*p! (mildly offensive)

pendejo/a idiot (mildly offensive)

¡Qué asco! Gross!

Farra party; can also be used as a verb, "*farrear*," meaning "to party"

Chupar to drink alcohol (literally "to suck")

chuchaqui hungover (from Quechua)

¡Dale! A bit like "hit it!" (when encouraging someone to catch a wave, for example). Used without emphasis, *dale* can be used to mean "ok, I agree."

¡De ley! ¡De una! Absolutely!

¡Pilas! A bit like "look sharp!" or "let's go!" Can also be used as an adjective; i.e., *Tengo que estar pilas mañana* (I have to be sharp tomorrow).

¡Ya sabe! You know it!

Perhaps the most Ecuadorian slang word is imported from English: *man* translates as "guy"; e.g., *el man* (the guy) or *estos manes* (these guys). It can also be used to refer to a woman; e.g., *la man* (the woman), and can be suffixed with *-ito/-ita*, as in *este mancito* (this little guy).

TERMS OF ADDRESS

When in doubt, use the formal *usted* (you) as a form of address.

I *yo*
you (formal) *usted*
you (familiar) *tu*
he/him *él*
she/her *ella*
we/us *nosotros*
you (plural) *ustedes*
they/them *ellos* (all males or mixed gender); *ellas* (all females)
Mr., sir *señor*
Mrs., Madam *señora*
Miss, young woman *señorita*
wife *esposa*
husband *esposo*
friend *amigo* (male); *amiga* (female)
boyfriend/girlfriend *novio/novia*
son/daughter *hijo/hija*
brother/sister *hermano/hermana*
father/mother *padre/madre*
grandfather/grandmother *abuelo/ abuela*

GETTING AROUND

Where is . . .? *¿Dónde está …?*
How far is it to . . .? *¿Que tan lejos está …?*

(very) near/far *(muy) cerca/lejos*
How many blocks? *¿Cuántas cuadras?*
the bus station *la terminal terrestre*
the bus stop *la parada de bus*
the ticket office *la boletería*
I'd like a ticket to . . . *Quisiera un boleto a …* (*un ticket* is also common)
return *ida y vuelta*
Where is this bus going? *¿A dónde va este bús?*
What time does it leave? *¿A que hora sale?*
From which platform? *¿De que anden?*
Stop here, please. *Pare aquí, por favor.*
the taxi stand *la parada de taxis*
take me to … *llévame a …*
the boat *el barco/el bote/la lancha*
the airport *el aeropuerto*
reservation *reservación*
baggage *equipaje*
the entrance *la entrada*
the exit *la salida*
from . . . to . . . *de…a…*
by/through *por*
from *desde*
the right *la derecha*
the left *la izquierda*
straight ahead *derecho; recto*
in front *en frente*
beside *al lado*
behind *atrás*
the corner *la esquina*
the stoplight *el semáforo*
a turn *una vuelta*
here *aquí*
over here *por acá*
there *allí*
over there *por allá*
street/avenue *calle/avenida*
highway *carretera*
bridge *puente*
address *dirección*
north/south/east/west *norte/sur/ este/oeste*

ACCOMMODATIONS

Do you have a room for tonight? *¿Tiene una habitación para esta noche?*

May I (may we) see it? *¿Puedo (podemos) verlo?*

What is the rate? *¿Cuál es el precio?*

Is that your best rate? *¿Es su mejor precio?*

Is there something cheaper? *¿Hay algo más económico?*

discount *descuento*

Does it include breakfast? *¿Incluye el desayuno?*

a single room *una habitación sencilla* or *individual*

a twin room *una habitación con dos camas*

a room with a double bed *una habitación matrimonial*

with private bath *con baño privado*

with shared bath *con baño compartido*

hot water *agua caliente*

shower *ducha*

towels *toallas*

soap *jabón*

toilet paper *papel higiénico*

blanket *cobija; manta*

sheets *sábanas*

air-conditioning *aire acondicionado*

fan *ventilador*

key *llave*

manager *gerente*

FOOD

I'm hungry/thirsty. *Tengo hambre/sed.*

breakfast *desayuno*

lunch *almuerzo*

daily lunch special *el menú del día*

dinner *cena*

It's really delicious! *¡Es muy rico!*

the bill *la cuenta*

menu *carta*

order *pedido*

glass *vaso*

fork *tenedor*

knife *cuchillo*

spoon *cuchara*

napkin *servilleta*

drink *bebida*

coffee *café*

tea *té* or *agua aromatica*

carbonated water *agua con gas*

noncarbonated water *agua sin gas*

beer *cerveza*

wine *vino*

milk *leche*

juice *jugo*

sugar *azúcar*

cheese *queso*

eggs *huevos*

bread *pan*

salad *ensalada*

fruit *fruta*

lime *limón*

fish *pescado*

shellfish *mariscos*

shrimp *camarones*

meat (without) *(sin) carne*

vegetarian *vegetarian/a*

vegan *vegano/a*

chicken *pollo*

pork *chancho*

beef/steak *res/bistec/lomo*

bacon/ham *tocino/jamón*

SHOPPING

money *dinero*

cash *efectivo*

Do you accept credit cards? *¿Aceptan tarjetas de crédito?*

How much does it cost? *¿Cuánto cuesta?*

Do you have any change? *¿Tiene cambio?*

expensive *caro*

cheap *barato; económico*

more *más*

less *menos*

a little *un poco*

too much *demasiado*

HEALTH

Help me, please. *Ayúdeme por favor.*
I am ill. *Estoy enfermo/a.*
Call a doctor. *Llame un doctor.*
Take me to . . . *Lléveme a . . .*
hospital *hospital; clínica*
drugstore *farmacia*
pain *dolor*
fever *fiebre*
headache *dolor de cabeza*
stomachache *dolor de estómago*
nausea *náusea*
to vomit *vomitar*
medicine *medicina*
antibiotics *antibióticos*
pill/tablet *pastilla*
ointment/cream *crema*
bandage *vendaje*
Band-Aid *curita*
sanitary napkins *toallas sanitarias*
tampons *tampones*
birth control pills *pastillas anticonceptivas*
morning after pill *píldora del día después*
pregnancy test *prueba de embarazo*
condoms *preservativos; condones*
dentist *dentista*
toothache *dolor de muelas*

COMMUNICATIONS

telephone call *llamada*
cell phone *celular*
SIM card *chip*
phone credit *saldo*
pay phones *cabinas*
I would like to call . . . *Quisiera llamar a . . .*
Internet café *cyber*
a computer, please *una maquina por favor*
@ sign *arroba*
copies *copias*
scan *escaneo*
print-out *impresión*
post office *Correos Ecuador*
letter *carta*

envelope *sobre*
stamp *sello de correo*
airmail *correo aereo*
delivery *entrega*
registered *registrado*
package/box *paquete/caja*

AT THE BORDER

border *frontera*
customs *aduana*
immigration *inmigración*
passport *pasaporte*
identity card *cédula*
profession *profesión*
marital status *estado civil*
single *soltero/a*
married *casado/a*
divorced *divorciado/a*
widowed *viudado/a*
travel insurance *seguro de viaje*

VERBS

The infinitives of verbs have three possible endings: *ar, er,* and *ir. Many verbs are regular:*

to buy *comprar*
  I buy; you buy (formal); you buy (informal); we buy; they buy *yo compro; usted compra; tu compras; nosotros compramos; ellos/ellas compran*
to eat *comer*
  I eat; you eat (formal); you eat (informal); we eat; they eat *yo como; usted come; tu comras; nosotros comemos; ellos/ellas comen*
to climb *subir*
  I climb; you climb (formal); you climb (informal); we climb; they climb: *yo subo; usted sube; tu subes; nosotros subimos; ellos/ellas suben*

Some common verbs that can be conjugated using the pattern above for *ar, er,* and *ir* verbs are:

to pass, to spend (time), to happen *pasar*
to owe, must, should, ought to *deber*

to stay, remain *quedar*

to speak *hablar*

to carry, bring *llevar*

to arrive *llegar*

to leave, abandon, to let, allow *dejar*

to call, to name *llamar*

to take, drink *tomar*

to live *vivir*

to watch, look at *mirar*

to look for *buscar*

to wait for, to hope *esperar*

to love *amar*

to work *trabajar*

to need *necesitar*

to write *escribir*

to give *dar* (regular in the present tense except for *doy*, "I give")

to do or make *hacer* (regular in the present tense except for *hago*, "I do/make")

to tell or to say *decir* (regular in the present tense except for *digo*, "I tell/say")

Some of the most useful verbs are irregular:

to have *tener*

I have; you have (formal); you have (informal); we have; they have *yo tengo; usted tiene; tu tienes; nosotros tenemos; ellos/ellas tienen*

to come *venir* (similarly irregular: *vengo, viene, vienes, venimos, vienen*)

to be able to *poder*

I can; you can (formal); you can (informal); we can; they can *yo puedo; usted puede; tu puedes; nosotros podemos; ellos/ellas pueden*

to go *ir*

I go; you go (formal); you go (informal); we go; they go *yo voy; usted va; tu vas; nosotros vamos; ellos/ellas van*

Ir can be used to express the simplest future tense, the same as in English; i.e., "I am going to eat" would be "Voy a comer"; "you are

going to eat" would be **"usted va a comer."**

Spanish has two forms of "to be." Use *estar* when speaking of location or a temporary state of being: *"Estoy en casa."* ("I am at home.") *"Estoy enfermo."* ("I'm sick.")

I am; you are (formal); you are (informal); we are; they are *yo estoy; usted está; tu estás; nosotros estámos; ellos/ellas están*

Use *ser* for a permanent state of being: *"Soy doctora."* ("I am a doctor.")

I am; you are (formal); you are (informal); we are; they are *yo soy; usted es; tu eres; nosotros somos; ellos/ellas son*

NUMBERS

0 *cero*

1 *uno*

2 *dos*

3 *tres*

4 *cuatro*

5 *cinco*

6 *seis*

7 *siete*

8 *ocho*

9 *nueve*

10 *diez*

11 *once*

12 *doce*

13 *trece*

14 *catorce*

15 *quince*

16 *dieciseis*

17 *diecisiete*

18 *dieciocho*

19 *diecinueve*

20 *veinte*

21 *veinte y uno* or *veintiuno*

30 *treinta*

40 *cuarenta*

50 *cincuenta*

60 *sesenta*

70 *setenta*

80 *ochenta*

90 *noventa*
100 *ciento*
101 *ciento y uno* or *cientiuno*
200 *doscientos*
500 *quinientos*
1,000 *mil*
10,000 *diez mil*
100,000 *cien mil*
1,000,000 *millón*
half *medio* or *la mitad*
one-third *un tercio*
one-quarter *un cuarto*

TIME

What time is it? *¿Qué hora es?*
It's 1 o'clock. *Es la una.*
It's 3 in the afternoon. *Son las tres de la tarde.*
It's 4am *Son las cuatro de la mañana.*
6:30 *seis y media*
quarter to 11 *un cuarto para las once*
quarter past 5 *las cinco y cuarto*
midnight *medianoche*
midday *mediodía*
an hour *una hora*
a minute *un minuto*
a second *un segundo*
after *después*
before *antes*

DAYS, MONTHS, AND SEASONS

Monday *lunes*
Tuesday *martes*
Wednesday *miércoles*
Thursday *jueves*
Friday *viernes*
Saturday *sábado*
Sunday *domingo*
today *hoy*
tomorrow *mañana*
yesterday *ayer*
January *enero*
February *febrero*
March *marzo*
April *abril*
May *mayo*
June *junio*
July *julio*
August *agosto*
September *septiembre*
October *octubre*
November *noviembre*
December *diciembre*
a week *una semana*
a month *un mes*
spring *primavera*
summer *verano*
autumn *otoño*
Winter *invierno*

Courtesy of Bruce Whipperman, author of *Moon Pacific Mexico*. Amended for Ecuadorian usage by Bethany Pitts.

Suggested Reading

HISTORY AND POLITICS

Almeida Chávez, Mónica, and Ana Karina López Ramón. *El Séptimo Rafael.* Quito, Ecuador: Dinediciones, 2017. A deep journalistic investigation into Rafael Correa Delgado, president of Ecuador 2007-2017. In Spanish.

Becker, Marc. *The FBI in Latin America: The Ecuador Files (Radical Perspectives).* Durham, NC: Duke University Press, 2017. An examination of FBI documents that reveals the nature of U.S. imperial ambitions in the Americas.

Becker, Marc. *Pachakutik: Indigenous Movements & Electoral Politics in Ecuador.* Lanham, MD: Rowman & Littlefield, 2012. An overview of one of the Americas' most powerful social movements, the Confederation of Indigenous Nationalities of Ecuador (CONAIE).

De la Torre, Carlos. *The Ecuador Reader: History, Culture, and Politics.* Durham, NC: Duke University Press, 2009. An excellent collection of short, readable articles by Ecuadorian authors, politicians, and journalists on various topics such as agriculture, politics, women's rights, religion, etc.

Lavinas Picq, Manuela. *Vernacular Sovereignties: Indigenous Women Challenging World Politics.* Tucson, AZ: University of Arizona Press, 2018. Highlights the important, unrecognized role of indigenous women in politics, focused on Ecuador.

Perkins, John. *Confessions of an Economic Hitman.* London: Ebury Press, 2005. Explosive account of the economic pressure applied to South American governments by the United States. It claims that Ecuadorian president Jaime Roldós Aguilera was assassinated in a CIA conspiracy.

FICTION

See the *Background* chapter for recommended literature by Ecuadorian authors.

Burroughs, William S. *Queer.* New York: Viking Penguin, 1996. A companion piece to Burroughs's first novel, *Junky* (1953), *Queer* describes a fictional addict's escapades during a pilgrimage from Mexico to Ecuador in search of ayahuasca.

Resau, Laura, and María Virginia Farinango. *The Queen of Water.* New York: Delacorte Books, 2011. A poignant novel for young adults based on a true story of an indigenous girl sold to a mestizo family as a servant.

Sepúlveda, Luis. *The Old Man Who Read Love Stories.* Boston, MA: Mariner Books, 1995. In the Ecuadorean jungle, an elderly widower who finds comfort in reading romance novels joins in the hunt for an enraged ocelot.

209

TRAVEL AND MEMOIRS

Bemelmans, Ludwig. *The Donkey Inside*. New York: Paragon House, 1990. Portrait of Quito and its people during World War II, by the French author of the famous *Madeline* children's series.

Michaux, Henri. *Ecuador: A Travel Journal*. Evanston, IL: Marlboro Press/Northwestern, 2001. A short, quirky account of the Belgian-born author's travels in Ecuador in 1927.

Poole, Richard. *The Inca Smiled: The Growing Pains of an Aid Worker in Ecuador*. Oxford, UK: Oneworld Publications, 1997. The story of a British volunteer in Ecuador in the 1960s.

von Däniken, Erich. *The Gold of the Gods*. London: Souvenir Press, 1973. The story of a 1969 expedition to Ecuador's Cueva de los Tayos and the discovery of ancient gold artifacts inside.

CULTURE

Cuvi, Pablo. *Crafts of Ecuador*. Quito: Dinediciones, 1994. Beautifully photographed book on Ecuadorian crafts.

Miller, Tom. *The Panama Hat Trail: A Journey from South America*. Washington, DC: National Geographic Books, 2002. A book about the famous misnamed hat, as well as Ecuadorian history and culture.

Nikolovski, Goce. *Taste of Ecuadorian Cuisine (Latin American Cuisine Book 10)*. Morrisville, NC: Lulu Press, 2017. Collection of over 200 traditional Ecuadorian recipes.

WILDLIFE & THE NATURAL WORLD

Noboa, Andrés Vásquez. *Wildlife of Ecuador: A Photographic Field Guide to Birds, Mammals, Reptiles, and Amphibians*. Princeton, NJ: Princeton University Press, 2017. An all-in-one guide to mainland Ecuador's wildlife.

Ridgely, Robert, and Paul Greenfield. *The Birds of Ecuador: Field Guide*. Ithaca, NY: Comstock, 2001. The bible of birding in Ecuador, with 800 pages of color plates and descriptions of Ecuador's 1,600 species.

Internet Resources

GENERAL ECUADOR WEBSITES

EcuadorExplorer.com
www.ecuadorexplorer.com
Useful online guide.

Ecuador Travel
www.ecuador.travel
Ministry of Tourism site.

Andes Transit
www.andestransit.com
Useful site to check bus schedules.

QUITO

Quito Official Travel Information
www.quito.com.ec
City tourist office's website, with comprehensive information.

NEWS AND MEDIA

BBC
www.bbc.com/travel/
south-america/ecuador
BBC Travel page on Ecuador.

El Comercio
www.elcomercio.com
Quito-based national daily newspaper, in Spanish.

El Universo
www.eluniverso.com
Guayaquil-based national daily newspaper, in Spanish.

The Guardian
www.theguardian.com/world/
ecuador
The Guardian offers the most comprehensive international coverage of Ecuador.

TRAVEL ADVICE

British Foreign Office Travel Advice
www.gov.uk/foreign-travel-advice/
ecuador
Information on entry requirements, security, and health in Ecuador.

U.S. Department of State Ecuador Country Profile
http://travel.state.gov
Click on *Find International Travel Information* and then *Country Information*.

VOLCANOES AND NATURAL DISASTERS

Instituto Geofísico-Escuela Politécnica Nacional
www.igepn.edu.ec
Up-to-date information on volcanic and seismic activity, in Spanish.

Smithsonian Institution Global Volcanism Program
www.volcano.si.edu
Profiles on the world's volcanoes, searchable by country.

LANGUAGE

Cultures of the Andes
www.andes.org
Kichwa language links, songs, and pictures.

CONSERVATION

Acción Ecológica
www.accionecologica.org
Ecuador's most well respected environmental organization (in Spanish).

Amazon Frontlines
www.amazonfrontlines.org
NGO defending indigenous rights to land, life, and cultural survival in the Amazon.

DECOIN (Defense & Ecological Conservation of Intag)
www.decoin.org and http://codel-coecuador.com
Information on the struggle to defend one of the world's most biodiverse regions from mining.

National System of Protected Areas
http://areasprotegidas.ambiente.gob.ec/en
Information on Ecuador's national parks and protected areas.

Protect Ecuador
http://protectecuador.org
Wealth of information on the horrors of mining in Ecuador, with some excellent maps.

HUMAN RIGHTS
Freedom House
https://freedomhouse.org/country/ecuador
Profile on freedom of speech and democracy in Ecuador.

Human Rights Watch
www.hrw.org/americas
Information on human rights issues in Ecuador.

Index

List of Maps

Front Map

Quito

Excursions

Photo Credits

More Guides for Urban Adventure

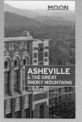

ASHEVILLE & THE GREAT SMOKY MOUNTAINS

BOSTON

BUENOS AIRES

CHICAGO

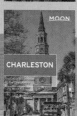

CHARLESTON

CLEVELAND

LOS ANGELES

MEXICO CITY

MONTRÉAL

NASHVILLE

NEW YORK CITY

OSLO

PORTLAND

QUÉBEC CITY

REYKJAVÍK

SAN DIEGO

SAVANNAH

SEATTLE

VANCOUVER

WASHINGTON DC

Gear up for a bucket list vacation

MOON

TRIP OF A LIFETIME

ANGKOR WAT

MOON

BARCELONA & MADRID

JESSICA JONES

MOON

TRIP OF A LIFETIME

GALÁPAGOS ISLANDS

MOON

JAPAN

JONATHAN DE HART

MOON

TRIP OF A LIFETIME

MACHU PICCHU

RYAN DUBÉ

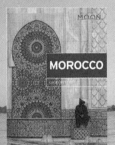

MOON

MOROCCO

MOON

NEW ZEALAND

JAMIE CHRISTIAN DESPLACES

MOON

NORWAY

MOON

TRIP OF A LIFETIME

PATAGONIA

WAYNE BERNHARDSON

MOON

ROME, FLORENCE & VENICE

MOON

USA NATIONAL PARKS

THE COMPLETE GUIDE TO ALL **59 PARKS**

BECKY LOMAX

MOON

CAMINO DE SANTIAGO

SACRED SITES, HISTORIC VILLAGES, LOCAL FOOD & WINE

BEEBE BAHRAMI

or plan your next beachy getaway!

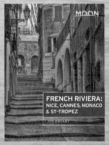

Be bold and go beyond...

These savvy city guides include strategies to help you see the top sights *and* find adventure beyond the tourist crowds.

OR TAKE THINGS ONE STEP AT A TIME

Moon's pocket-sized city walks with fold-out maps are the perfect companion in cities abroad!

MAP SYMBOLS

▤ Expressway	○ City/Town	✈ Airport	⚲ Golf Course			
▤ Primary Road	◉ State Capital	✖ Airfield	🅿 Parking Area			
▤ Secondary Road	◉ National Capital	▲ Mountain	⬭ Archaeological Site			
----- Unpaved Road	★ Point of Interest	✦ Unique Natural Feature	⬥ Church			
— Feature Trail	• Accommodation	⚑ Waterfall	⛽ Gas Station			
------- Other Trail	▼ Restaurant/Bar	♠ Park	◎ Glacier			
·········· Ferry	■ Other Location	⬛ Trailhead	▨ Mangrove			
▤ Pedestrian Walkway	▲ Campground	⛷ Skiing Area	▨ Reef			
▥ Stairs			▤ Swamp			

CONVERSION TABLES

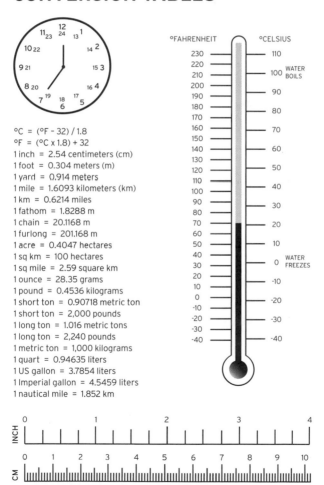

°C = (°F − 32) / 1.8
°F = (°C x 1.8) + 32
1 inch = 2.54 centimeters (cm)
1 foot = 0.304 meters (m)
1 yard = 0.914 meters
1 mile = 1.6093 kilometers (km)
1 km = 0.6214 miles
1 fathom = 1.8288 m
1 chain = 20.1168 m
1 furlong = 201.168 m
1 acre = 0.4047 hectares
1 sq km = 100 hectares
1 sq mile = 2.59 square km
1 ounce = 28.35 grams
1 pound = 0.4536 kilograms
1 short ton = 0.90718 metric ton
1 short ton = 2,000 pounds
1 long ton = 1.016 metric tons
1 long ton = 2,240 pounds
1 metric ton = 1,000 kilograms
1 quart = 0.94635 liters
1 US gallon = 3.7854 liters
1 Imperial gallon = 4.5459 liters
1 nautical mile = 1.852 km

MOON QUITO
Avalon Travel
Hachette Book Group
1700 Fourth Street
Berkeley, CA 94710, USA
www.moon.com

Editor: Kimberly Ehart
Acquiring Editor: Nikki Ioakimedes
Series Manager: Kathryn Ettinger
Copy Editor: Deana Shields
Production Designer: Rue Flaherty
Cover Design: Faceout Studios, Charles Brock
Interior Design: Domini Dragoone
Moon Logo: Tim McGrath
Map Editor: Mike Morgenfeld
Cartographers: Albert Angulo, Brian Shotwell
Proofreader: Ashley Benning
Indexer: Greg Jewett

ISBN-13: 978-1-63121-714-2

Printing History
1st Edition — December 2019
5 4 3 2 1